THE GOVERNMENT OF BEANS

KREGG HETHERINGTON

# THE GOVERNMENT OF **BEANS**

*Regulating Life in the Age of Monocrops*

DUKE UNIVERSITY PRESS · DURHAM AND LONDON · 2020

© 2020 DUKE UNIVERSITY PRESS
All rights reserved
Designed by Matthew Tauch
Typeset in Arno Pro by Westchester Publishing Services

Library of Congress Cataloging-in-Publication Data

Names: Hetherington, Kregg, author.
Title: The government of beans : regulating life in the age of
monocrops / Kregg Hetherington.
Description: Durham : Duke University Press, 2020. |
Includes bibliographical references and index.
Identifiers: LCCN 2019041805 (print) | LCCN 2019041806
(ebook) | ISBN 9781478006060 (hardcover) |
ISBN 9781478006893 (paperback) | ISBN 9781478007487
(ebook)
Subjects: LCSH: Soybean industry—Paraguay. | Soyfoods
industry—Paraguay. | Sustainable agriculture—Political
aspects—Paraguay.
Classification: LCC HD9235.S62 P345 2020 (print) |
LCC HD9235.S62 (ebook) | DDC 338.1/733409892—dc23 LC
record available at https://lccn.loc.gov/2019041805
LC ebook record available at https://
lccn.loc.gov/2019041806

Cover art: Police guarding soybean field, Paraguay, 2013.
Photo by Edgar Vázquez.

# CONTENTS

# ACKNOWLEDGMENTS

This book was ten years in the making, and it has caused me to accumulate more debts than I can fathom. The usual caveats apply: all the mistakes here are mine. And yet I've never before felt just how totally beholden authorship is to the ecosystems (social, intellectual, and more-than-human) in which it thrives. It's an awesome luxury to be able to do something as all-consuming as write a book, probably a luxury that is unsustainable. But here I am; I've written another one, and below are some of the hundreds of people who gave me a boost along the way.

I relied heavily on three researchers who helped me with portions of this project: Marco Castillo, Alejandra Estigarribia, and Sofia Espíndola Oviedo. They came and went over the eight years of research, but at many different moments they were deeply involved not only in data collection but in conceptualization of the research problem itself. Long discussions, which you will catch a glimpse of in chapter 6, were integral to the analysis as it went on. What is harder to show is the cumulative effect of those discussions as they took place over several years, and even harder to show the affective collateral of working so closely together. All three of them became very dear friends; if nothing else came of this project, that would have been enough.

The project would also have been impossible without the generosity and openness shown to me by a surprising number of bureaucrats who worked in the Paraguayan government between 2008 and 2012. We interviewed over 120 people for the book on tape, many of them several times, and many others allowed me to tag along during the workday and look over their shoulders. Most of these appear in the book with pseudonyms, so I can't name them here. But three in particular are obvious, and were also the most generous from the beginning. I originally contacted Miguel Lovera, Inés Franceschelli, and Sylvia González with some trepidation, knowing how much the project might depend on their blessing. Not only were they enthusiastic, but they actively participated in the project for many years, constantly ready to help out and return over old ground, to teach me as I slowly came around to seeing things the way they did, thinking deeply with me as the project matured and the landscape changed. I couldn't have asked for more generous interlocutors in the field, and while all of them have given me their approval on specific parts of the text, I hope that they find themselves fairly represented when they see the whole.

The same is true for a large group of farmers on both sides of a seemingly intractable social and political divide, who invited me into their homes. For the sake of preserving their anonymity, their names also do not appear here, though I still count on the support and generosity of two families in particular: Antonio Galeano and his kids, Derlis, Sonia, Diego, and Mariza, and Jorge Galeano, Demesia Rodríguez, and Leticia Galeano. In Asunción, Noni Florencio, Antonio Castillo, Carolina Castillo, and Thomas Jönsson make it all work. A gaggle of other frequent interlocutors, from whom I continue to learn constantly, are too many to name, but here's a short list: Jazmín Acuña, Carolina Álvarez, Perla Álvarez, Alicia Amarilla, Lucas Bessire, Paola Canova, Joel Correa, Ana Estigarribia, Jorge Estigarribia, Ramona Fischer, Christine Folch, Adriana González Brun, Lawrence Morroni, Andrés Olmedo, Isa Olmedo, Roni Paredes, Adelina Pusineri, Sonia Rodríguez, Luís Rojas, Javiera Rulli, Carly Schuster, Gustavo Setrini, Reto Sonderegger, and Miguel Stoeckel. Tomás Palau, who passed away toward the beginning of this project, is sorely missed.

Several of my colleagues and students did me the invaluable service of reading early, tortured drafts of this manuscript, and giving me feedback, without which the book would have been even more of a soup of half-formed inanities than it is now. They are Andrea Ballestero, Alex Nading, Alix Johnson, Alejandra Melian-Morse, Mark Doerksen, Chantal Gailloux,

Aryana Soliz, Elie Jalbert, Kassandra Lockyer-Spooner, Kristina Lyons, Émile St-Pierre, and Mathieu Guérin. Students in the writing group at the Concordia Ethnography Lab, particularly Marie-Eve Drouin Gagné and Tricia Toso, were excellent companions for the longest months of this project. Others dropped comments along the way, after reading or listening to pieces of the text, which rattled around and eventually affected the words here. The ones that gave me the most (productive) trouble came from Aaron Ansell, Akhil Gupta, Alex Blanchette, Anders Blok, Andrea Muehlebach, Andrew Barry, Andrew Matthews, Anne Spice, Antina von Schnitzler, Ashley Carse, Atsuro Morita, Austin Zeiderman, Bart Simon, Brian Larkin, Brian Noble, Carlota McCallister, Carolina Cambre, Casper Bruun Jansen, Chris Kortright, Cori Hayden, Cymene Howe, David Howes, Diana Bocarejo, Diane Nelson, Dominic Boyer, Donna Haraway, Drew Gilbert, Eduardo Kohn, Elaine Gan, Eleana Kim, Fabiana Li, Gastón Gordillo, Gretchen Bakke, Heath Cabot, Heather Swanson, Ignacio Farías, Isabel Stengers, Jake Kosek, Jeremy Campbell, Jill Didur, Jim Ferguson, John Hartigan, John Law, Jorge Pantaleón, Julie Soleil Archambault, Jun Borras, Kaushik Sunder Rajan, Kevin Gould, Kim Fortun, Kristin Asdal, Lesley Green, Lindsay Dubois, Lisa Stevenson, Liz Fitting, Manuel Balán, Mario Blaser, Meghan Morris, Michael Huner, Nais Dave, Natasha Myers, Nikhil Anand, Nora Nagel, Orit Halpern, Pablo Lapegna, Pauline Gardiner-Barber, Penny Harvey, Sarah Besky, Sarah Muir, Tina Hilgers, Tone Druglitrø, and Zachary Caple. Still others are the sort of long-term interlocutors without whom I would find it very hard to think at all, especially Marisol de la Cadena, Anna Tsing, Martin French, Ramón Fogel, and Tania Li.

It's an ongoing pleasure to work with Duke University Press, particularly Gisela Fosado, who continues to support me in all of my projects. Pieces of the chapters ahead have appeared in other places, although always in quite different form, and I especially appreciate the rigorous blind reviews I received there. These other places include *Cultural Anthropology, Current Anthropology, Indiana Journal of Global Legal Studies, Journal of Latin American and Caribbean Anthropology, Environment and Planning D: Society and Space*, and chapters in *How Nature Works* (editors Sarah Besky and Alex Blanchette, 2019), and *A Routledge Companion to Actor-Network Theory* (editors Anders Blok, Ignacio Farías, and Celia Roberts, 2019). The funding for most of this came from the Social Sciences and Humanities Research Council of Canada, the Fonds de Recherche du Québec, Société et Culture, and institutional support from Concordia University, Dalhousie University, and the Centro de Estudios Rurales Interdisciplinarios in Asunción. Workshops funded by Wenner Gren and the Society for Advanced Research were also key places where I worked out some of the ideas that drive the book.

None of this work would be possible without the inspiration, collaboration and endless patience of Danielle, Sadie, and Dylan.

# Governing the Anthropocene

A t dawn on June 15, 2012, a detachment of heavily armed riot police approached an isolated land occupation in the district of Curu-guaty in northeastern Paraguay. They were met by a small delegation of men from the camp, representatives of a local organization of landless *campesinos* who had been fighting for the right to settle there for generations.[1] That fight had recently intensified because land was becoming more scarce, because forests were almost gone, and because the massive ranch that claimed to own the land was beginning to plant soybeans, a crop that in Paraguay had come to represent the annihilation of a certain rural way of life. Tensions were complicated by the fact that the national government at the time, led by leftist president Fernando Lugo, claimed to prioritize rural welfare, land reform, and environmental regulation. And yet here were the police, armed as if for war, marching against a precarious encampment of families on the edge of a small stand of trees.

It is impossible to say exactly why, but a firefight ensued, and by the time it was over, six police officers and eleven campesinos were dead, with dozens more wounded or in jail. Within days, the "Massacre of Curuguaty" had been turned into a national crisis, and by the end of the week, the president had been removed from office in what his supporters called a "parliamentary coup."

Rural activists were stunned. It was hard enough to comprehend how a president they considered an ally might have allowed such a violent eviction to take place. Now they had to contend with the prospect that that ally was gone altogether, replaced by something far more sinister. The new president, installed the following day, immediately began to dismantle the tepid regulations that Lugo had enacted around the use of pesticides and genetic materials that were central to the soy boom. As Lugo's replacement made the rounds declaring his friendship with soy farmers, he also mobilized the national police to protect crops from landless farmers.

As with any event of this sort, there are many ways to tell the story, many ways to sort out the main characters and attribute responsibility. The courts tried to construct their version of the story through a trial, but after seven years, all charges were dropped. Campesinos and human rights lawyers described the trial as a farce from the beginning. But behind its failure lies another possibility: the Massacre of Curuguaty wasn't really amenable to the sort of storytelling in which people and their intentions occupy the main stage. Because while it was clearly a criminal event, the specific actors and actions were also participants in a larger, far more complicated drama whose contours were always present even if they were hard to make out.

Since the early 2000s, rural activists had been developing this larger story, which turned on a simple idea: *la soja mata* (soy kills). Those three words were useful as a slogan, yelled during marches and scrawled on banners and concrete all over Paraguay. But they also brought with them an analysis of a growing list of deaths, human and otherwise, for which soy could be held responsible. The Massacre of Curuguaty fit the story perfectly, confirming fears that as soy expanded, it robbed campesinos of their ability to harvest and live from their own preferred crops, undermined an old project to build a functioning welfare state, and made it impossible to imagine a government that responded to their interests.

This book tells the story of those soybeans, the way they transformed Paraguayan lives, both human and nonhuman, how they inspired a governmental response, and why that response failed so dramatically. Like all ethnography, it is a local story—a story of local people and plants, of histories of power and ecological entanglements, and of the travails of a small group of underfunded, inexperienced bureaucrats sincerely trying to make a difference. It is also a regional story of Latin America's attempts to revive leftist

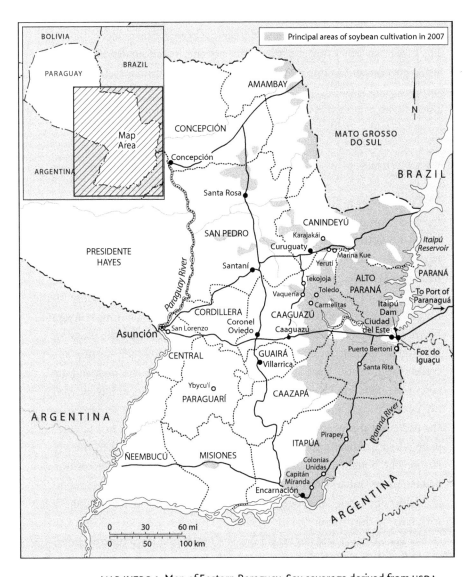

MAP INTRO.1  Map of Eastern Paraguay. Soy coverage derived from USDA,
*Paraguay Biotechnology Annual.*

politics in the early twenty-first century and the way that those attempts were thwarted by more cynical and destructive political rivals. And finally, it is a profoundly global story, a chapter in a century of expanding monocrops, of the destruction of ecosystems in the service of a specific model of human life. Like many other stories of the Anthropocene, it is about the difficulty of using government to mitigate the problems that government itself created during a quickly fading era when human well-being seemed to be achievable through the promises of limitless growth.

## WHY SOYBEANS?

This project began for me years earlier, when I was living in Paraguay and trying to come to terms with the breadth of what my campesino friends meant when they said "soy kills."[2] One of the people who worked hardest to educate me at the time was Ña Costanza, an activist who lived on sixteen hectares of land halfway down a long road known as Carmelitas.[3] Her farm, like those of others who considered themselves campesinas and campesinos, was a mix of cash and subsistence crops, fruit trees, and forest. When I went to visit, her husband was usually out in the fields with the oldest of her twelve children, tending cotton, peanuts, corn, beans, and cassava; she could spare time to chat and drink *terere* among the chickens, pigs, and the rest of her children. I went because Ña Costanza was kind, indulgent with my poor Guarani, and never tired of talking about injustice. And because she had good stories about soybeans. She had been one of the first to complain when her next-door neighbor had sold his farm, and when the soy farmer who bought it started to fumigate the crop using a small tractor. She had led three January 2005 attempts to prevent that tractor from getting to the field, convincing other neighbors to block the road with her, yelling "la soja mata" at the driver.

For Ña Costanza and her neighbors, soy represented a completely novel kind of agriculture. It had been present in Paraguay since the late 1970s but had been concentrated primarily in the easternmost districts of the country. By 2000, however, soy was by far the country's most profitable export, and the territory planted in soy was expanding westward at a rate of almost two hundred thousand hectares per year. The crop was grown on relatively large farms using high-end machinery and an increasingly complex portfolio of chemical inputs, meaning that soy was exclusive: it created fabulous wealth for a minority of farmers and dispossessed the rest of farmland and forest.

Moreover, it turned huge areas of the mixed landscape that the rural poor had once coveted into something alien—a blanket monocrop crawling with giant machines and soaked in pesticides. Land takeovers and pollution led thousands to move out of the countryside, finding refuge in the growing slums of Asunción, Buenos Aires, and São Paolo. Smallholder colonies, once the symbol of Paraguayan progress, began to shrink as households packed up and fled, abandoning cotton fields and gardens to bulldozers, fire, and then soybeans.

Ña Costanza argued that her neighbor's small plot of soybeans marked the beginning of an invasion—*la punta de la lanza* (the tip of the spear) that would destroy her community. Down at the end of Carmelitas, the first families to come into contact with soy farms complained constantly of the smell of pesticides and the headaches and rashes that accompanied spraying. The previous year, an eleven year-old boy had died near the Brazilian border after being sprayed by his neighbor. And just to the north, soy farmers had paid local police to evict campesinos (among them Ña Costanza's son) and burn down their houses. To the east, just across a small stream, the county of Toledo had almost no trees left; one small settlement there had disappeared completely as the land was covered in soybeans, while the town of Toledo built silos bigger than anything anyone had ever seen. Ña Costanza's family, like all of her neighbors, was too poor to plant soy. Instead, almost all of the beans were planted by Brazilian immigrants who had settled on the Paraguayan side of the border region and were now suddenly hungry for land. The combination of wealthy immigrants and soybeans seemed almost unstoppable—like the wind, Ña Costanza said. And if anything, this was the most unsettling effect of them all: the winds had changed. When they blew from the east they were stronger and hotter and carried noxious smells.

On the ground, the approaching beans were creepily homogeneous, a dense carpet of waist-high shrubs that grew together, turned brown almost overnight, and then disappeared over a few days of harvesting. Their uniformity matched the specs of the machinery that tended them, their genetics engineered to withstand a constant chemical assault that killed all other plants. Soybean farmers needed heat, sunlight, and relatively well-irrigated soil, but what they mainly needed was horizontal space with few obstructions (trees, water towers, pesticide regulations, or protesters). And this made it a particularly voracious driver of what has been called a "global land grab," a rush to bring larger and larger arable areas of the planet into the production of industrial monocrops.[4]

Far from the field, soy was an ideal "flex crop," whose value arose from the many different kinds of processing to which it could be subjected.[5] Soy grown in Paraguay rarely stayed in Paraguay, but was already a ubiquitous if largely invisible part of modern life in many other countries. It was the world's most common vegetable oil, and its by-products were used in processed food for everything from preservatives to adhesives. Outside of the food chain, it was turned into glue, grease, putty, varnish, fuel, plastic, linoleum, cement, clothing, foam stabilizer, and explosives.[6] Its biggest use, however, was feeding animals destined for slaughter. When soybeans were crushed and the oils extracted, the remaining meal was the single-most-important ingredient in animal feed worldwide.[7] Modern chicken and hog farming and the cattle feedlot industry could not exist without the annual global production of some 350 million tons of soybeans, a figure that kept growing every year.[8]

All of this made the soy of "soy kills" a complicated social, political, and environmental actor. In conversations like those I used to have with Ña Costanza, soy was not merely an object but also a reference to something— some larger force, process, or social ailment—that radically defied objectification. Its violence was generally slow, moving at the pace of unpleasant smells, toxic accretions, and cancer clusters.[9] In the capital city, where so much of the regulatory politics actually took place, many activists had a clearer sense of the global structural stakes of the industry, the way it turned Paraguay into an extractive frontier for wealth accumulated elsewhere. But few of those activists had ever seen or smelled a soy field. So as it moved between campesinos and their urban allies, "la soja mata" could be incredibly polysemic, evoking in different contexts land loss, sickness, deforestation, climate change, neoliberalism, labor migration, global capitalism, Brazilian imperialism, agribusiness, biological manipulation, violence, poverty, injustice, and the loss of a way of life.

The mass noun "soy," which in Spanish and Guarani takes a definite article—"la soja"—made it easy to talk in these nonspecific ways. One could easily blame "la soja" for all of these things without specifying in what way it bore responsibility. What were its units? Was it made up of beans or silos and machinery or transnational companies or farmers? Did the wheat that farmers planted in rotation with soy or the Roundup herbicide they sprayed on it constitute part of "la soja," or were they a separate problem?[10] Because these questions never had stable answers, soy was less like an object than what Timothy Morton calls a "hyperobject," a massively distributed thing that defies anyone's ability to know it but nonetheless remains present, exerting an agency beyond human control.[11] In this book, therefore, I treat soy less as a crop species or a commodity than as a character whose way of being in the world was complex enough to at times seem benign, at others terrifying, at others totally inscrutable.

The first part of the book, "A Cast of Characters," tells the story of the rise of soy as a national political actor. But it also makes the case that soy is a character of the Anthropocene, in two specific ways. The first is literal: the Anthropocene is an age of monocrops. Soy, like other extensive, mechanized crops, drives climate change and mass extinction. It demands deforestation and in so doing degrades the soil's ability to absorb carbon. It is energy-intensive, requiring massive inputs of fuel, fertilizers, and pesticides and is destined to feed a growing global meat industry that is one of the world's largest producers of greenhouse gases.[12] Soy also drives species extinction by destroying habitat and requiring the industrial-scale annihilation of other creatures that it recategorizes as pests.[13] As with other environmental processes, the speed and violence of these changes is geographically uneven: they accrue first in frontiers of extraction like Paraguay, while in other parts of the world they are felt mainly as a form of inexplicable market abundance in cheap meat and other goods.[14]

Second, soy is a character of the Anthropocene because of the way that it participates in a particular historical conundrum. At the moment it appeared, soy seemed like a crisis—a violent event overtaking people's homes and lives. And yet like climate change, soy was also a perverse echo—the return, in monstrously inverted form, of a series of progressive promises made decades earlier. To the extent that soybeans present a problem for life, they do so as the result of a crisis in the notion of human welfare that was articulated after the end of World War II and spread to places like Paraguay through international development promoters. This period is often referred to as the great acceleration because of the sudden intensification in the use of fossil fuels and the advances it made possible in the standards of living of a certain portion of the human species.[15] In agriculture, this era is known, somewhat ironically, as the Green Revolution, a time when huge investments in agrarian technology and intensified land use contributed to a diminution of hunger and an increase in national economic growth, all the while destroying forests and other complex ecologies. One reason it is so hard to figure out how to respond to agricultural destruction is the same reason that decarbonizing the economy is so difficult: the government systems we rely on to protect people and other living things from the ravages caused by economic growth are impossible to disentangle from the same systems that promote that growth.[16]

## WHY GOVERNMENT?

Paraguay's rural activists were hardly alone in thinking that the best way to mitigate the harm caused by soybeans was to appeal to the national government. It is a common premise of the global environmental movement that activities that produce widespread harm need to be governed in the public interest by a strong regulatory state. This premise is based on the idea that the state is the only apparatus able to effectively know and intervene on behalf of the common good in a world beset by complexity and uncertainty.[17] In Paraguay, the promise of the state was structured around a diagnosis of its past debilities: the state apparatus had been controlled by a single party for the preceding sixty-one years and for most of that time by a notorious army general whose friends still wielded enormous political influence and were heavily invested in agriculture. By extension, it was possible to believe that capturing the state from those interests might make it possible to limit soy's destructiveness and revive an old promise of rural welfare.

In 2008, activists received a rare opportunity to try this hypothesis out. As part of Latin America's "left turn," Paraguayans elected as their president a soft-spoken rural bishop, Fernando Lugo, who received support from a ragtag coalition of opposition groups, technocratic reformers, Marxist sociologists, environmentalists, and peasant organizations.[18] Soybeans did not figure prominently in Lugo's official platform, but for his rural supporters, his promises about integrated land reform and rural welfare were set against a backdrop of killer soy.[19] Lugo's power to deliver on these promises was of course quite limited, but he did appoint a number of activists and environmentalists to top bureaucratic offices to see what they could do in the regulatory trenches of the agricultural state.

I refer to this group of activist bureaucrats, a small subset of Lugo's coalition, as the Government of Beans. Their four years in office constituted a kind of regulatory experiment, testing the hypothesis that a stronger state could curb the excesses of the soy industry. These new functionaries were concentrated in the Secretariat of Environment, the Ministry of Public Health and Social Welfare, the Institute for Rural Welfare (IBR), and most controversially in the obscure National Service for Plant and Seed Health and Quality (SENAVE).[20] They spent those four years trying to find ways to address the problems caused by the soy boom using the information-gathering and regulatory capacities entrusted to their offices. But the enthusiasm and ambition of these activist bureaucrats far exceeded the limited resources at their disposal.

Activists in Lugo's government called what they were doing a *proyecto estado* (state project) that revolved around four ideals uniting leftist and centrist political movements.[21] The first of these was social democracy, promoting a relatively interventionist role for state regulators in supporting welfare (health care, education, old-age security, and access to land) and social justice (social inclusion and environmental and labor rights). The second is what commentators in the 1990s called ecological modernization, which proposed that large-scale environmental harms could be solved by studying and regulating them.[22] The third was transparency, built on the claim that inequality and violence resulted primarily from the corruption and incompetence of past governments, vices to be solved by institutional reform.[23] And the fourth was the assertion of national sovereignty, particularly in relation to the United States and Brazil, two countries long accused of imperialist meddling in Paraguay.[24]

In each of the four dimensions, antisoy activists believed their state project could even stop the spread of soybeans. Soy was a detriment to social welfare, and campesinos felt they needed the state to protect them from it. Soy was an environmental predator, and it needed to be regulated by the state to prevent it from further destroying the environment. Soy was the result of government corruption, and once a clean government was in place that actually applied environmental laws, soy's excesses would be reduced. And soy was a product of Brazilian imperialism, since the crop was planted predominantly by Brazilian migrants living in the border region. The Paraguayan state was "absent" in these areas, activists often said, and by reasserting national sovereignty, Paraguayans would regain control over soy and its destructiveness.

It should come as no surprise, of course, that the promise of state regulation was extremely hard to achieve. Many anthropologists have pointed to the magical qualities of state thinking—the way it creates a notion of unity and coherence around the threat of violence while in practice that coherence is always vanishing or becoming fractious, multiple, and self-contradictory.[25] Morton describes the state as a hyperobject, because not unlike Paraguayan soy, it seems to be both everywhere and nowhere at once, impossible to completely locate or control but also impossible to ignore, an entity with its own kind of brutal agency.[26] And this is more or less how the

Government of Beans played out—as a bright promise that slowly became bogged down in the particulars, in the sticky relations between tools and objects, and in the ever-multiplying complexities of the task at hand.

In fact, the problems that lay ahead for the Government of Beans were prefigured by previous, less ambitious, regulatory failures in agriculture. One of these, at the very outset of the soy boom, is particularly instructive. In 2000, the government had banned the use of Roundup Ready soybeans, a new, genetically modified variety that had just begun to appear in Paraguayan fields. Following the lead of environmental regulators in Brazil, the sitting president had declared a moratorium on the use of any genetically modified seed pending further study of its environmental risks. Yet only a few years later, the Ministry of Agriculture recognized that at least 90 percent of the national soy crop consisted of Roundup Ready plants: practically the entire crop was illegal. The violation was so egregious that it became a joke among regulators, who referred to Roundup Ready soybeans as "soja Maradona," after the Argentine soccer player famous both for his ability to work his way through any team's defense and for having won a World Cup on the basis of an illegal hand goal.[27] Just as that famous "hand of God" goal had made a mockery of the idea that soccer was to be adjudicated by a neutral arbiter, soy had powers that, for good or for bad, had made a mockery of Paraguayan state sovereignty. Of course, there are many nonsupernatural reasons the ban never worked, but none of them completely accounts for the regulatory difficulties that soy caused over the course of Lugo's tenure.

Indeed, the Government of Beans was always shadowed by the possibility that the entire notion of regulation on which it was based was upside-down. As many bureaucrats told me during this research, even as they were trying to find ways to curb the soy industry, they worried they had in fact been co-opted into doing the opposite, acting as functionaries in an *estado sojero* (Soy State), not unlike a petrostate in the thrall of a single, destructive industry. Regulators may have wanted to believe that the state was made to protect people's right to live well in a healthy environment but often found themselves protecting soy itself, enforcing laws that were meant to strengthen the crop and promote its expansion. The problem perhaps was less state absence than regulatory capture or even more fundamentally that the entire regulatory apparatus had been built by the soy sector to service its own interests.[28]

The title of this book, *The Government of Beans*, is meant to evoke this tension, since it can be read in two ways—as a body either controlling or controlled by beans. At times it was possible to keep these two state projects distinct, and in these cases I use different names to flag the distinction: the Government of Beans refers to regulatory attempts to limit soy's expansion, whereas the Soy State refers to the way the soy industry used the state to help it expand. Often, however, it was very hard to distinguish them. For instance, Paraguay was often compared with Argentina, where the soy boom was almost as dominant in the national economy. There, the successive governments of Néstor and Cristina Kirchner chose not to limit soy but rather to tax it heavily and to use the money raised to help fund the expansion of welfare services. That model was similar to the way leftist governments in the region used revenue from oil, gas, and mining in a process that environmental critics labeled "neo-extractivism."[29] But although many Paraguayans promoted the Argentine model, a series of historical, territorial, and ethnic dynamics made the prosoy and antisoy positions much harder to reconcile in Paraguay.

This produced a pervasive sense that the instruments of state power did not quite fit the problem at hand. The lack of fit was at times existential, as in the conflict between the Government of Beans and the Soy State, but most of the time it was more mundane, a problem of regulatory pragmatics.[30] Regulation is the application of laws to the real world, and as in the courtroom, the gap between any rule and the real, messy situations to which it is supposed to apply becomes the place of judgment, where rule and situation need to be translated into adequate mirrors of each other. This gap and the discretion it affords the inspector, the lawyer, or the judge are one of the crucial sites for the exercise of exceptional power, or sovereignty.[31] But to the extent that sovereignty seems like a spatial exercise—closing gaps between abstractions and actualities—regulatory pragmatics shows that the whole practice of law occurs through the progressive unfolding of responses between bureaucrats, politicians, lawyers, citizens, and the many nonhumans who are subject to regulation but have interests of their own. In the Government of Beans, even the smallest bureaucratic action, like an inspector filling out a report, could become part of a long game, a war of position about the future of the nation. Each step of regulation was about trying to change the conditions under which a dimly anticipated set of future actors would have to act, knowing the whole time that other actors and other projects, working at different tempos and in different time frames, were also affecting those future conditions.[32]

As a result, the apparatus of the state always seemed out of phase with the phenomenon that regulators and activists were trying to regulate.[33] Consider a mundane example: farm inspectors were unionized employees whose workday ended at three o'clock in the afternoon, and in fact, any farm inspection report drawn up after that time was not considered legally valid. Activists wishing that the inspectors would work a little harder often complained that "the soy doesn't stop working at 3:00 p.m." These little struggles over how to think about the time of regulation, plant growth, and human labor were further overwhelmed by the slow movement of legal procedures. In the time it took to put a crop of beans in the ground, tend it, harvest it, and sell it (around four months), it was difficult for a regulatory agency to mount a full response: to spot a problem, generate an official denunciation, allow due process to occur, and then sanction the farmer. Meanwhile, the whole process might be derailed by any number of conspiracies brewing within the government or the global economy or among fungal spores in Brazilian soy fields. Specific beans came and went, while the law took its time. And the reverse was also true: regulations changed, along with interpretations of those regulations, and those tasked with policing them came and went while soy remained and expanded, riding out inspections, court cases, scandals, elections, massacres, and coups.

The great experiment of the Government of Beans ended in a series of dramatic and unforeseeable events. In the wake of the Massacre of Curuguaty, Lugo was overthrown and his appointees were run out of their offices; many regulations they had passed were suspended and documents they had generated were burned. It was not the first time a government project had failed, and it would be easy to say that the violent capture of the state was only another iteration of a long-standing Paraguayan tradition. But experiments all have their peculiarities, and their failures leave remains from which future experiments will be built. In the immediate aftermath of the Government of Beans, those remains suggested a new way of thinking the long history of agrarian destruction.

### AGRIBIOPOLITICS

One of the curious details of drama of the Government of Beans was the way that it made visible previously obscure bureaucratic offices, revealing them as sites of deep underlying tensions. The most important of these was SENAVE, the phytosanitary agency dedicated to governing the health of plants. If you've never heard of such an office, then you are like most Paraguayans prior to the Lugo's election. It is one of those technical state agencies that normally evades public attention, and its purview includes making sure that seed sellers maintain germination standards, that farmers comply with wind limits on spraying chemicals, that bugs do not cross borders in truckloads of produce. It is a vital piece of all modern agriculture regimes, and participation in global markets is impossible without it, yet it rarely shows up in popular discussions of agrarian problems, much less coup plots. In retrospect, however, there was no more obvious place for the Government of Beans to play out, and untangling why that is offers a perfect window on the rise and intractability of modern monocrops.

The history of phytosanitary regulation looks a lot like classic biopolitics, the term Michel Foucault used to describe techniques for governing human life that emerged in the eighteenth and nineteenth centuries.[34] For Foucault, biopolitics ushered in a period of governing human life at the scale of the population, which could be helped to thrive through territorial interventions in reproduction and health, or allowed to die. Phytosanitary regulation works through a similar logic, as a way of governing the populations of crop plants living in a given territory and making sure that conditions are right for agriculture to prosper. Not surprisingly, both forms of regulation appeared around the same time and for similar reasons. The same conditions of densifying human populations that gave rise to public health also made it necessary to secure large-scale food production. The grain monocrops that emerged at this time were as vulnerable to pests as human populations in cities and required analogous governmental intervention at a scale beyond any single farm.

Until the early twentieth century, it was not uncommon to think of these two problems together, not just because they formed a singular system related to food security but also because so many analogies flowed easily between phytosanitary regulation and public health. Each one promoted health by controlling reproduction, killing invasive life forms, and limiting the movement of infected and susceptible organisms by instituting borders, quarantines, barriers, and buffer zones. Once modern agrichemicals (the phytosanitary equivalent of medicine) were added around World War II, these techniques made possible the massive boom in global agricultural production known as the Green Revolution. Although contemporary analysts began to separate human and plant health into fundamentally different categories, the Green Revolution was always justified in biopolitical terms, a project to "feed the world" that reimagined a target population at the scale of humanity.[35] But even as it created the possibilities for the emergence of a universalist understanding of human welfare, the Green Revolution was accomplished by opening new frontiers, enabling a new wave of settler colonialism, and destroying forests and indigenous lives to make room for the large-scale production of singularly aggressive plants.

As I argue in the third part of this book, the Green Revolution also coincided with an epistemological shift in the way Europeans conceived of biopolitics, leading to the odd difficulty that Foucault and a generation of his followers had in talking about agriculture. Until the war, human and plant health regimes were often thought of together. And yet after the war they were increasingly thought of as completely distinct. That rift enabled a further blind spot in the way they thought about human welfare. As Europe and North America built robust new welfare states based on industrial growth, they encouraged countries in Latin America and Asia to invest in agricultural development on the promise that this would eventually equip them to emulate the North. The familiar story of biopolitics remained largely blind to the way that northern welfare states were built in part on the violent extractive frontiers being opened in other parts of the world at the expense of other forms of life.

To respond to this theoretical difficulty in talking about the relations between the government of human and plant health, I have started referring to the conflict over soybeans in SENAVE as "agribiopolitical." In a longer genealogy of agribiopolitical arrangements, it becomes clear that soy was in many ways a continuation of previous developments (indeed, many have called it part of the Second Green Revolution).[36] For instance, most campesinos who complained about the soy boom had been the beneficiaries of a previous cotton boom. In their respective moments, both soy and cotton had benefited a great many humans and by different metrics had lifted Paraguay itself out of poverty.[37] Yet in other ways, soy and cotton were profoundly different. Prior to the 1990s, smallholders often marched in favor of greater access to pesticides, arguing that their well-being depended on killing off the various critters that affected their cotton and therefore their sometimes precarious foothold in modern economic life. By the time the Government of Beans came around, many of these same movements were demanding not that the state protect the crops that promoted their welfare but rather that the state protect them from crops that were killing them. For a small but growing population, soy was an invasive species in the full sense of the word, something foreign to the nation and an assault on its sovereignty and well-being.

The failure of the Government of Beans to respond adequately to campesinos' plight is symptomatic of the difficulty contemporary state apparatuses have in dealing with other characters of the Anthropocene. As Anna Tsing has pointed out, monocrops are emblematic landscapes of late capitalism, spaces of industrial killing that aim to simplify life into its most scalable, commodifiable forms.[38] They are also failures of imagination, products of a seeming paralysis in the way we think with nature—what Vandana Shiva has memorably called "monocultures of the mind."[39] I propose agribiopolitics in the same spirit—that is, as a way of opening up noncanonical agrarian histories that offer a different appreciation of the relations at play in global agriculture and of the perverse role of nation-states within those relations. Agencies like SENAVE are, after all, managers in a global system of mass killing of insects, weeds, fungi, and crop species that global capitalism deems suboptimal. This puts such agencies at the center of a much larger conversation about the relations among agriculture, settler colonialism, ecocide, and genocide.

## ETHNOGRAPHY IN THE ANTHROPOCENE

This book tells a story of how the dilemmas of the Anthropocene challenge governmental form; in the same way, they challenge the theoretical and narrative conventions of ethnography. One of the roles of theory for the social sciences is to provide a coherent language to describe complex phenomena and in so doing to transcend the phenomena themselves. But while I draw extensively from this analytic tradition, it was clear almost from the beginning of this project that such an analytic approach would itself be out of phase with the phenomenon I was researching. I might attempt to diagnose or evaluate governmental failure, but the exercise would be disingenuous. If anything, evaluation—the idea that building singular narratives of failure was the key to future success—seemed to miss the enormity of the problem at hand.

So while this book shares a lot of interpretive resources with political economy, science and technology studies, and Foucauldian genealogy, it does not attempt to resolve the well-known tensions between these approaches in a new synthesis.[40] The text is divided into three parts, each broadly addressing a different conceptual problem. In part I, I ask how soybeans became political. In part II, I explore why the Government of Beans backfired. And in part III, I take in a much longer history and ask how the Government of Beans is symptomatic of the Age of Monocrops. Each one deploys a distinct analytic language to tackle these questions. Furthermore, each section evokes a distinct ethnographic mood through which

Paraguayan activists and regulators lived. In the lead-up to Lugo's election, I dwell on the pervasive sense of agrarian injustice that characterized rural politics as soybeans became prominent actors. During the Government of Beans itself, I look at the day-to-day grind of trying to actualize the great promise of regulation that arose after the election. And after Lugo's fall, I capture something of the pessimism that engulfed the same people and political movements and brought back a sense of *longue durée* inevitability.

But even these three frames only partially strive for internal coherence, and the relations between individual chapters are purposefully disjointed. The book moves through a series of stuttering attempts to understand particular situations that are never entirely resolved. If one of the purposes of ethnography is to evoke the experience of its main characters, then part of what I want readers to feel is the way that bureaucrats and activists struggled to understand their own unstable condition. Each project undertaken remained slightly incomplete, each new urgency redefined the frame of what the Government of Beans was all about. Many projects were simply left unfinished, questions left unanswered as people were removed from their jobs, records were lost, or new crises engulfed the interpretive frame. To evoke this, each chapter tells a story or a parable using different characters. But the chapters are also deliberately short, ending before I am able to sew up the excessive loose ends. In that sense, then, the book is an attempt at writing the Anthropocene, experimenting with available languages, tools, scales, and tempos through a series of cascading situations.[41] Like its protagonists, it never presumes to have found a stable answer but simply tries to keep up with its objects.

It is not unusual in the social sciences today to encounter attempts to represent worlds as multiple and heterogeneous. But a brief comparison might help to illustrate how much more unsettled the world of the Government of Beans is—not just at an ontological level but also at a conceptual level—than most of these depictions. One of my models going into this project was Annemarie Mol's brilliant book, *The Body Multiple,* which argues not only that things are ontologically multiple but also that our attempts to understand them add to this multiplicity.[42] I often felt during the Government of Beans that this was the most hopeful version of what technocratic intervention might look like. As Mol shows, there are times when the multiplicity of technical objects *works*. In the case she studies, different medical specialists working in a Dutch hospital produce ontologically distinct versions of the disease atherosclerosis. And yet despite radical differences, clinicians and pathologists coordinate to produce a system that hangs together well enough to diagnose and treat patients reasonably effectively. My optimism that environmental governance might work in a similar way linked me to the regulators I studied, all of whom knew that the task—or tasks—ahead would be monumental but nonetheless believed that they were worth trying, in fragmentary but coordinated fashion, using whatever tools and training they had at hand.[43]

Yet when the Government of Beans ended in a massacre and a coup, it finally became clear why the analogy could not hold. The idea that one could hold multiplicity together analytically may work well in specific contexts such as a hospital in a wealthy country, where divergent knowledge practices are underwritten by an uncontroversial project to promote patient welfare. But in a field where the welfare of one population is constructed at the expense of another, where expertise around certain plants relies on the annihilation of others, and where all the actors are enmeshed in long-standing struggles to control not only resources but the offices charged with redistribution, the grounds for coordination are far more unsettled. One could of course point out that the Dutch hospital's notion of welfare is itself dependent on frontier violence occurring elsewhere and on a history of colonialism that extracts resources from places like Paraguay, shipping them along old colonial navigation routes to the port of Rotterdam. These questions are not absent from Dutch politics. In fact, in 2014, a Dutch think tank published a report worrying about Paraguay's growing resistance to monocrops when the Dutch economy depended on an estimated eight million tons of Paraguayan soybeans annually.[44] But those worries do not generally crash in on the hospital, and the work of treating diseases functions locally only because the violence that made it possible in the first place remains offstage.

In the Government of Beans, there was no offstage because every attempt to regulate agriculture connected beans, farmers, and regulators into intractable Anthropocenic conspiracies and made obvious how the devices of government were always at some level complicit in the destruction they sought to mitigate. Soy is not a multiply enacted object but a hyperobject that thrives in the violent morass of neocolonial extraction. This book demonstrates some ways in which governmental practice at times made soy seem knowable or controllable. It is astonishing, for instance, how much government infrastructure goes into assuring that one can reliably measure and report the moisture content of a given sample of soybeans. But for those wishing to measure the rise in cancer rates around soy fields, the effects on rural welfare of the ever-present smell of herbicides, or the link between farm size and unemployment, the infrastructure is far less reliable. These things are harder to know because they make it harder to separate the question of what objects are being measured from the question of who controls the instruments that define those objects and the history of who killed whom to get control of those instruments. These difficulties do not necessarily make the task of measurement or regulation impossible, nor do they doom all similar governmental experiments to failure. But they do make the Government of Beans a cautionary tale about a particular story of government promise and about how fraught the terrain of experimentation has become.

# PART I    A CAST OF CHARACTERS

According to his own self-aggrandizing autobiography, Pedro Nicolás Ciancio was the first person to plant soy in Paraguay in 1921.[1] Ciancio's parents were Italian immigrants who had arrived in the years following the devastating War of the Triple Alliance (1865–1870) to establish themselves as one of the elite families of national reconstruction. Ciancio traveled to Italy as a young adult and studied medicine and nutrition there, before returning to Paraguay on a mission to improve his country, still war-torn, impoverished, isolated, and rural. Using the liberal terminology of the day, Ciancio considered Paraguay to be "barbaric" and in need of civilization through economic, moral, and physical improvement.[2] He found the answer to all of these ailments in a little-known Asian legume that he brought from Brazil and began to cultivate in a rural plot next to his clinic.

A medical doctor and agronomist, Ciancio's thought epitomizes what I've come to think of as agribiopolitical. For him, the life of plants and the life of human bodies were intimately connected, and their relationship was central to the health and vitality of the nation-state. From the 1920s onward, he dedicated his life not only to the many agricultural, medical, and culinary experiments required to make his case, but also to publicizing both his diagnosis of Paraguay's social ills and the fabulous qualities of his preferred cure. In an op-ed, "The Bio-philosophy of War," Ciancio channeled Thomas Aquinas, arguing that violence in general, and Paraguay's two devastating wars in particular, were the result of hunger. In a speech to President Felix Estigarribia in 1939, he took his diagnosis even farther: "We are sick—at least in part—with a tendency for laziness and malevolent and harmful verbosity; thirsty for pleasures and drunk with vanity; luxury and alcoholism are booming; we squander everything; our religious faith is soft, and respect and courtesy are on the decline."[3] In response to all of this, he proposed soy, a plant that would banish slothfulness, jump-start the economy, improve the soil, and foster more liberal international trade. Soy's astonishing nutritional qualities would make Paraguayan bodies more robust, and its chemical versatility and market potential could spur Paraguay's long-awaited industrial revolution.

Thomas Jefferson is supposed to have said, "The greatest service which can be rendered any country is to add a useful plant to its culture; especially a bread grain."[4] Whether he knew the line or not, Ciancio clearly saw himself as a heroic figure in this cast, and made it his life's project to turn Paraguay into a "veritable soy granary" for the world.[5] Moreover, his proposed agrarian transition bore all the hallmarks of the Green Revolution that was about to overtake the region: the soy boom would be centered on government-supported campesino agriculture, in which poor families would plant small plots of soy by hand, consuming some of it themselves and selling the rest of it for industrial export. This would ensure the broadest distribution of nutritional and economic benefit, and turn Paraguay into a soy-based welfare state.

For his efforts, and in recognition of his tireless zeal, several of his colleagues dubbed him the Christopher Columbus of Soy. But his crusade was a complete failure during his lifetime. The president whom he lobbied so earnestly was only moved, apparently, by one of his proposals: to add soy meal to military rations as a cheap source of protein.[6] President Estigarribia, an agronomist himself before he became a marshal in Paraguay's war with Bolivia (1933–1936), approved the ration plan in 1940, anticipating the need to use plants to make Paraguayans more violent rather than more peaceful. Later that year, Estigarribia passed a new constitution giving the executive almost unlimited powers, then promptly died in a plane crash, giving rise to fifty years of dictatorships.

By the 1950s, Ciancio was in the final years of his life, a frustrated visionary, still telling anyone who would listen about what he called the "queen of the legumes." Even though his written work adheres to the blustery style of all of the big men of his generation, it's also heavy with melancholy:

In truth, since [I began planting soy] I have had to continue preaching with increased ardor and enormous patience, as I have encountered obstacles, indifference, incredulity, censure (that though hidden is no less bitter) and the most cruel and scornful mockery! . . . Poor soy! How many stones in your long path! They have pierced you with their thorns along the way. It doesn't matter. It was necessary to bleed from your wounds to attain the goal! . . . But neither the immense resistance, nor the solitude, have ever diminished the light of my faith in this crusade, or in the ideal of a richer and more cultured country that has fed my thoughts and labors.[7]

It's not surprising that between the accolades, he was also mocked as "Dr. Soy" by his contemporaries. In passages like this one, he seems uninterested in dissociating his own suffering from the suffering of the plant that he clearly loved. Whatever the reasons, Ciancio never got the audience he wanted with the early architects of Paraguay's Green Revolution, and after his death soy all but disappeared from the countryside for almost two decades.

So Ciancio is only a minor character in the cast of the story you're about to read. His vision remains only one of a number of possibilities that didn't quite play out, part of the detritus of an earlier agribiopolitics that few people ever picked up. As it turned out, soy didn't need a human champion to become Paraguay's most dominant plant, just a series of improbable events that had little to do with anyone's plans for welfare, nation building, or even nutrition. Soy found other characters to settle with, both human and nonhuman, as it migrated into Paraguay during moments of geopolitical crisis. And it developed a far more complicated agribiopolitical relationship with the state than Ciancio had envisioned. By the time Paraguay had become a "veritable soy granary for the world," the relationship between plant health and human health had become something that Ciancio would have found completely foreign, and likely tragic. But to understand how we got there, I need to tell you about a number of other characters, including plants, people, and governmental apparatuses, that did accompany the soy revolution, even if somewhat accidentally.

# CHAPTER ONE

# The Accidental Monocrop

One of the most curious historical characteristics of Paraguay's soy boom is how unplanned it was. Pedro Ciancio's lobbying on behalf of soy happened just as a massive international investment in crop improvement and production might have made his vision possible, but Paraguayan policy makers chose to direct those investments into completely different plants. This would turn out to have profound consequences for how soy would later be regulated, with whom it would become associated, and how it would affect rural Paraguayans when it expanded. So our story about soy begins without soy, when the US government and the Rockefeller Foundation first enrolled Paraguay in the great global agribiopolitical experiment known as the Green Revolution.

The story goes that in 1943, the US offered Paraguay a major agrarian development project called STICA in an attempt to woo the country away from its wartime Nazi sympathies.[1] The program had both geopolitical and humanitarian pretensions: by improving agriculture in countries like Paraguay, the Rockefeller Foundation believed that they could reduce hunger and create the basis for welfare among the poorer nations in the region, while the US government could also use the program as an incentive to create political alliances.[2] Over the course of the Green Revolution, the

US government would repeatedly intervene militarily in Latin America, in countries like Guatemala, Nicaragua, Chile, and El Salvador, when it was unable to impose its agendas there. But Paraguay proved to be far more pliant, especially after 1954, when General Alfredo Stroessner took power. Using the technical infrastructure provided by STICA and other development resources that became available in the 1960s, Stroessner and his allies in the ruling Colorado Party embarked on an ambitious rural welfare program that transformed the sparsely populated eastern frontier into an agro-export powerhouse.

During that period, Paraguayan development centered on two crops that recur throughout this book: cotton and wheat. Cotton was a populist crop, seen as appropriate for smallholders, and was combined with a colonization program that sent landless campesinos from central departments out into the forested eastern half of the country to create small farms there.[3] The plan was carried out by the new Institute for Rural Welfare (IBR), which formalized new smallholder colonies and worked to provide campesinos with the implements needed to plant and export cotton. Cotton thus served to cement Stroessner's regime, by extending a new bureaucracy throughout the countryside and enrolling thousands of campesinos as clients. Though it ultimately failed to deliver most of its promises, it did radically change the way campesinos lived in many of Paraguay's eastern departments, particularly San Pedro, Caazapá, and Caaguazú. Perhaps most importantly, it kept the promise itself alive that one day Paraguay's rural poor would be able to count on a state that provided for their welfare as citizens. In part as a result of this program, Stroessner remained in power for the next thirty-five years, consolidating a huge support base in the countryside and coming to be known as the US's most reliably anticommunist regime in the region.[4]

There will be much more to say about cotton and land reform later in the book. But first we need to look at the other crop the regime tried to develop, wheat, which followed a completely different political and territorial logic. Unlike cotton, wheat was seen as appropriate for the midsize farms of European immigrants living in their own colonies closer to the Brazilian and Argentine borders in the southeastern department of Itapúa. Agronomically, wheat was a bit of an odd choice for a country that everyone knew was too hot and humid for existing varieties. Moreover, almost the entire population sustained itself on cassava and corn. But wheat had a certain mystique that cassava could never have. It was a favorite plant of the Green Revolutionaries worldwide, and, perhaps most importantly, like the immigrant communities themselves, wheat fit the rather Teutonic aesthetic aspirations of the Paraguayan elite.

When pressed, more than one of the old agronomists from the wheat program told me that General Stroessner himself had chosen wheat to be the poster plant of Paraguayan agriculture. He had been born to Bavarian immigrants in 1912 in the southeastern city of Encarnación during a substantial wave of immigration from Germany, Ukraine, Poland, and Italy. During his vacations, they said, Stroessner used to return home to fish along the Paraná River, and dream of seeing the area transformed into fields of golden grain. And so, to please the dictator and to participate in the global excitement around the new agrarian miracles, the scientific leaders of Paraguay's Green Revolution set as their highest aspiration to become a nation self-sufficient in wheat.[5]

A great deal of Paraguay's agrarian infrastructure was built with mechanized, midsized wheat farmers in mind.[6] The STICA program sent aspiring Paraguayan scientists to the US and Central America, training world-class experts in crop improvement to run Paraguay's new crop research facilities. The ministry built its flagship agricultural research station at Capitán Miranda, right in the heart of wheat country, and set about making varieties of wheat that behaved in Paraguay as wheat behaved in Germany. Paraguay was visited by wheat specialists from all over the world, and most Paraguayan scientists claimed to have trained at one point or another with Norman Borlaug, the father of the Green Revolution, whose invention of high-yield wheat had won him the Nobel Peace Prize.[7]

On its own limited terms, the program was a success: Paraguay began exporting wheat in 1986 after surpassing self-sufficiency. Wheat's biggest impact on Paraguay, however, was as a gateway crop to soybeans. Wheat is a winter crop that requires a lot of nitrogen, and soy is an ideal companion to plant in the summer. Cheap to plant and easy to grow, soy makes inert nitrogen available to other plants through a process called fixing, carried out by bacteria in root nodules. By planting soy in summer, wheat farmers took care of most of their fertility needs, and the beans were sold at a modest price across the border in Brazil, which had a growing internal market for soya oil. By the late 1960s, this rotation was already well established among European wheat cooperatives around Encarnación, even though the market for soy itself was still relatively marginal.

And then a series of events happened in the Northern Hemisphere that would transform the soy industry throughout South America. Since the end of World War II, the United States had dominated the global soybean market.

It had begun to plant soy at large scales to produce army rations, and soon after the war the crop was converted into livestock feed, facilitating a sudden intensification in poultry and pork production. But US dominance would change in the course of a single season in 1972.[8] Following a catastrophic crop failure in the Soviet Union, the US government approved the sale of 24.2 million tons of grain to their Cold War rivals, much of it on credit. The Soviet Grain Deal, as it is known, had enormous repercussions for global agricultural trade, creating market shortages across the rest of the world, and leading to an average increase in global food prices of almost 50 percent.[9] The worst-hit of these commodities was soybeans, which quadrupled in price over the next ten months. Facing the possible collapse of the US meat industry, in 1973 the US temporarily embargoed all soybean exports. The adjustment had the desired effect in the short term, bringing domestic soy prices back down. But it immediately created a shift in global markets, particularly Japan, which began a concerted effort to find a new, more stable supplier for soy. The Japanese found that potential in Brazil, which already produced soy at a modest scale. Brazil's military government seized the opportunity and began a bilateral agreement with Japan to convert the *cerrado* lowlands into fields of soybeans. In a few years, Brazil became the world's largest exporter of soy meal, and transformed its own national diet by flooding it with cheap soya oil, the by-product of meal production.[10]

Paraguay's first soy boom began, therefore, as a peripheral effect of the US embargo and the arrival of Japanese development money in Brazil. Only a few years after the wheat program had really established itself, wheat farmers found that their summer cover crop was much more valuable than their main crop, and a lot easier to grow. International soy prices, which in 1970 had been around $1 a bushel on international markets, had by 1975 settled at around $7 a bushel, and the growing investment in soy planting and processing in Brazil had created an almost insatiable market only a few kilometers away. The relationship between soy and wheat had reversed. Wheat, destined for the domestic market, acted as a winter cover crop for the real cash cow: soy destined for export.[11]

By the late 1970s, Paraguay's economy was booming, registering over 12 percent growth in some years.[12] Soy was not the only reason for this. Cotton was still more significant, as was the construction, with Brazilian financing, of the massive Itaipú hydroelectric dam. But soy alone, which had barely registered as a national product in 1970, accounted for almost 10 percent of the country's exports by 1980.[13] By the turn of the twenty-first century, with the dam finished and cotton prices in decline, soy took an increasingly prominent role in the national economy. Over the next five decades, as the US exported its feedlot model around the world, and as biochemists found increasingly exotic uses for soybean oil, demand for Paraguayan soy continued to expand.

## THE MIGRANT COMPANION

So soy was present in Paraguay as a companion for wheat when global realignments in the 1970s created a market opportunity for anyone willing to risk everything on this curious new crop. But our story is still missing soy's primary human companion, and the peculiar ethnic imaginary that the plant would soon begin to foster. As I've said, the first communities to plant soy in Paraguay at any scale were the European immigrant colonies clustered in Itapúa along the Argentine border. Settled over the first half of the twentieth century, these communities industrialized a range of agricultural products for export along with wheat, including cotton, corn, cassava, sugar, tung oil, and *yerba mate*.[14]

European colonies in wheat country were part of a wider dynamic of immigration in South America, as governments pursued a strategy of agricultural modernization that involved attracting European migrants and displacing their own native populations.[15] In Itapúa, they were largely isolated from national politics, which remained, until the rise of Stroessner, a game played mostly by elite families in and around Asunción. Their isolation from state infrastructure led them to build their own collective enterprises, German-style farm cooperatives that supported diverse forms of production and socialized financial investment and risk. Eventually many of these consolidated into a massive single cooperative known as simply Colonias Unidas, which became the most significant economic actor in the area.[16]

But these were not the immigrants who would make soy boom. Colonias Unidas was highly successful, but its risk aversion kept farms diversified. The same was true of the Japanese colonies that settled just west of Colonias Unidas after World War II, and the Mennonite colonies to the northwest.[17] The rapid conversion of the landscape into soy required a different sort of farmer, one that was a little less set in their ways, and it happened that just such farmers were moving into the department north of Itapúa, Alto Paraná, at exactly that moment.

In the late 1960s, just before soy prices skyrocketed, Stroessner's government had begun to pursue new diplomatic relations with Brazil, including opening up the eastern border region to Brazilian settlers.[18] Paraguay made large stretches of forested land there available to colonization companies that recruited poor farmers from southern Brazil and offered them cheap land on the Paraguayan side of the border. Many of these newcomers had not been in Brazil for more than two generations, and most had German names, part of an earlier colonization effort in Brazil that had by then reached saturation.[19] Poor, insular, and distrusted by Paraguayans and Brazilians alike, these migrants came to be called Brasiguaios, and for decades would live in a gray zone between the two countries.[20] It was these marginalized migrants who first gambled on soy in a serious way. Some were desperate, having lost land in Brazil, and were looking for any new place to rebuild, while others were attracted by a speculative frontier in a land renowned for its cheapness and fertility. Or perhaps, as many of these people say themselves, it was the gaucho culture of southern Brazil, a culture of individual tenacity, tolerance of risk, and extremely hard work, that made them so successful.[21]

However we want to understand the relationship between Brasiguaios and soybeans, their companionship flags a key agribiopolitical characteristic of twentieth-century Paraguay: specific crops are always linked to specific languages, nationalities, and ethnic identities. I therefore use the word "companion" here not merely to signal a more-than-human relationship in agricultural stories but also to point out the way crops become implicated in histories of ethnic conflict. Much is riding on these seemingly casual associations of Europeans with wheat, Paraguayan campesinos with cotton, and especially Brasiguaios with soybeans, all the more when nationalist projects of rural welfare are in the air. It will take some time to tease out all of these implications, but they are never far from the frame.

For now, suffice it to say, it was from these once-isolated Brasiguaio towns that soy erupted, not as a rotation crop among others, but as a full-blown monocrop. Stories of rapid enrichment drove immigration faster. According to the national census, in 1981 there were already 300,000 Brazilians living in the three departments bordering Brazil. A decade later the number stabilized at around 410,000 people, many of those now naturalized or descended from the early pioneers.[22] They emulated the cooperative financial model of Colonias Unidas, but this time with soy monocrops in mind. By the end of the 1990s they had mechanized soy production throughout Alto Paraná, the northern parts of Itapúa and the eastern half of Canindeyú, and they were busy building larger and larger farms with more impressive machinery every year. In short order, soybeans, with

Brasiguaios as their companions, had become a demographic, economic, and environmental force.

## THE INDUSTRIAL MONOCROP

Brasiguaio pioneers did not have it easy. Coming from poverty in Brazil, and into a country where they often encountered suspicion and hostility, all of the accounts I heard from Brasiguaios about this period were stories of great hardship, hard work, and xenophobia.[23] But to me the most striking pioneer trope that emerged repeatedly was of struggle to convert the forests into soy fields. One person with whom I spoke at length was Ronaldo, a farmer who arrived as a kid in 1971 just before the first soy boom began. Forty-five years later, still speaking in a thick Portuguese accent, he tried to impress on me how difficult life had been for his father after moving the whole family from Brazil. There they had lived in extreme poverty, with a small plot of land on rolling hills that wasn't much good for anything but ranching. But when they got to Paraguay, they were totally isolated. He told me, "Everybody suffered when we were here. There was nothing. Have you seen how big the trees used to be around here? We cut those by hand. It could take days for one tree. We built our house by hand. And when we started planting soy, it was with machetes and hoes. Everybody suffered, and many people went home."

In this motif, which I heard repeated by many men of Ronaldo's generation, relief from suffering was linked to deforestation. The huge trunks he referred to, by way of contrasting his relative wealth today, are almost nowhere to be found in the border region. Over the 1980s and 1990s, as soy expanded, forests were removed at a faster rate than almost anywhere in the world.[24] When in 2004 the government passed a draconian measure called simply the Zero Deforestation Law, there wasn't much left to protect.

While there was certainly no hint of nostalgia for the trees in Ronaldo's story, deforestation was the first step in an agronomic transformation that would soon bring serious problems for farmers. By the mid-1980s, the loss of forest cover turned many fields to rivers during Paraguay's impressive summer rains, leading to rapid erosion of topsoil. Soy farmers solved this by adopting novel no-till farming techniques: instead of plowing the land after a harvest, exposing the soil to erosion, farmers would spray the entire field with Roundup, a broad-spectrum herbicide that killed everything in the fields. Once dead stalks were bent over, soy could be planted directly between the stalks, which continued to hold the soil in place. Because it dramatically reduced erosion, no-till technique was considered a major advancement in agricultural conservation.[25] But it also required mechanization and vastly increased reliance on herbicide, and because it increased input costs, it also favored larger, more intensive farms.[26]

As the soy monocrop expanded, it inevitably began to require new forms of care and protection. Monocrops, for all of their impressiveness, are fragile things.[27] The effort required to simplify the landscape, to create giant populations of genetically identical plants, inevitably attracts intruders that prey on those varieties or thrive in their midst, and the larger the scale of the problem of plant health becomes, the more farmers need large-scale phytosanitary interventions, primarily the use of chemical pesticides. Killing off biological intruders in soy fields then creates its own problems. By the early 1990s, Paraguayan soy fields were full of herbicide-resistant weeds (especially *lecherita*, a particularly hardy milkweed), and a new range of caterpillars and beetles (*chinches*), which required frequent doses of cypermethrin. In the late 1990s, soybean rust, an aggressive and highly mutagenic fungus whose spores clouded the region during the hot months, demanded fungicides. By then, most soy farmers were dousing their fields regularly in cocktails of agrochemicals, including several herbicides and insecticides and up to five different fungicides. During this period, pesticide use in Paraguay was largely unregulated, and irregular customs reporting makes it almost impossible to know how much of these chemicals was being used.[28] But it's clear that in addition to the expansion of the crop, the use of chemical pesticides skyrocketed.

Then, in 1999, the whole production package shifted again, with the biggest invention since no-till agriculture: genetic modification (GM).[29] Roundup Ready soybeans, the first commercially available GM seed in the world, were an ingenious technology of intensification. Roundup Ready is so named because the plant is impervious to Roundup herbicide, which otherwise kills almost all plants in any given field. Farmers could thus dispatch most weeds by spraying Roundup, even while soy was growing. This in turn made it easier to mechanize fields, and decreased farmers' labor costs. Genetic modification set up Paraguayan soy, and the communities that planted it, for a second boom.

Once again, there will be much more to say about the way that soybean communities, and other crops, expanded over territory, first killing off other organisms that got in their way and then systematically killing the new beings that appeared in their midst. For now, though, it is this moment that

I am most interested in dwelling on, the moment Roundup Ready soy seemed to have resolved the main impediments to soybean expansion, and produced a new hunger for land among Brasiguaio settlers and their descendants. By then, though, there was very little forest left for soy to expand into, and it began, instead, to come up against the colonies of Paraguayan campesinos whose agricultural lives looked completely different, and rather more vulnerable, than the mechanized wave of the soy frontier. That is where soy would confront an entirely new set of characters, whose increasingly organized objection to the soy boom would eventually give rise to the Government of Beans.

# CHAPTER TWO

# Killer Soy

A t 7 a.m. on January 2, 2003, Petrona Villasboa de Talavera sent her eleven-year-old son Silvino out with his cousin to the local corner store. It was already very hot and a key point in the day when both domestic and agrarian work was being carried out in anticipation of the midday heat. So as Silvino was riding his bike home along the dirt road, his neighbor, Hermann Schlender, was out spraying his soybeans. Schlender happened to drive too close to the road just as Silvino was passing the field, and one of the wings on his sprayer passed over Silvino's head, dousing him in a mix of herbicide and insecticide. Later that night, the whole family fell ill with debilitating stomach cramps, vomiting, and diarrhea. Everyone recovered after a few days, except Silvino, who experienced severe distress after another neighbor sprayed his crops in a field that came within seven meters of the Talavera house. He was finally brought to a local health post on the seventh, where the doctor diagnosed him as having been poisoned with organophosphates, a potent insecticide. He was dangerously dehydrated, but the health post had no saline solution with which to treat him, so he was transferred to another health center and finally to a regional hospital, where he died that afternoon.[1]

All of this happened in the small campesino colony of Pirapey, which lies on Highway 6 just north of Colonias Unidas, and just south of the area where soy was expanding most aggressively. Silvino's family had been one of the first to arrive in the area in the 1970s as part of the agrarian reform. Like most of the rest of the population that called itself campesino, they spoke Guarani at home but did not consider themselves indigenous. Instead, they were mestizo, quintessential national figures, part Spanish, part indigenous, and wholly modern. The agrarian reform had provided an opportunity to move to Pirapey as pioneers, to claim fertile land and build cotton colonies as part of a national development promise. Yet unlike the majority of such colonies, Pirapey was close to the Brazilian border, so campesinos there had witnessed the growth of the soy industry around them. And they were the first to realize that, even as the cotton boom faded and agrarian promises moved to soybeans, they would be completely excluded from this new crop. The need for capital to invest in machinery, and the control of the burgeoning industry by Brasiguaios, made it impossible for them to participate in the new agricultural revolution happening all around them.

By 2003, campesino activists in various parts of the country told me that pesticide poisoning was an increasingly common occurrence as soy expanded into areas populated by the rural poor.[2] But the frequency of these problems (along with forced evictions, water contamination, and the increasingly unpleasant odors on the wind) was not enough to amplify the complaints about soy beyond the political circuits of campesinos and their supporters. This is what made Silvino's death vital to the story of soy's rise: it was the first time that conditions lined up just right to send a case to criminal court, and from there to amplify it into a major political disruption.

The unprecedented nature of the case can be read between the lines of the prosecutor's filings, who for months tried to find a legal category to fit the crime he believed had occurred. On March 24 of that year, he charged Schlender and his neighbor with "producing common risks," a form of criminal negligence, in the boy's death. Under pressure from environmentalists, the prosecutor soon added the charge of "mistreating the soil," though he never provided evidence to back up this charge. Only two months later, he added culpable homicide.

The increasing seriousness of the charges speak to the way that the Silvino case became a flashpoint, first for rural activists and urban leftist professionals, and soon for international environmentalists and human rights lawyers. Within a few months, the controversy surrounding Silvino's death had moved beyond the courtroom, and it would haunt the struggle over soy and the rise of the Government of Beans for at least the next decade. Silvino's name and picture were tied to the emergent slogan for rural activists, "la soja mata." And as much as soy farmers tried to dismiss it, when the slogan began to appear on sidewalks and walls in Asunción, it became clear that soy had become entangled in a whole new set of agribiopolitical associations. By the end of the trial, Silvino, soy, and the state's role in protecting the welfare of the rural poor from pesticides had become matters of national concern.[3]

## FROM NATURE TO EVENT

Until Silvino's death, campesino activists had always had trouble articulating their critique of soy. Despite the comparatively rapid advance of the frontier, soy's violence was generally slow, in the sense meant by Rob Nixon: it moved through a series of "calamities that patiently dispense their devastation while remaining outside of . . . flickering attention spans."[4] For those living near the fields, the frontier had its moments of more obvious destruction: the bulldozers and fires used to remove the forests and the remnants of old farmsteads, the forced evictions of recalcitrant squatters, and the occasional assassination of a community organizer. But then it would quickly settle back down into the apparently lazy rhythm of the crop, the movement of the sprayer trundling around behind a tractor, with its precarious-looking wings that won it the nickname "mosquito." Even among most campesinos, the original impulse was not to complain too loudly. At that time, the most common criticism I heard was about the smell of pesticides wafting into people's homes, from the ubiquitous saccharine smell of Roundup to the rotting-flesh smell of 2,4-D. Since most had come to these places as pioneers themselves, or were only a generation removed from settlement, they were used to the smell of fire, of gasoline, and of some potent pesticides they themselves used on their cotton. All of these had for a long time been taken as signs of progress. And for a population that had endured poverty, military repression, and the arbitrary violence of local strongmen, it was hard to get anyone to complain publicly about smells or the other small, incremental changes that soy brought with it.

This is not an unusual situation, of course. Most environmental injustices occur in impoverished communities, where they combine with other problems, and few of them motivate collective political action.[5] Campesino colonies, even when they were the vanguard of national development, were always zones of poverty and precarity, replete with a host of endemic problems, such as poor health and diet, labor insecurity, poor education, crumbling infrastructure, and high rates of infection, injury, violence, and infant mortality. None of these rose, as Beth Povinelli puts it, to the level of events, because they were the cumulative effects of abandonment.[6] The unpleasant smell of pesticides, the disappearance of local forests and animals, the dry wind, and, increasingly, the rashes, headaches, and nausea, just added themselves to the general, cumulative effects of poverty. Each rash, each day spent inside hiding from the smell of 2,4-D, was merely a quasi-event, part of a list of nuisances that confounded response.[7]

So what made Silvino's death so different? As the prosecutor soon found out, even the death of a young boy is difficult to render as an event. The prosecution's legal strategy was to narrate the event as a specific incident of negligence leading to his death, a clear dramatic scene with only a handful of actors, in which responsibility could be easily apportioned. The defense's strategy was to disqualify the scene's eventfulness by complicating it to the point that it receded into a background jumble of relations which could not be parsed.

The name for this jumble of relations was very specific: Silvino had not died from Schlender's negligence but rather from unspecified natural causes, probably malnutrition or food poisoning.[8] In some ways, then, the trial recapitulated what Bruno Latour has called the "modern constitution," the ontological premise that human and natural causes belong to different realms.[9] The natural cause takes a death from the realm of injustice and returns it to the realm of the legally uneventful.

And yet the natural causes being evoked here move us beyond the modern constitution, because from another perspective they are in fact diseases of poverty. As proof of the likelihood of malnutrition or food poisoning, the defense described Silvino's rustic living conditions, particularly what it claimed was the inadequate sanitation in Silvino's mother's rudimentary kitchen. It was impossible to attribute criminal responsibility to Schlender because nothing had actually happened that could be separated from the background conditions of the scene itself. Yet even in the neutral phrasing of the "natural cause," the defense knew that it was playing a sleight of hand, tacitly blaming Silvino's mother and the condition of poverty that she represented.

In his remarkable ruling for the prosecution, the judge in the initial trial also evoked poverty as a key part of the situation but shifted the relationship between the natural cause and human responsibility. "We are not talking about a 'normal' person, who is healthy and well-nourished, whose defenses to agrochemicals would be different in such circumstances," he wrote.[10] For him, Silvino's poverty was a background condition that added to the responsibility of those spraying dangerous substances. What the defense called a natural cause, the judge turned into the context for Schlender's negligence, which ultimately became the event causing Silvino's death. On both sides, therefore, the case revolved around the contrast between two temporal modes: nature, a stable state in which the particulars are inseparable from background conditions; and event, one in which the particulars produce their own interpretive context, a necessity for distributing responsibility.

The defense knew that its strategy was sound and on appeal continued to disqualify Silvino's victimhood based on his poverty. When the case reached its second appeal, in 2005, the defense attacked the physical evidence that had been presented by the prosecution. In lurid detail, backed up by the explanations of eleven biochemists, the defense went after both the clinical assessment of local doctors and the various substances extracted from Silvino's corpse and from surviving family members. None of the original lab reports could be trusted, they argued, because the materials had been mishandled from the outset. A full necropsy hadn't been performed on Silvino's body because the family didn't have the resources to do so right away, and, per Paraguayan custom, he had been buried within twenty-four hours of his death. Tissue samples were only taken, therefore, after the body had been in the ground for a week. The local doctor had written in his report that he suspected Silvino had been poisoned with organophosphates, but none of these were found on Schlender's farm. The defense went on to mock the doctor's incompetence:

> We need to signal some points that make us suspect the professional ability of this witness: (a) as the first professional to attend to Silvino Talavera, the doctor in question was in charge of him for several hours, during which the patient was totally dehydrated. But he was completely incapable of giving him even basic saline, something that even a beginner in first aid would know. (b) Even though he claimed that this was a poisoning, he didn't perform a basic gastric lavage, for which all he would have needed was water and soap. (c) When he was designated to carry out the autopsy and take samples, *he added saline to the containers*, for which he was later deemed *negligent*, since it caused the samples to be lost.[11]

In other words, if Silvino's death itself couldn't easily be attributed to his poverty, then at least all of the evidence of poisoning could be disqualified based on the poverty of the clinics in which it was gathered, their unstable access to saline, and their lack of forensic training. They even suggested the new possibility that Silvino had died because of medicine administered by the doctor after the improper diagnosis and proposed corroborating this through a third exhumation and autopsy.

The family came in for even less subtle disqualification, as trace amounts of chemicals in their blood were attributed to the family's lack of personal hygiene, their inability to wash their clothes daily, and their inadequate storage of household insecticides. Silvino's body and the household he lived in were too poor to offer a reliable account of events, and so too was the town's minimal public health infrastructure. Even the judges who initially found for the prosecution would later be accused of being parochial and corrupt. The true stakes of the "natural cause" argument now become sharper. In the first instance, nature, including poverty, was a state of uneventfulness. Having lost this argument, the defense returned again, arguing that poverty made everyone and everything around Silvino's body incapable of bearing witness to that event. They were disqualified for living in conditions in which expertise, or even reliable subjectivity, was impossible. Not only did poverty and ignorance kill Silvino, poverty and ignorance also made the network around Silvino incapable of speaking on his behalf.

This episode tells us a lot about why criminal courts, on their own terms, are not very good at dealing with economic inequality or environmental injustice. The distinction between the natural and the eventful is not just a matter of perception, it's a partition of time that's held in place by the courts themselves. The poverty of a victim is a perfect alibi, because it not only distributes causes across a range of sites, it also undermines the validity of the knowledge of those affected.[12] The silencing of the families of victims could be compounded in less subtle ways as well: Silvino's uncle Serapio, a local organizer in his own right, was stabbed to death three days before the trial.[13] And yet sometimes conditions line up just right and certain people are able to find new forms of articulation that cause a more fundamental rupture in the distribution of justice. The Silvino Talavera case, and the double disqualification of campesino suffering on the soy frontier, would eventually lay the groundwork for the radical proposal of Fernando Lugo's government: not only that rural welfare and environment needed to be regulated together, but that those who most needed that regulation could be a political force in their own right.

Silvino's death was an event, then, to the extent that it fundamentally disrupted the state of affairs that had to that point been thought of as natural.[14] But events are also made, since no specific situation is eventful until it has been rendered part of a sequence, narrated in such a way that it comes to explain a difference between a before and an after.[15] Events are a cuts in time, occasions for new forms of relating that simultaneously produce a rupture in other forms of relating. In so doing, they produce a temporal distinction between a past and a future, and a specificity that allows them to be reiterated. Or, as Isabelle Stengers puts it, an "event . . . brings the future that will inherit from it into communication with a past narrated differently."[16] For that reason, eventfulness itself is always a site of struggle.

A brief discussion of a technical aspect of Roundup Ready soybeans helps to make this clear. The biotech industry that created them is built around the ability to patent living organisms that they have engineered. More precisely, though, biotech patents genetic "events," the name for any identifiable gene mutation that reiterates itself through an organism's reproduction. Thus, Roundup Ready soybeans bear the genetic echo of a temporal rupture in the soybeans' genealogy, produced and patented by Monsanto engineers. Such events could of course be narrated in a lot of ways, and the relations that figure in the story could be made more or less complex to take in the full scope of circumstances and actors involved in making possible the corporation, the laboratory, and science itself. But the genetic engineering patent is a result of a second displacement, a cutting down of relations to narrate it coherently.[17] That cutting is far from neutral, elevating certain actions and actors and disqualifying others in a way that not only obscures history but controls the way that future resources will be distributed. The people cleaning the lab in off hours may be fundamental to the production of a patentable genetic event, but because they are left out of the story told by the patent, they have no claim on its future iterations.

But genetic modification was eventful beyond the strictly genetic sense. When these new food crops first appeared in the 1990s, they also produced knowledge controversies around the world, with environmentalists arguing that genetic modification posed risks to human health, to crop biodiversity, to independent farms, and even to ecosystems broadly. In a series of cases brought before the Environmental Protection Agency in the United States, crop scientists argued that genetic modification did not substantially change the nature of the organisms in question and therefore should not be subjected to further regulatory restrictions. Essentially, they argued that genetic modification may have produced a genetic event sufficient for the recognition of property rights, and thereby the emergence of new forms of capital, but not an environmental nor public health event, which would entail further regulation.[18]

The same argument played out differently in different jurisdictions. For instance, in Europe, where the relationship between human health, agriculture, and the environment has historically engendered more bureaucratic intervention, activism around genetically modified organisms (GMOs) created far more disruption and resulted in comparatively restrictive regulation.[19] As Stengers puts it, the struggle over GMOs was paradigmatically eventful, not just because it produced various regulatory changes within the EU, but because it "made both scientific experts and . . . politicians think, as if a world of problems that they had never posed was becoming visible to them."[20]

The Silvino Talavera case was caught up in this moment of global dispute over genetic modification, and it too concerned whether new forms of agriculture should be considered eventful, and therefore regulatable, or not. The actual verdict in the case, after two rounds of appeals, was ambiguous. The judge dismissed the charges of homicide and mistreating the soil, but sentenced Schlender to two years in jail on the charge of criminal negligence causing death. He then immediately suspended the sentence, allowing Schlender to return home. For Schlender's allies, this was a sign that the judge knew them to be right, but that he had bowed to public pressure and issued a symbolic guilty verdict. For Silvino's family, and the now massive network of lawyers, activists, and supporters gathered around them, the suspended sentence compounded the injustice. But injustice or not, they had accomplished what in retrospect was a far more impressive goal: they had created an event, a disruption in the standard way of thinking agribiopolitics, that would continue to reiterate, sometimes in the form of haunting, the conversation about soy from then on.

## THE EMERGENCE OF KILLER SOY

How had this happened? If, as campesinos contended, soy had killed before this, then part of what made Silvino's death eventful was the moment in which it happened, and the place. The town Silvino was born in was an agrarian reform colony, as I've said, but it was also a specific one, created in 1976 by Stroessner's military regime as a way to dismantle the leadership of a Christian base movement called the Ligas Agrarias.[21] After killing, jailing, and exiling many of the movement's top ranks, Stroessner had used the land reform to relocate people from the strongest areas of resistance. And while it worked in the short term, many of these communities still had important ties to radical land rights organizations. Petrona Villasboa, Silvino's mother, was a member of one such organization, called CONAMURI, which mobilized to support her when Silvino fell ill the second time.[22] Other political relations were available for the response as well. The truck that brought Silvino to the health clinic belonged to an alternative agroforestry school called CECTEC, whose head, Andrés Wehrle, had taken refuge in Itapúa in the 1980s after Stroessner branded him a communist. All of these people were well versed in political organizing against a dictatorship that also operated through slow violence and only occasionally produced an actual corpse. They knew how to spot an opportunity and to move people accordingly.

Silvino's death did not, in other words, become eventful on its own. Rather, eventfulness was the result of the careful recruitment of allies and materials that together suggested a new language through which to understand soy. Villasboa and Wehrle first called on the environment secretary of their district, a relatively new position in municipal administration, and that person, inspired by a sense of sudden importance, spent the following two days with the local doctor, ensuring that blood and urine samples were taken from all the family members. By the following week, a district attorney was searching the homes of Silvino's two neighbors to collect pesticide samples and exhumed the body for further tissue samples. Pieces of evidence began to accumulate. Blood samples showed that the family had been exposed to some sort of cholinesterase inhibitors and found traces of Roundup and a solvent called phenol. All of this was collected as evidence for the case, and though most of them would later be discounted in court, they had already begun to work outside of the court, amplified by a growing network of supporters that soon included other campesino organizations, lawyers in Asunción, and even activists from Argentina and Holland.[23] The cumulative effect of all of these details was the emergence of a whole new language that would allow the event of Silvino's death to echo through subsequent encounters between activists and soy.[24] It was the Talavera case that made everyone in Paraguay know the meaning of "Roundup," its generic name *glifosato*, and other chemicals that had not previously existed to them: cypermethrin, organophosphorus, phenol.

Even more impressive was the way that new names for agricultural objects and activities began to mark growing antagonism around soy. This linguistic shift was one of the first things I had to learn as I moved out of activist circles at the beginning of this project. If among activists I was used to hearing about the dilemmas around *agrotóxicos* (agrotoxins), I learned that among soy farmers, the term was *agroquímicos* (agrochemicals). The same went for the word *transgénico* (transgenic), which replaced the more neutral *biotecnología* (biotechnology). Perhaps the most striking of these was the word *sojero* (soy farmer), which the industry insisted was a misnomer; instead, they called themselves *productores* (producers). Industry spokespeople were irritated by the term "sojero" because it distilled a massive, complex industry that included wheat, corn, canola, rice, and meat, down to a single, controversial crop. Soja itself had taken on new meanings, and suddenly appeared, even in the urban imagination, as chemically intensive fields surrounding tiny, permeable shacks full of children. Whether one agreed with it or not, most Paraguayans would soon begin to understand what was meant by "la soja mata"—soy kills.

The irruption of this new language had a dramatic and lasting effect on soy farmers. Fourteen years after Silvino's death and many years after I stopped hearing about Silvino in activist circles, I still found soy farmers talking about it in the eastern border region. I never brought up the case during interviews, but it sufficed for me to ask about why soy was controversial, why people were so opposed to genetic modification, or why government regulations had become more stringent over the years. "Well," many would say, "there was this case of a young boy . . ." These farmers believed that they were the victims in the case, which had pitted new social movements against them, created the regulatory landscape they were still fighting, and even helped elect a president they despised. Silvino had died of "natural causes," they told me (usually with awkward caveats like "that doesn't mean it wasn't a tragedy"), and belief to the contrary was a sign of both Paraguayan ignorance and suspicious political leanings. I have no doubt that most of them were sincere in this. But what was most striking to me was how little the language had changed, how so many people were still trying to relitigate the case or exorcise Silvio's ghost, trying to reconstitute a natural state of affairs they felt they had lost.

Perhaps the most telling version of the Talavera story is the one given to me by Paolo, a soy farmer to whom I often turned for his incisive analysis of national debates. After recounting Silvino's story to me, he said, "I want to be perfectly clear. The death of any child is a tragedy. There's no one who will deny that, and I don't mean to take anything away from the family." Then he paused and offered the following carnivalesque rebuttal:

I have an idea that would put this to rest once and for all. . . . I would set up a sprayer, full of Roundup and cypermethrin, right in the middle of the Plaza Uruguaya [in Asunción]. I'd get a public medical examination, showing exactly what was in my blood and my urine, and anything else you'd want to know. And I would come riding in on a pink Cadillac, two girls in bikinis at my side. I'd drive right under the nozzle of the sprayer, take off my shirt and let them spray me for a full ten seconds, to get me good and wet, much more than any boy who accidentally passes under a nozzle. And a week later, we'd get a full battery of medical tests on my body and show that nothing remained, that I was in perfect health.[25]

The Cadillac in the Plaza Uruguaya is a rich image for anyone familiar with Paraguayan politics. The plaza is a park in downtown Asunción, across from the train station, and historically used as place for rural protesters to gather, and often camp, before they set out on marches to make demands on the state. Driving a pink Cadillac into the center of that square would clearly be read as class mockery. But it's the form of this story that matters most. Paolo was convinced that the science would bear him out, convinced, as so many soy farmers were, that one could drink Roundup without suffering any ill effects. But the science in itself was not good enough. It would have to be made eventful, a spectacle. Silvino's death had caused a disruption that could not be mended—it could only be disrupted again with another event.

Meanwhile, for activists, the disruption was only the beginning. Silvino's death had brought killer soy into view, a moment of agribiopolitical clarity that outlined a whole new set of material relations that required response. But if the criminal trial helped to produce this disruption, it was far from an ideal venue to discuss the role of soy in rural hardship. After all, even though soy was everywhere present in the case, the court could not attribute responsibility to beans, only to specific people, and the harms it could investigate were similarly restricted to a single death. If soy had previously been diffuse enough to qualify as nature, like poverty, when it emerged it was not as some fully formed actor ready to be known. Instead, the soy of "la soja mata" always stood for an excessive assemblage without clear limits, not to an object, but a hyperobject implicated in a great variety of harms and causes.[26] Responding to it meant moving beyond the courtroom, with its restrictive ontological scripts, and into the realm of legislation. More specifically, it would mean figuring out the relationship between soybeans and that other hyperobject with which they had been struggling for generations: the nation-state.

# CHAPTER THREE

# The Absent State

S oy, once it emerged into public view during the Silvino Talavera trial, could be many things to many people, but one of the constants was its fraught relationship with the Paraguayan state. Among campesino organizations, two conceptions of soy helped drive this home: in the first, soy fields were described as a "desert," and in the second, rural problems in general were blamed on an "absent state." The desert was not just devoid of life; it was somehow outside of legitimate political community.[1] When campesinos said that the state was "absent," however, they had a very specific conception of the state in mind, one whose primary function was to protect their well-being and promote rural welfare through land reform and the support of smallholder agriculture. That conception of the state was part of an agribiopolitical promise that had animated campesino life for decades, and to the extent that it remained unfulfilled, Paraguayans liked to say that the state had not yet arrived in the countryside. The idiom of the promise of welfare, as in so many parts of the world, had been nationalist, a sense that the state was responsible for protecting a population vaguely defined not just by citizenship but by a set of ethnic and cultural traits that properly belonged within Paraguay's borders.

But nationalist campesinos were not the only ones to see a basic antagonism between soy and the nation-state. Sojeros also believed that soy thrived on less regulation, less political intervention, and, often, fewer Paraguayans. Of course, when sojeros disdained the state, it was not as a long-promised ideal entity protecting citizens, but rather what they saw as an actually existing assemblage of corrupt and inefficient bureaucrats with an unpredictable allegiance to Paraguayan national culture. The reasons these two constituencies saw soy and the state as incompatible did not completely map onto each other, nor were either of them fully coherent. But the general sense that soy and the Paraguayan state were natural antagonists animated politics on both sides, and structured the fraught way in which the Government of Beans came into being.

To get a sense of just how agriculture could be inflected with divergent national imaginaries, it suffices to visit the two largest agrarian expositions on Paraguay's social calendar. The first, known simply as La Expo, held every July on the outskirts of Asunción, was established in the 1940s by the Asociación Rural del Paraguay, a group of elite landowners, ranchers, and Colorado Party politicians. Along with the usual show of sturdy cows, fancy-looking goats, and Ferris wheels, La Expo is a hodgepodge of national folklore, traditional foods, and Guarani polka music. Any company with the money to participate can do so provided they are draped in the red, white, and blue of the Paraguayan flag. Politicians make appearances and give speeches in Guarani and Spanish, and elite Asunceños go to see and be seen among relics of a romanticized rural past. Contemporary campesino agriculture is not really on display, and in general the site is exclusive of the rural poor. But when they do show up, campesinos recognize the national symbolism, the kinds of political patrons that they rely on, and a style of wealth to which many aspire.

Since 1993, however, La Expo has been mirrored by a new expo that takes place in May in Santa Rita, the de facto capital of soy country and only about forty kilometers from Pirapey, where Silvino Talavera used to live.[2] Expo Santa Rita was originally created by an organization called the Centro de Tradiciones Gauchas "Indio José" as a fund-raiser for cultural activities promoting the gaucho culture of Brazilian immigrants. But as soy grew over the next decade, the event morphed into a showcase for high-end machinery, banks, agrarian consultants, and luxury consumer items like Harley-Davidson motorcycles. And though it has become more inclusive of Paraguayan identity over the past decades, the space remains decidedly Brasiguaio: the first language of Expo Santa Rita is Portuguese, the headline acts are invariably *sertanejo* country singers from Brazil, and the audience is full of blond hair, white Stetsons, and plaid shirts tucked into jeans. If La Expo in Asunción seems to speak to a feudal past, an exclusive space with awkward reminders of Paraguayan political history, Expo Santa Rita is all about the future. The city even calls itself La Ciudad del Progreso, and the soy and Portuguese are impossible to disentangle from the shiny harvesters and the anticipation of great wealth.

Expo Santa Rita's unabashed celebration of the soy boom and Brasiguaio culture made the city a focus of anxieties about Paraguayan sovereignty. The first major work to explore this anxiety was a 2005 volume edited by Ramón Fogel and Marcial Riquelme, *Sojero Enclave: Poverty and the Weakening of Sovereignty*.[3] The volume's primary aim was to raise concern about the correlation between the soy boom, the expulsion of campesino farmers, environmental degradation, and the cultural shift in border areas. In one telling table, for instance, Riquelme compared 2002 census data for districts in Candindeyú, to show a correlation between soy, Portuguese, and declining populations.[4] By contrast, he showed, little soy was being planted in districts where Guarani and Spanish still predominated and the population was still growing. The former districts were closer to the eastern border, while the latter were closer to Asunción. At the epicenter of it all, Riquelme put Santa Rita, a district where Portuguese was spoken in the primary schools and City Hall.[5] The loss of Paraguayan languages and the declining population all meant that Paraguay was losing sovereignty in soy-farming areas.[6] In his own chapter, Ramón Fogel added other forms of death to the equation, invoking Silvino Talavera and decrying ecocide in soy areas.[7]

Riquelme defined sovereignty as "the capacity of a nation-state to exercise its control over its territory."[8] What offended Riquelme was both the incapacity of the state to protect its citizens and its environment and the fact that people spoke Portuguese in public schools. The absent state was indexed not just by weak regulatory institutions, but by the absence of national culture, both of which were being engulfed in soybeans. Santa Rita's proximity to the border with a far more powerful county made this absence seem all the more dire. But at its core was a concern that a loss of sovereignty inevitably weakened the state's ability to deliver on the promise of rural welfare.

Benedict Anderson famously posited that nationalism emerged from the crucible of Latin American independence from Spain, as different factions of the creole elite tried to work out the relationship between military control and cultural identity.[9] Paraguay was somewhat exceptional in this regard, as most historians think the tension between culture and territory was resolved relatively quickly after Gáspar Rodríguez de Francia declared independence for Paraguay in May 1811. Francia became Paraguay's first dictator, creating a new republic by closing all borders, making Guarani a national language, and trying to homogenize the population with decrees against the intermarriage of elites. All of this was made possible by Paraguay's relative geographic isolation as a landlocked outpost of the Spanish Empire. Argentina considered it a province, but its remoteness from Buenos Aires allowed Francia to exercise extraordinary control over the population in the outskirts of Asunción.[10] Even in the period of liberalization that followed Francia's death in 1840, Paraguayan nationalism was fierce, and was the primary force that later drove hundreds of thousands of Paraguayans to their deaths in the suicidal war against Brazil, Argentina, and Uruguay that effectively destroyed the republic between 1865 and 1870.[11]

In a fascinating analysis of the prewar period, Michael Huner shows that for Paraguayans, the nation's other was not only other nations but also the forest (ka'aguy, literally, "under the trees").[12] This is significant in relation, for instance, to Argentina, where the bush was imagined as *desierto*, a kind of empty frontier that would inevitably be filled by the Argentine state. Paraguay's ka'aguy, on the other hand, was a nonstate space in a different sense. It was profane (that which lay outside of the sacred ground of the church), racialized as indigenous, and legally indeterminate, neither fully part of Paraguayan territory nor part of any other nation-state. Paraguay was what Augusto Roa Bastos called "an island surrounded by land," fiercely sovereign without being entirely clear on where its borders lay.[13] Even when Paraguay declared war on Brazil, it was not officially over a border dispute, but as a protest against the annexation of Uruguay. So while the Paraguayan nation certainly played a crucial role in the ill-fated declaration of war, territorial sovereignty was not what that nation was all about.

The precise location of Paraguay's territorial borders would become briefly important at the end of the war, when Brazilian forces occupied Asunción for seven years. Argentina objected to Paraguay being annexed to Brazil, and both sides eventually agreed to take a portion of territory for themselves while granting Paraguay sovereignty over the rest. The border between Brazil and Paraguay was established along the Paraná River, but very few people calling themselves Paraguayan lived anywhere near that border. Moreover, as Asunción struggled to emerge from the devastation of the war, it deepened the separation of state and territory. Asunción reconstituted its economy by borrowing from the British Exchequer, using state land as collateral.[14] This began a cycle of borrowing and land sales that would end in 1885 with the state selling off over 79 percent of national territory.[15]

The upshot of all these sales was that Paraguayan forests ended up being owned by a handful of foreign companies. In the eastern border region, the three most important of these were a British firm called La Industria Paraguaya, run by Paraguayan politicians, a French investor named Domingo Barthes, and a Brazilian company known as Matte Larangeira.[16] These massive estates were extractivist enterprises that gathered forest products, primarily yerba mate, for export. The estates primarily operated on a system of debt slavery that ensnared indigenous and other transient laborers in the collection of yerba. Small cities such as Villarrica became centers for recruiting yerba collectors who would effectively leave behind their rights as citizens when they disappeared into the forests for years at a time.[17] Well into the 1960s the area of the *yerbales* was still forested, even though the market for yerba had waned, and with it the brutal labor regime.

It was onto this forested territory, a site of waves of historic violence, that Stroessner projected his own nation-building project, refiguring the territory as "land without people" and beginning a systematic appropriation and redistribution of forested space.[18] In 1963, he inaugurated the Institute for Rural Welfare (IBR), whose mandate was to redistribute forest estates to Paraguayan citizens.[19] Supported by the Alliance for Progress and the new agricultural development infrastructure of the Green Revolution, the regime expropriated parts of La Industria Paraguaya and other absentee-owned land, distributing it in smaller plots on credit to anyone willing to work it. This was how colonies like Pirapey were created, as landless families from the dense central departments around Asunción moved eastward into the forests of Caaguazú, San Pedro, Alto Paraná, Itapúa, and Canindeyú. The land reform was therefore a potent mix of three projects for the regime: it produced a new model of rural welfare by fostering export production by smallholders, boosted the national economy by bringing land into production, and rectified the historical taint of the previous century's land sales.

By the end of the 1960s, expropriation and deforestation were the hallmarks of Paraguayan sovereignty on a frontier that moved ever eastward in an explicit echo of Brazilian, Argentine, and US frontier colonialism. This March to the East, as the regime's propagandists called it, established the communities that for the latter part of the twentieth century became iconic of the Paraguayan nation: poor, Guarani-speaking mestizos whose future well-being would be connected to the reclamation and transformation of Paraguayan territory. For most of these colonizers, the Brazilian border had little to do with this story, because the edges of national territorial aspiration remained in the ever-receding forest. If campesinos still used the word "ka'aguy" to describe the vegetation in these areas, they also adopted the old Argentine frontier rhetoric of the "desierto" to evoke a national space waiting to be conquered.

The propagandists of the March to the East were more quiet about a parallel process in which they were also involved. In regions closer to the Brazilian border, most of the land expropriated by the government was sold to private colonization companies.[20] Some of this went directly to Brazilian speculators, like Geremia Lunardelli, who created Santa Rita, while other land was handed out in large parcels as patronage to Paraguayan military officers, who would in turn sell it to colonizers.[21]

This part of Paraguay's agrarian development did not operate through the same aspirations for rural welfare, nor did it mobilize the same nationalist rhetoric. So, for instance, the Estatuto Agrario of 1963, which made all of this colonization possible, quietly repealed an existing law against selling land to foreigners within one hundred kilometers of the border. At the same time, because colonization was not being managed directly by the IBR, the Paraguayan state was slower to set up an institutional presence in the new agrarian colonies being created in these regions. For later critics like Riquelme, this amounted to a relinquishing of national sovereignty in the border region, and this was particularly galling because Paraguay was still very much under threat of Brazilian annexation.

Paraguay's March to the East was in part a response to Brazil's own March to the West, a colonization program that relocated small farmers displaced by land concentration closer to the coast. By the time Brazilians began entering Paraguay, competition for land in the border states of Mato Grosso, Paraná, and Santa Catarina was already fierce. Paraguay's apparently empty, and extremely cheap, forests were right next door. If the Paraguayan government saw this as a potential for economic growth, the Brazilian military dictatorship saw it as an opportunity to exercise what it called "living borders."[22] As the author of Brazil's security doctrine put it, "A living border (or a border in tension, when they are linked to political economic or military interest) is submitted to the pressure of the stronger state. That pressure is always real, and is felt in the cultural and economic expansion of the stronger side toward the weaker. In periods of tension, that pressure can take on a military character."[23] The quote, part of a speech delivered in 1966, came right after a dispute over the positioning of the border had led to Brazilian troops deploying to the Guairá Falls on the Paraná River north of Santa Rita.[24]

That brief military conflict was quickly resolved as the two states pursued a series of bilateral agreements, particularly the building of the Itaipú dam, which flooded the falls. But for nationalists, the newfound friendship between Brazil and Paraguay was always unequal, a reason for constant vigilance over what went on in this border region. So when soy arrived, spreading through the fields around Santa Rita and other rapidly growing migrant settlements, it inevitably came to be seen by some nationalists as a manifestation of Brazil's living border thesis and a direct threat to Paraguayan sovereignty.[25] Soy, like ka'aguy and desierto, would come to signify the absence of the state. But if ka'aguy and desierto had been spaces of aspiration, soja indicated a space whose promise had been lost to Brazilian expansion.

## LIBERTARIAN SOY

As I mentioned at the outset of this chapter, Brasiguaio settlers had their own reasons to see a negative relationship between soy and the state. In my interviews throughout the eastern border region, an overwhelming majority of soy farmers expressed their disdain for Paraguayan people and institutions. In dozens of these conversations, Brasiguaios characterized Paraguayan workers as lazy, politicians as corrupt, and Paraguayan culture in general as backward and violent.[26] Many theories circulated openly as to what precisely Paraguay's problem was, from the particular racial mix of the population to aspects of the Guarani language that made them incapable of rationally conceptualizing time. Some were framed in almost sympathetic ways, pointing to a history of dictatorial repression that made people mean, introverted, and ignorant. There were many exceptions to this rule, particularly in my conversations with the second generation of these immigrants, but the early wave of settlers in this region overwhelmingly treated Paraguayan culture as something retrograde and did their best to shield themselves from its influence. Fearful of Paraguayan cultural contagion, many of Santa Rita's pioneers maintained family homes on the Brazilian side of the border in Foz do Iguaçú, traveling into Paraguay weekly to build farms in the forest but not deigning to contaminate their children with Paraguayan citizenship or schooling. Indeed, many of that early generation of pioneers remained Brazilian and moved back when they retired, to enjoy the benefits of a Brazilian pension and medical system, having resisted paying taxes to the Paraguayan state their whole lives.

Brasiguaio disdain for Paraguayan culture amplified an underlying political libertarianism, an adamant opposition to state intervention and taxation. If most campesinos complained of the absent state, believing that life would generally be better if government were more responsive to their needs, most sojeros—and hence most Brasiguaios—insisted that the more absent the state was, the better. Instead of cultivating ties with Paraguayan institutions and political benefactors, they developed relationships with input companies and grain multinationals. In fact, even while they refused to pay export taxes, it was sojeros themselves who brokered an agreement with Monsanto in 2004 to pay the company a royalty of 4 percent (of gross earnings) for the use of their Roundup Ready seed. That same year, Syngenta (which also produced and distributed soybean seed) published an infamous ad that showed a map of South America free of national borders, with the region between Argentina, Paraguay, and Bolivia covered in a homogenous green blob, the "United Republics of Soy."[27] The state could only appear on such a map in negative terms, with soy representing a vibrant, progressive, wealth-creating force, and the state representing red tape and backwardness.[28]

And yet this image of soy and the state as opposites of each other missed a key aspect of the way soybeans lived on the border. National borders are of course not mere limits or demarcations of national sovereignty, but also crucial spaces of selection, judgment, and speculative comparison.[29] The border marks a specific set of differences that can become the basis for economic speculation, or what economists call arbitrage.[30] Thus, the farmer who establishes a family home in Foz do Iguaçú but a farm in Santa Rita is exploiting these differences creatively, combining what they see as the cultural benefits protected by the Brazilian welfare state on one side of the border with the cheap land and labor available on the other side. The difference in the values of these goods (culture, land, labor) within such close proximity to each other is made possible by the border itself.

Stroessner's dual development strategy was based not on erasing the border, but on exploiting the opportunities for arbitrage that the border enabled. In an era in which many countries were attempting to modernize by limiting imports (the strategy known as import-substituting industrialization), Stroessner's government sought to integrate the country into regional trade networks by fostering closer economic ties with Brazil. The Itaipú dam, built using mostly Brazilian capital but mostly flooding Paraguayan forests, was a key part of this. Another was the building of the Friendship Bridge across the Paraná River between the two countries, and the creation of a tax-free trading zone on the Paraguayan side. Paraguay was granted customs privileges at the Brazilian port of Paranaguá, giving Paraguayan exporters a new access to the Atlantic that didn't go through Argentina.[31] Even during the dictatorship, when it was notoriously isolated in political and cultural terms, Paraguay became an open economy, with a high ratio of imports and exports to overall GDP.[32] This simultaneous openness and closedness was not contradictory but complementary, since it was precisely Paraguay's relative isolation that made it a useful site for international speculation.[33]

Opening up trade also created the condition for flows of more mundane goods that turned the border region into one of the most important thoroughfares of contraband and money laundering in the world. This trade speculated not only on differences in the value of goods and services but on differences in policing and taxation. Paraguay's lack of export taxes, compared to the high taxes of its neighbors, meant that there was an advantage for Argentine and Brazilian exporters to smuggle their goods into Paraguay and export them from there. Contraband cigarettes and VHS tapes, produced in and around Ciudad del Este, and the cheap electronics, watches, and women's underwear smuggled in from the Middle East and Southeast Asia found their way into South America through Paraguay, before being moved to the much larger black markets in Brazil and Argentina.[34] These would much later be joined, further north along the border, by significant flows of drugs (Bolivian cocaine and Paraguayan marijuana) and weapons (small arms from the United States).

All of these conditions meant that the Brasiguaio population planting soy on the Paraguayan side of the border was not merely an extension of Brazil but quite its own thing, thriving on a series of comparative advantages that only border life could produce.[35] Even for sojeros living on the Brazilian side, there was an advantage to linking Paraguay into their export chain through a series of creative, quasi-legal uses of the border. Brazilians with relatives on the Paraguayan side were known to draw credit from the Paraguayan Development Bank (loaned, in the early 1980s, at half the interest rate of Brazilian credit), which they would use to grow soy in Brazil. They could then smuggle the soy into Paraguay across the border and register it as Paraguayan, to avoid paying export tax when they crossed it officially back across the border to truck it to the port at Paranaguá.[36] These practices continued in some form until at least the early 2000s (as did similar practices on the Argentine border).

All of this points to the fact that soy's relationship to the Paraguayan state was far more ambivalent than either the absent-state or antistate position suggests. If there's any place that the state's capacity to limit and control is at its strongest, it's around the border. But it doesn't follow that soy's vitality and the state's enforcement of its border relate to each other negatively. Even in moments like the 1990s, when the Paraguayan regulatory state was in greatest disarray, when contraband and money laundering seemed to flout any notion of a functioning border, soy thrived not despite the border but because of it. It was the border that produced differences in policing, land values, regulation, taxation, labor rights, fertility, bureaucratic cultures, migration histories, and language that all became opportunities for the arbitrage on which soy thrived. Behind the image of soy's antistatism, therefore, was an implicit agribiopolitics that relied on government to hold these territorial advantages in place.

This makes it all the more curious that by the time of Silvino Talavera's death, both sojeros and their opponents had come to see soy and the Paraguayan state as opposed to one another. For Fogel and Riquelme, and progressive nationalists like them, the state was the continuing disappointment of a welfare promise that seemed to be growing more remote as Brasiguaio soy fields spread westward from the border. For many in the soy industry, any promise of further regulation threatened a fragile comparative advantage they had carved out beyond Brazilian territory. And so as soy and its detractors became increasingly visible, both sides came to see national regulations as a key site of struggle.

# CHAPTER FOUR

# The Living Barrier

The first time I drove along the highway and back roads around Pirapey in 2017, I was struck by the high dense walls of vegetation, usually of sugarcane or elephant grass, that separated soy fields from roads. These barriers first appeared in Paraguayan law in 2004 and from then on could be found throughout the country, though in most departments they were thin and infrequent. What surprised me in Itapúa, near where Silvino died, was how thick and imposing these barriers were, sometimes closing off dirt roads and hiding soy completely from passing traffic. Referred to in Paraguay as the *barrera viva*, or living barrier, this piece of green infrastructure remained the most obvious marker on the landscape of a decades-long struggle to rethink the relationship between plant health and human health in response to Silvino's death. It was part of a long game to build a bulwark against soy's advance, behind which the state might still be able to nurture the welfare of its citizens.

The barrera viva standing between soybeans and vulnerable citizens is another key character in the drama ahead, but to explain why it took this form and how it came to be where it was, I need to show how politics moves from places like Pirapey, where the state was said to be absent, to

Asunción, where the laws were made, back to Pirapey, where those laws came to be inscribed back on the landscape, in this case in the form of elephant grass. Versions of this same movement in and out of the capital will recur throughout this book as one of the most entrenched territorial problematics of modern governance in Paraguay. But it is not only spatial: the movement from field to office building and back again also entails a translation from the material relations of soy, pesticides, and sick bodies to the abstraction of rules, and back again. And it is also a displacement that crosses class and livelihood, as the campesinos and sojeros intimately concerned with soy's violence ally with lawyers, politicians, and bureaucrats who inhabit the world of rule making, so far from the soy fields themselves.

The story of the barrera viva began with an attempt to bridge this distance. Shortly after Silvino's death, his mother's friends in CONAMURI reached out to a lawyer in Asunción named Silvia González, a committed activist in campesino land struggles and defender of human rights, who ran a small but successful advocacy NGO out of the Catholic University.[1] González was one of the main lawyers involved in the case as it worked its way through appeals over the next three years. But as I met with her on repeated occasions in Asunción's poshest restaurants, where other tables were occupied by her powerful political enemies, I was also aware of the great gulf between campesino activists and their urban professional allies. González spoke little Guarani and moved in a world of NGOs, universities, and international consultancies that supported campesino struggles from a relatively safe, salaried distance. She was a quintessential example of what I have come to call a "new democrat," an Asunción professional of the left, steeped in opposition to the dictatorship and support for campesino struggles, but who moved in class and cultural milieus that excluded them.[2]

Yet these characteristics, mixed with González's lawyerly doggedness, made her a formidable ally for campesino organizations wishing to push back against soy. Even as she worked on the criminal trial, she began to look for legislative ways to transform Paraguayan agribiopolitics more fundamentally. Working from her office across the plaza from the Paraguayan Congress, she wrote a new law that would curtail soy farmers' use of pesticides, especially around vulnerable populations, and instill a number of mitigating practices like the living barrier. The project, and the political fight to make it law, took over four years. And everything about it, from the awkward country-city alliance that brought it about to the tensions it created between sojeros and environmentalists, was a prelude to the election of Fernando Lugo and the Government of Beans.

When Silvia González set out to overhaul the agrarian legal regime, the Paraguayan government did very little to control the use of agrochemicals. The existing pesticide law, Law 123/91, had been created in 1991 to make Paraguay conform to agricultural best practices during a flurry of international attention to regional environmental problems. Agriculture had changed dramatically in the following decade, and so had global food safety standards, leaving Paraguay's legal regime out of touch with the soy boom.[3] But outdated legislation was hardly the biggest hurdle. The government had no reliable way to monitor or police the use of these chemicals, and though everyone knew that the quantity of pesticides being used was increasing astronomically with the spread of soy, most of the importation and distribution happened at the margins of the formal market. Attempts to improve this situation fell to more informal regulatory actors, to leaflets and seminars offered to farmers by the World Wildlife Federation, the Canadian International Development Agency, production cooperatives, and the pesticide brokers themselves. While González's work therefore centered on an attempt to write a new pesticide bill, her larger ambition was to bring the state to the soy fields, and to build there an agribiopolitical apparatus capable of protecting people's health from the new dangers around them.

So let's consider for a moment just how monumental such a state-building project actually is. The legislation for such a system would have to include, at the very least, a comprehensive set of guidelines for evaluating the health and environmental risks of any given material, and infrastructure to carry out both field trials and epidemiological trials in a highly dynamic environment. A frequently updated list of permissible chemicals would need to be accompanied by guidelines for best practices. Funding would be needed (through either fees or taxation) for an inspection infrastructure (including certification programs and regional offices) and a legal regime allowing those inspectors to enter farms and demand information. One would also need to build a network of public laboratories capable of analyzing samples and a department of epidemiology in the Ministry of Public Health. Finally, all of this would need to be enforced by a punitive regime, including inspectors, police, and prosecutors to force compliance with the guidelines.

Elements of everything on this list already existed, scattered throughout the bureaucracy in some less-than-ideal form. All of these offices had been built over decades of single-party rule, and were therefore controlled by Colorado Party operatives who were openly hostile to González and people like her.[4] The project could therefore not be about conjuring an apparatus out of midair. The outdated list of chemicals, the ad-hoc NGO guidelines, and the infrastructure of the existing Department of Plant Health would all need to be consolidated into a new kind of system, and hundreds of functionaries would have to be convinced to change the practices in which they had all been trained, and on which many of them had gotten wealthy.

The event of Silvino's death had dispelled the naturalness of slow violence and made room for the emergence of a new public that thought of pesticides not as a question of agrarian production but as a problem for human health. And this created an opportunity to change the agribiopolitical calculus inscribed in the law. But when the main characters in this book decided to respond to soy through regulation, the temporal scales and rhythms at play became wholly different: the coming and going of political fads, the unexpected irruption of new events, the maddening inertia of bureaucratic work, and the manic frenzy of the electoral cycle.

## LAWS, DECREES, AND PRESIDENTS

Bear with me for a moment while I get a bit technical, but some familiarity with legislative procedure is essential to understand how volatile the barrera viva would become. There were two primary ways to change the regulatory field. The most obvious, but also the most difficult, was to draft a new law and try to get it passed through two houses of Congress, both of which were controlled by the Colorado Party, and then get it signed by a Colorado president. The second strategy was to appeal only to the President, to pass a regulatory decree that would amend the law already in place (Law 123/91). An executive decree would be far more limited in its scope, and it would also be easily overturned by subsequent governments, so this was clearly the lesser of the two options, but it was also much easier. González decided to hedge her bets and started two projects in parallel. On the one hand, she enlisted the help of Oxfam and WHO to begin public consultations aimed at rewriting the law.[5] In the meantime, she participated in the drafting of an executive decree to clarify articles of Law 123/91.

But none of González's efforts would have had much effect had they not also lined up quite naturally with the electoral cycle. The year Silvino died was an election year in Paraguay, and most of the country was looking forward to replacing the sitting president, Luís Ángel González Macchi, who had ascended to the post through a particularly sordid back door. During the 1998 election, he had been elected to the Senate as part of the Colorado Party's closed candidate list. He had soon after been chosen president of the Senate, a role that often changed with shifting internal party alliances.[6] That position put him third in line to the presidency in March 1999, when the vice president was assassinated and the president was sent into exile for suspicion of conspiracy in that assassination.[7] González Macchi served the remaining four years of the presidential mandate and is primarily remembered for historic levels of unpopularity and gross embezzlement during some of the worst years of Paraguay's long economic recession.

By contrast, the man the Colorados had chosen to succeed him in the 2003 elections, Nicanor Duarte Frutos (known simply as Nicanor), was wildly popular. Nicanor was a brilliant populist. He liked to play up his own rural roots, and spoke a fluent, biting Guarani in the bombastic style of a long legacy of Colorado *caudillos,* or strongmen. But he was also a lawyer with keen knowledge of how government worked, and he could play the role of the professional technocrat. On April 20, 2003, fifty-five years after the Colorados first took power, Nicanor easily won the presidential election. Even before he assumed the office that August, he set up a team to plan the modernizing of outdated institutions and legislation. Into that process stepped Silvia González, along with hundreds of other lobbyists around Asunción, intent on taking advantage of the opportunities this presented.

The first months of Nicanor's presidency were beset by soy-related conflicts. From September 2003 to January 2004, forty-two accusations of pesticide poisoning made it to the national newspapers, and the last of these incidents left two people hospitalized.[8] Wanting to appear to be doing something about the situation, Nicanor called an ad hoc committee together on February 4 to study the existing legislation and see if there were any quick solutions that would palliate rural tensions. At the table were campesino leaders, Silvia González and environmentalists from other national NGOs, representatives of the major production cooperatives, and two technicians from the Department of Plant Defense, the predecessor to SENAVE. After two short days of discussion, they decided that the most immediate problem was that the guidelines for regulating Law 123/91 dealt only with aerial fumigation, and that midsized farmers like Hermann Schlender, who used a tractor, were not covered by the regulations. They came up with a list of recommendations for reforming the regulation by decree, and this was quickly signed by the president on March 18.

Decree 2048/04, which regulated Law 123/91, instantly added several new instruments to the pesticide law, including rules about notifying neighbors before spraying, the maximum wind velocity above which one could not spray, security specs for pesticide storage, labor standards around agrochemical application, and maintenance requirements for equipment. Importantly, approval of new chemicals and techniques would now be supervised by representatives of both the Ministry of Public Health and Welfare (MSPyBS) and the Secretariat of the Environment (SEAM). But by far the most contentious issue was the creation of two completely novel regulatory instruments meant to enforce a separation between soy and people. First, farmers were expected to leave an unsprayed security buffer, or *franja de seguridad*, around all fields that bordered on roads, houses, and public places. Second, they were expected to plant barreras vivas, the walls of vegetation with which I started this chapter, to prevent pesticide drift in the same places.

The key provision of the decree was Article 13:

> In cases where crops run alongside populated, communal roads subject to pesticide application, barreras vivas are required to avoid possible contamination, drifting to third parties, and following these recommendations:
>
> The minimum width of the barrera viva must be 5 meters. Species used for the barrera viva must possess dense foliage and a minimum height of 2 meters.
>
> Where no barrera viva is present, a franja of 50 meters will be left alongside roads, where pesticides shall not be applied.[9]

Years later, González and others told me that they had always thought this and other provisions of 2408/04 were weak, but it was a definite victory nonetheless, and they could now work on overhauling Law 123/91 in its entirety.

Representatives of the soy industry, on the other hand, felt as though they'd been cornered. Hector Cristaldo, the most prominent soy lobbyist in the country (and therefore González's clearest adversary), who was also at the table, told me this was the last time that he would be surprised in this way.

It was the third of December, Global Anti-agrotoxins Day, named for an accident that happened in a factory in India. . . . That day in 2003 they published a picture of a boy on the cover of *Última Hora*, with his face all burned. They said it was the result of fumigation with toxins. . . . It turned out later that it was pemphigus, a skin disease. But it was done. The decree was approved under pressure from that situation, that established a franja . . . barreras vivas and all that.[10]

The barreras were "a Paraguayan invention," he told me, "the product of a very well-organized campaign." The heightened public anxiety around pesticides had forced them to let it pass, but the barrera viva article was so obviously absurd, and so potentially harmful to such a key industry, that he expected it would never be enforced. Nonetheless, the decree was a warning shot, and in subsequent years the soy industry began to fortify its own lobbying efforts. Seeing the need for a stronger political voice on the national scene, nine different associations of farmers, processors, exporters, and cooperatives banded together and formed the Unión de Gremios de la Producción (UGP) in 2007, and named Cristaldo as their spokesperson.[11]

In 2007, González finally managed to bring her new pesticide bill to Congress to overhaul the law completely. The bill included a strengthening of barrera and franja provisions that had first appeared in the decree. The key article expanded the franja to one hundred meters (two hundred if aerial crop dusters were used), and the barrera now needed to be four meters thick and three meters high. This time the UGP hit back with a media campaign and a prepared congressional response. They argued that the provision would make it impossible for smaller farms to use tractors, since the buffers would take up too much of their fields. In the aggregate, they claimed, enforcing such a law would reduce soy coverage by 40 percent nationwide. Co-opting language that campesinos often used against sojeros, the UGP said that buffers were a land grab by environmentalists intent on destroying the industry.[12] When Congress was discussing the bill, they also managed to block all demonstrators from the chamber on the argument of a Colorado congressman, Julio Colmán, that the bill was an "incitement to class warfare." González, who managed to get into the hearing through her own friendship with one of the deputies, remembers the scene well: as campesinos demonstrated outside for the passage of the bill, she found herself on the balcony sitting among well-known soy farmers and lobbyists. She knew from their demeanor that the bill had no chance of being passed and, sure enough, it was quashed without being read.

It seemed as though that might be the end of the story. But there was one more game in play that was much larger than any of these particular actors. The antisoy forces were not naive enough to think that their law would pass, nor even that if it passed it would be enforced. After all, they believed that the government, and its regulatory agencies, were controlled by corrupt oligarchs in the pocket of soy interests. So it is not surprising that many of the people involved in drafting the new legislation and organizing rallies around the Silvino Talavera case were also implicated in preparing for the 2008 presidential election to replace Nicanor. Against all odds, they won that election, completely changed the relationship between soy and the state, and extended the fight over barreras vivas another four years.

## FROM DECREES TO ENFORCEMENT

The historical legacy of Fernando Lugo's election was completely contradictory. It was simultaneously an unprecedented upset in the long-standing hegemony of the Colorado Party and an anomalous blip that left few traces in Paraguayan law. Congress was still firmly controlled by the Colorados, and Lugo's electoral coalition with the Liberal Party (Partido Liberal Auténtico Radical) meant that even in the executive branch, most ministries were controlled by Liberals who opposed regulatory overreach.[13] Lugo did appoint close New Democratic allies to the ministries of Finance and Public Health, but conceded the largest ministry, Agriculture, to the Liberals, who appointed a minister with close ties to the UGP. Moreover, Lugo didn't make any changes to the personnel of SEAM, and SENAVE went to a Liberal pesticide salesman who had previously served as the president of the Paraguayan Soy Association.[14] None of this presaged any strong changes in the way that the government regulated the soybean sector.

Once the dust had settled from the election, the UGP set about trying to stabilize their position through a bit of legislative jujitsu. A year into Lugo's mandate, they took González's old pesticide bill, the one they had campaigned against in 2007, and reintroduced it to Congress with slight, but very telling, modifications. In the new version, farmers were no longer required to notify the public before aerial fumigation. Neither the Ministry of Public Health nor SEAM had a role in pesticide regulation (the entire law fell under the jurisdiction of SENAVE). The security buffer was removed entirely from the law, and the barrera viva rules became less strict. A flurry of legislative amendments ensued, but González admits that she was outmaneuvered, and that the UGP ultimately got the amendments that they wanted. The sixteen-day legislative drama surrounding this bill is the stuff of legend on both sides, with each accusing the other of dirty backroom tactics, including surreptitiously exchanging pages of the text after it had been read and before it was signed. The stories I've heard contradict each other so completely that I won't try to make sense of them here, except to say that over those sixteen days, the height, width, and density of barreras vivas changed repeatedly. In the end, the new law required a barrera of two meters in height and five meters in width, with no stipulation about the density of foliage.[15]

The co-opted version of the pesticide bill became Law 3742/09 in the final days of the 2009 legislative calendar. González was not, however, ready to concede defeat. The new law had not yet been regulated by executive decree, and so as far as anyone could figure out, Decree 2408/04 (which Nicanor had passed to regulate Law 123/91) was still in effect.[16] And Decree 2408/04 still contained stricter language about barreras vivas. For the next two years, this generated widespread confusion in the bureaucracy and throughout the countryside: How could a decree regulate a law that had been written after the decree was signed? How could one interpret such a decree if some of its principles were in tension with law itself? Was the franja de seguridad still in effect? Did barreras vivas need to be dense or not? In other words, until Lugo signed a new decree, two potential interpretations of the law remained in effect, one supported by the soy industry and the other supported by Silvia González and other activists in Lugo's coalition.

The walls of elephant grass, corn, sugarcane, and eucalyptus that sometimes flanked Paraguayan soy fields, and sometimes didn't, in the years ahead were the most visible symptom of these months and years of wrangling in Asunción, of the movement of documents, arguments over words, and even, as we'll see, over commas. The barriers were the perfect symbol for the presence or absence of the state in the countryside, not only because they were patchy and ambiguous themselves, but because their relationship to articles of law was open to nearly endless interpretation. One of the great battles of Lugo's time in office would concern who had to plant barriers and what they would look like. And so it's not surprising that the office charged with interpreting and enforcing the pesticide law, SENAVE, would itself become a critical site for the tensions as they unfolded.

# CHAPTER FIVE

# The Plant Health Service

U ntil Lugo's election, SENAVE, the state agency tasked with enforcing pesticide laws, was a quiet place, one of a string of technical offices with virtually interchangeable acronyms. The agronomists and pesticide salespeople who ran it, and the soy farmers and industry representatives who were its primary clients, preferred things that way. Lugo, however, completely overturned this state of affairs when he named a left-wing scientist, Miguel Lovera, to preside over the institution. As soon as Lovera got the call, he phoned Silvia González and asked her to head up his legal department. Appointing bureaucrats was one of Lugo's few discretionary powers, and while all such appointments were bound to stir some controversy, this one turned out to be one of the defining moments of his term in office. Rural activists and environmentalists had been outflanked in their attempts to change laws, so Lugo effectively put them in charge of interpreting and enforcing the law instead.

Like González, the new head of SENAVE was quite different from the campesinos in Lugo's rural coalition. He was the son of a radical doctor and had lived for many years in Europe, where he finished his doctorate in plant biology before returning to Paraguay to try to make a living in academia or international consulting. But he spoke Guarani well, and a certain gruff affability won him trust from campesino leaders, who saw him as an honest defender of their interests. He had already shown his bona fides by upsetting the soy lobby as an outspoken critic of deforestation and GMOs. And because he was not a career bureaucrat or politician, he could make a credible claim to be incorruptible.

Most Paraguayans had no idea that Lovera's appointment might be a high-stakes affair, but the soy lobby immediately interpreted it as a threat to a tense agribiopolitical arrangement that they had spent years cultivating. Before he had even assumed the post, the UGP had begun a media campaign to discredit him. The country's primary newspaper, ABC *Color*, ran daily stories denouncing the appointment, offering Hector Cristaldo space to make the UGP's case.[1] Some of these stories painted Lovera as a charlatan who was unfit for a technocratic job, while others accused him of being a dangerous criminal with links to a burgeoning Marxist guerrilla movement.[2] The precise problem with Lovera didn't matter so much as the signal that an enemy had appeared in their midst. And with this, Lovera agreed. In our very first meeting, only two weeks after he'd assumed the job, he was frank with me, likening his own head office to an outpost in enemy territory. The hundreds of functionaries who now worked for him were either Colorados or Liberals, and until he became their boss, they had all answered to the UGP's program. As many others would tell me, the UGP treated SENAVE like their "patio," and Lovera was spoiling it for them.

Yet Lovera immediately faced a fundamental and unsurprising question: What can anyone actually do from a position in the bureaucracy to change fundamental relations of power between politicians and economic actors? Did he have any real ability to affect what was happening in soy fields, or did the very structure of the agency itself ensure that anyone appointed to that position would only serve a structure already in place? The drama surrounding Lovera's experimentation with these questions will have to wait until part II. But first I need to introduce SENAVE as a character in its own right, and to try to explain why it is so difficult to spot the locus of agency in regulatory work.

## THE MAKING OF A REGULATORY INSTRUMENT

SENAVE was a product of the neoliberal realignments that embroiled Paraguay in the new development and trade relationships following the end of the Cold War. After the coup against Stroessner in 1989 and the first democratic elections in 1992, Asunción was overtaken by international development banks and organizations offering aid programs promising "good governance" and "transparency."[3] Among these was the Inter-American Development Bank (IADB), which throughout the Cold War had worked closely with the regime to support the Green Revolution goals of improving crops. Now, in the age of neoliberal development policy, it had decided that the key to solving Paraguay's poverty lay not in improving agriculture but in fighting corruption and bureaucratic inefficiency. And so in 1994, the IADB proposed a bold new plan to reform the Ministry of Agriculture, to dismantle the bureaucracies that the bank had helped to create, and to rethink how government related to agriculture altogether. Instead of directly fostering the development of plants such as wheat, cotton, and soy, the Ministry of Agriculture would now be rationalized to deliver technical services to the private sector. The plan presented to the government in 1994 involved creating a series of new autarchic agencies, semiautonomous offices housed within the ministry but with their own executive structure, applicable laws, and budgets.[4] One of these technical agencies was SENAVE, which was to govern all things phytosanitary.

The IADB argued that a new phytosanitary agency would open up markets by helping Paraguayan exporters to comply with the Codex Alimentarius, the tome of international standards for pesticide use.[5] Yet despite the international pressure, Paraguay was very slow to implement the IADB project, and it all but sat on the shelf at the Ministry of Agriculture's technical planning office for the next decade. The industry had little interest in institutional change. During the 1990s, soy farmers exported most of their product to Brazil and Argentina, and international shipping went through the port at Paranaguá, where producers could rely on Brazilian inspectors. The potential costs of changing regulatory infrastructure far outweighed—or seemed to outweigh—the potential benefits of more streamlined quality control. Not until 2002, when an export crisis forced the soy industry to change its practices, did the laissez-faire attitude toward phytosanitary regulation become harder to sustain.

The crisis centered on opposition to Roundup Ready soy in Brazil. Paraguay had banned the planting of GMOs in 2000, but almost every bean planted there was Roundup Ready anyway. A similar ban was also in effect, with more success, in three Brazilian states, including Paraná, which controlled Paraguay's export corridor. But in 2002, the governor of Paraná extended the GMO ban to include not just beans being planted but beans entering or transiting through the state, a decree that effectively closed the main trucking route from the Paraguayan border to Paranaguá.[6] Sensing a potential collapse in their access to European markets, Paraguayan production cooperatives began pressuring the government to adopt the IADB's old reform proposal, to build SENAVE, to show compliance with the Codex nationally, and to make it easier to bypass Brazilian politics.[7]

All of this coincided with the political opening discussed in chapter 4: the election of Nicanor Duarte Frutos. At the same time as Silvia González began lobbying for the creation of a pesticide law, various soy interests were lobbying for the creation of SENAVE. The first few months of Nicanor's presidency were key to preparing the playing field for the next decade of agrarian politics. Just as the first parts of the Government of Beans were being built through the legislative restrictions on soy production (primarily its use of pesticides), so too was another set of structures being put in place whose primary goal was to improve export opportunities for those producers.

I don't wish to give the impression that the industry moved in lockstep around these changes. As I've said, most farmers were suspicious of state involvement at all, and many soy farmers grumbled about SENAVE's creation at the time, just as many resented the need to pay royalties to Monsanto when Roundup Ready soybeans were legalized.[8] But at the level of the national crop and especially for the big players, these problems were all offset by the benefits of new markets. Contracts with overseas buyers could now be negotiated more easily, as Paraguayan producers could get their compliance with standards verified locally. Ports on the Paraguay and Paraná rivers could now be brought into compliance with export standards, removing producers' dependence on Paranaguá. In only a few years, the bulk of the soy that had been traversing the Brazilian border on the way to the Atlantic now started going down the Paraná River into Argentina, a boost in shipping volume so immense that Paraguay soon developed the third-largest fleet of tugboats in the world.[9] Multinational seed companies such as Monsanto and Syngenta, and grain conglomerates such as Cargill and Archer Daniels Midland (ADM), all set up offices in Ciudad del Este, and began building silos, crushing facilities, and ports. Small producers I talked to in the border area who had initially opposed this change said it took a mere two years to win them over to the far more favorable export conditions that it fostered. And over the next decade, the area planted in soy increased by another 50 percent, while overall national production doubled in tonnage.[10]

Already we can see that the notion that soy and the state were somehow opposed to each other was at least partly backward. Far from limiting soy, the creation of a bureaucracy to regulate the industry was all about expanding the crop. Nor was this a story of government being captured or co-opted by industry: the industry had, for all intents and purposes, created the regulatory structure through their own lobbying organizations. In fact, the whole episode undermines any clear distinction between government oversight and industry self-regulation. Instead, it shows the state as an extension of the increasingly well-organized beneficiaries of the soy boom. In other words, SENAVE was a stronghold of what I've taken to calling the Soy State, that cornerstone of an agribiopolitical apparatus without which it would be impossible to sustain three million hectares of beans.

### WHAT DOES REGULATION DO TO BEANS?

To get at how SENAVE helped the soy industry, and why they considered Lovera such a threat, it helps to shift the scale of analysis to the mundane procedures of regulatory practice that occur every day in SENAVE offices. For this I chose a simple example: the measurement of soybean moisture content. Moisture affects the value of the beans, since the water must be removed during processing, and too much water increases the likelihood that beans will rot in a silo or vessel. Everyone who buys, sells, or otherwise handles beans is interested in how much water they contain. As loads of beans move from truck to silo, back to truck, then into boats or warehouses, SENAVE mandates that their water content must be measured by a trained technician, bearing a SENAVE badge, and using a properly calibrated moisture meter (a machine a little larger than a car battery). All along the soy chain, certified technicians from private logistics companies charge a small fee to dip a ladle into the beans, crush the sample into a moisture meter, and produce a readout indicating what percentage of the sample's mass is water. The inspectors transfer this reading to a signed certificate bearing the SENAVE logo, which then travels on with the beans.

On the face of it, the moisture measurement (along with other similar rituals) creates a small choke point in the supply chain that forces producers into uncomfortable proximity with state agents. It reveals data about production and creates an added cost of shipment. Every soy farmer at some point has resented waiting and paying for these readings and fretted that the reading might decrease the value of their load. But the costly ritual is on balance highly valuable to them. Most of the time the moisture meter produces a certificate that expedites shipping and helps relationships along the chain. The more the various parts of the measurement have been standardized, the more reliable they've become. And thus, the SENAVE-standardized moisture meter makes it easier to scale up the industry, inviting involvement from larger corporate players like Cargill and ADM, whose margins depend on precise estimates of value, the stability of the products, and the cleanliness of mechanical equipment. In the end, the moisture meter creates one small bottleneck and cost while removing other larger ones.

While it may be tempting to think of such meters as devices that produce facts about soybeans, a more useful way to put it is that they qualify soybeans and make them able to do things they could not do prior to the availability of the qualifying ritual. To adopt a phrase from Bernadette Bensaude-Vincent and Isabelle Stengers, what the test does is produce "informed soybeans," matter augmented by information.[11] One bean may have the same percentage of moisture as any other bean, but once that percentage has been printed out and signed and stamped by a SENAVE-authorized technician, it is also something more, augmented by the accompanying documents. Like better genetics or growing conditions, the certificates improve soybeans and make them capable of new forms of movement. Informed soybeans store better and travel better because their organic potential for decay and rot can be better monitored across a larger agribiopolitical assemblage. From this perspective, SENAVE seems less like an overbearing state regulator, adding costs to an industry in order to protect citizens, than it does a rather prosaic piece of the production process, creating an enhanced organic product whose value has increased because it can be better monitored.

But while the UGP might have lobbied for the creation of SENAVE, it was also right to be vigilant. It had, after all, felt burned by the way Regulatory Decree 2048/04 had been passed, only a few months after SENAVE opened its doors, bringing barreras vivas and other problematic new characters into the institution's purview. For the time being it seemed likely that SENAVE would ignore those regulations the industry didn't like and that they could get them changed later, but there was always a danger that someone might try to ratchet those regulations into something more harmful to the industry. By conjuring the state in a mundane ritual happening all along the supply chain, every moisture meter, and every bottleneck that formed around it, presented new opportunities to actors over whom soy farmers and exporters had very little control. For instance, the moisture meter provided a surveillance point for collecting other sorts of information and an opportunity to extract more payments (either by increasing fees or demanding bribes). Even if SENAVE did not inspect for pesticide residue, the presence of the moisture meter made it much easier to imagine such inspections in the future and to demand that soy farmers pay for it. And SENAVE wasn't just inserting meters into the export chain; it also put in sieves to measure the size of beans as well as fumigation measures for containers, logbooks for crop dusters, and new safety equipment for handling pesticides. Each one of these represented a point where some other actor might intercede. And with that, soy producers became newly vulnerable to the contingencies of elections or to activist bureaucrats taking over the agency in charge. In other words, in every moisture meter, both the Soy State and the Government of Beans were present as possibilities.

## AGENCY, MEASUREMENT, AND SOVEREIGNTY

SENAVE epitomizes one of the central ambiguities of state agency. Even when it was indubitably present, the state could appear to be acting in the service of very different, often completely opposed, sets of interests. I've tried to give an overall feel for the way this ambivalence was felt in Paraguay by describing the state as a toss-up between two overlapping but antagonistic assemblages. One could of course name many, many more simultaneous projects beyond the Soy State and the Government of Beans that would complicate the story further, but in places like SENAVE, this specific ambivalence structured the mounting anxieties on all sides of the soy boom that helped bring Lugo to power and later brought him down.

What I've tried to show in this chapter, though, is that these anxieties are not merely the stuff of great political rifts in the imagination of the state, but that they also inhere in some of the smallest examples of bureaucratic action, in the mundane, everyday ways that functionaries carry out their jobs of measuring, standardizing, and certifying the stuff of agriculture.[12] In fact, part of the argument here is that far from being apolitical, these acts can become especially charged because it is at these moments of intimacy between regulators and the stuff on the ground that different state projects begin to intercede in the everyday. Small devices like the moisture meter are one of those points where the state descends out of the ideological arguments and gets stuck to the soybeans such that every bean from then on carries with it all of the ambiguities and dangers of state power.

In some fundamental way, every attempt to measure soy and to produce representations of it is constructive, enrolling soy in new connections, bringing more actors into its network. For Karen Barad, all attempts at description have this quality.[13] "Measurements," she says, "are causal intra-actions, physical processes. What we usually call 'measurement' is a correlation or entanglement between component parts of a phenomenon, between the 'measured object' and the 'measuring device.'"[14] To measure something is therefore to intervene in its existence, and also to allow it to intervene in the existence of the measurer. Soy demands a response from the state, and the state demands a response from soy, and, as they make these demands, each one comes to act differently in the world.

In the social sciences, the word "agency" has historically been contrasted with structure and denotes something like autonomous action. But we also use the word in everyday conversation to describe those governmental bodies that act as an instrument of power: e.g., SENAVE is a phytosanitary agency. But neither of these uses of the term quite captures the sense in which any agency's capacity to act depends on its relationship to the things upon which it is acting. This is what Barad means by intra-action.[15] For Barad, "'distinct' agencies are only distinct in a relational, not an absolute, sense, that is, agencies are only distinct in relation to their mutual entanglement; they don't exist as individual elements."[16] Pushing this further, she suggests we understand any statement about distinct agencies as an ontological operation, what she calls an "agential cut," which establishes a distinction between entangled agents as "measuring agencies (effect) and measured object (cause)," between that which is inside and that which is outside the object in question.[17] Agential cuts cannot be stabilized—to describe an agential cut is to make a further cut. Any way of representing is always open to being further represented, a measurement that can itself be measured.

For whom does the subcontracted technician with the moisture meter work? The soy industry, the public interest, the Colorado Party, or European importers? And what project is she helping to actualize? As the machine prints its little ticket, is it acting as part of the Soy State, increasing production, or is it infiltrating the industry with the possibility of the Government of Beans? The answer, of course, is that both of these projects, and many others besides, are operating simultaneously, and that in all of them a different arrangement of actors is possible. In such a highly dynamic space, every agential cut depends on other cuts, on responses to responses to responses. The moment one widens the lens even slightly beyond any specific measuring device, one encounters a buzz of other relations waiting to intercede in the future of the beans and the other people and things that surround them.

# CHAPTER SIX

# The Vast Tofu Conspiracy

The first time I presented this research in North America, an audience member who introduced herself as vegetarian asked me if this story meant she should stop eating tofu. Over the following years, some version of that question came up in almost every place I presented. In some cases the questioner would even point out that there was tofu in the room we were in, or waiting to ambush us at the reception, hidden in the ecumenical catered lunch favored at North American universities. The question bothered me at first, since it meant that I hadn't been clear enough that Paraguayan soy is all about meat; I had piqued someone's dietary anxieties over a misunderstanding. But I learned to savor these tofu moments, because they raised a kind of intimate dissonance in the context of the talk. Tofu was the listener's attempt to engage ethically with the story of Paraguayan soybeans by slotting it into the farm-to-plate narratives that dominate contemporary food politics. The frame might have led to a fixation on the wrong food, but the premise, that a listener's body might be an unwilling participant in an abhorrent global extractive industry of which they hadn't even been dimly aware, was hardly off-base.

The soy is everywhere—you just can't see it. It's in the chicken, the sauce, the packaging, the biodegradable cutlery, your clothing, the furniture, probably in the book you're holding, and maybe even the walls. At least you can see the tofu—it's on the end of your fork, so to speak.[1] But it's the unseen ways in which soy seeps into our everyday corporeal existence that are more difficult to reckon with. It makes any simple story about local actors and regulations seem almost impossibly quaint by multiplying the cast of characters ad infinitum.

The research behind this book was composed of long string of such tofu moments. I remember one night enjoying an open-air bebop show in Asunción with a number of friends and outspoken critics of soy. I made an offhand comment about how nice it was to hear this sort of jazz in Paraguay, and someone said, "We never had this before soy." I found comments like this unsettling. I could spend my whole day trying to understand how soy had become such a dominant character in Paraguayan politics, only to find it lurking ambiguously in the most unexpected places. On some days I wasn't sure it made any sense to talk about soy as an actor at all. On other days, the whole story would snap into place around a barrera viva, a moisture meter, a case of poisoning, and I'd redirect my questions toward this new moment of clarity. A little bit more digging would invariably make that one thing less distinct again, a shimmering effect of some other set of relations hiding just beyond my field of attention. I would organize my notes around it and promise to write a short chapter, and then I'd move on to the next thing that presented itself. The cast of characters kept growing.

Initially, the method felt like a terrible choice, or even a nonchoice, a desperate attempt to catch up to the objects of my research, which were constantly receding. But whether choice or not, just like the anxious question about tofu, the method began to feel appropriate to the project. Soy and the state were, after all, many things, as were the relationships between them and the relations upon relations. And so I reached out to three other researchers in Paraguay who could help me embrace the multiplicity even further. I asked them to do parallel versions of what I was doing: following up on particular actors and objects that were entangled with soy. Over the next five years, I did the bulk of the interviewing and participant observation in SENAVE, while the others followed other overlapping trails and other agential configurations. Marco Castillo, a sociology student, began compiling a history of the National Institute of Technology and Standardization (INTS). Sofía Espíndola Oviedo, the only person in the group who was fluent in Guarani and Portuguese, visited production cooperatives. Alejandra Estigarribia began digging into the office in charge of rural epidemiology.[2] Working as a team allowed us to produce moments of clarity more quickly, yet it also produced more vertigo as radical doubt also became more frequent.

More than anything, this collaborative method made me realize that I wasn't alone in feeling the vertigo. Just as I had long-standing ties to certain campesino organizations, Marco, Sofía, and Ale were all committed leftists with social and professional connections to Lugo's government and a deep desire to see it work. As the four of us moved among Lugo's newly appointed functionaries, we were also moving in a comfortable social space and easily accessing offices, like Miguel Lovera's, which would previously have been closed to us. What we encountered there were people like ourselves trying hard to make sense of the new sets of relations in which they suddenly found themselves, trying to figure out how to use their new position in the state apparatus to finally mitigate the problems they had long attributed to soybeans.

Many people spoke openly about how unsettled they were, politically and personally, by being in government. During one of my first interviews, a high-level state functionary described her first weeks on the job: "Here we are, sitting at the board table, and we're all from NGOs, and we're all used to saying, 'The state is the problem!' and then someone turns around and says, 'Wait a minute—we are the state!'" Almost every person who came into Lugo's governmental project at a high rank had grown up during the Stroessner years surrounded by militants, either in the pit of the national resistance movement or in exile in Argentina, Spain, or Sweden, planning Stroessner's overthrow from afar. In the twenty years since the coup that had ended Stroessner's rule, they had dedicated their lives to social movements and NGOs whose lifeblood was the critique of dictatorship. Thus, even as they tried to build institutions to protect those who had been abandoned on the fringes of soy fields, the project to strengthen state institutions invariably aroused fears of unseen forces, past and present, in the long shadow of authoritarianism.

## STANDARDIZED AUTHORITARIANISM

The ragged, epistemological edges of our project made themselves most keenly felt one day in December 2012, when Marco, Ale, Sofía, and I retreated to a cottage just outside of Asunción. Lugo had been deposed only six months before, and we were going over what we had done so far to figure out how we could continue the research. Marco was reporting to the rest of us on one of the projects he had undertaken, a description of the role of the INTS in the soy chain. Like SENAVE, INTS was a virtually invisible agency of the Ministry of Industry and Commerce, and none of us had really heard of it before we began to see its traces in the soy. Initially these traces took the form of colorful, holographic stickers winking from the sides of moisture meters and other technical equipment at the laboratories, silos, and trans-shipment centers that we visited. We soon began noticing the stickers everywhere—on gas pumps and grocery store scales. Marco had taken it on himself to produce a backstory for all of those stickers.

At our team meeting, he tried to give a first approximation of this story. The INTS had been created by the Stroessner government in 1963, but its real genesis began with the International Standards Organization (ISO), created in Geneva just after World War II. The ISO's stated aim was to promote peace through international trade and fight what it called "technical nationalism" and "technical barriers to trade" among European signatories.[3] In the 1960s, the ISO began expanding into Latin America by helping national governments to establish their own standards institutes. The expansion coincided with the Alliance for Progress, the Green Revolution, and the creation of the IADB, and presented itself as enabling development through export-led growth, all the while extending American Cold War interests throughout the region.

In one way, the creation of the INTS was only the national chapter of this globalization story. But it also participated in other stories. The year INTS was created, 1963, was already highly conspicuous to us (and it is already the second time it has appeared in this book), because it marked the end of a crucial period of consolidation of the Stroessner regime. Stroessner had taken the presidency in 1954, but had faced fierce opposition until at least 1959, when he violently suppressed student demonstrations and sent thousands of dissidents (including Marco's parents) into exile. Building on his new strength, Stroessner had passed a series of development-oriented reforms with the IADB, including creating the INTS and the Institute for Rural Welfare (IBR). These consolidated the regime's bureaucracy throughout the country, establishing it as a purveyor of services, a potential benefactor, and a fearsome surveillance apparatus.

Like all of the institutions created during this period of dictatorial institution building, the INTS had then gone into decline, neglected in the 1980s and 1990s during the final years of the regime and the bureaucratic chaos that followed Stroessner's ouster. Governed by a fractious executive board representing warring economic and political elites, the INTS's list of standards had become outdated, and the process for acquiring certifications had become arbitrary and sluggish. This became a problem primarily for international partners, who proposed a comprehensive reform of the agency.

So in 2001, Representatives of the European Investment Bank presented the government of Paraguay with a package of reforms, the Project for Strengthening the Competitiveness of Paraguay's Export Sector (FOCOSEP). The EU's justification for the project began with a diagnosis of Paraguay's economic problems:

> There is an insufficient culture of quality in the country, as well as weak institutions in this sector, which reduce its ability to enter external markets for products and services, even those for which it is well suited. . . . The benefits of globalization and economic integration have been limited in the country, in part because of its insufficient adaptation to the norms of access to international markets, weak public-private articulation and poor availability of information for public investments.[4]

In the ambitious language of development planners, therefore, FOCOSEP aimed to make the state more responsive to the export sector, to modernize the process begun in 1963.

Just like the IADB plan for SENAVE, which was happening in parallel, FOCOSEP's plan had languished until 2003, and just like SENAVE it had been revived by the Nicanor administration. In fact, one of Nicanor's first decrees was to disband the INTS's governing board and consolidate all power in the hands of its director, who then set about restructuring the institute according to EU recommendations.[5] Like SENAVE, INTS became autarchic, operating its own budget (separate from the Ministry of Industry and Commerce, to which it belonged) and generating its own income through certification fees. And like SENAVE, while the newly empowered INTS created new bottlenecks and costs for exporters, most of these exporters welcomed the new institutional presence. For soy farmers, it was easy to treat INTS as a service provider that ultimately enabled export by informing beans. Finally, in another echo of 1963, the consolidation of executive power and the strengthening of regulations had opened up new channels of international investment. In that first year of Nicanor's government, the International Monetary Fund, World Bank, United Nations Development Program, the European Investment Bank and IADB all bolstered their presence in the country and began to reinvest in the promise of Paraguay's export sector.[6]

All of these parallels between 1963 and 2003 also resonated with the frequent comparisons between Nicanor and Stroessner, both positive and negative. For critics, Nicanor was a new dictator; for backers (even reluctant ones), Nicanor got things done. Nor were these opinions mutually exclusive. A common narrative among Paraguayan agronomists, as well as German and American expats in the development community, was that even though they disliked Stroessner's dictatorship on principle, they considered it a golden age for rural development. The years of the democratic transition had, by contrast, been chaotic and unworkable, because priorities and personalities shifted too quickly to bring any project to fruition. For these people, Nicanor had been a breath of fresh air, even though they would have again preferred, in principle, for a more democratically minded party to be in power. Under both Stroessner and Nicanor the lines of force moving the government were clear, as was the steady support of international development funding.

At some level, none of this was surprising; it confirmed the overriding anti-imperialist narrative with which we were very familiar: European and American economic and political interests have historically preferred stable right-wing dictatorships to chaotic popular democracies. The history in Latin America of what Eduardo Gudynas, among others, has called "extractivism" is a history of strong, centralized governments trading away national resources to northern buyers in return for the resources needed to build authoritarian versions of the welfare state.[7] But if the morality of that story had always been easy to access when talking about the procession of power-hungry scoundrels who had until then occupied the Paraguayan presidency, it was much harder to figure out when talking to the functionaries, project coordinators, and technicians who were denizens of the apparatus. The closer we got to the technocratic details of how this extractivism occurred, the harder it was to pinpoint any clear villains. Most of the technocrats involved in the drafting of FOCOSEP, for instance, struck us as well-meaning people who genuinely wished for Paraguayans to benefit from globalization. Indeed, as we were to encounter again and again, many of these people who were nostalgic for Stroessner's bureaucracy, and supportive of Nicanor's institutional reforms, were also enthusiastic supporters of Fernando Lugo's state project.

Perhaps the most unsettling realization was how similar these people were to us and to our friends who had entered the bureaucracy during the Government of Beans. We too had ambitions for a stable understanding of what the state was about, what soy was about, and who was doing what harm to whom. We couldn't do any of that without being able to measure things reliably. And yet reliable measurement, it seemed, was reliable only to the extent that it used the infrastructure laid down by the INTS, the consensual language of extractivism, of soy, and authoritarian rule. As Pierre Bourdieu once argued, the state is not only the monopoly of force but also the condition of possibility for objectivity itself.[8] Every time we bandied about references to tonnage, toxicity, GDP, and acreage, we were speaking through a history of colonial and authoritarian violence.

## A VAST CONSPIRACY, AND A LOCAL ONE

It took Marco several hours to tell this story, and the more he got into it, the farther some of the connections he made seemed to stretch. For instance, in his reading on the history of the ISO, he kept being drawn to mentions of the Swedish Standards Institute (SIS), established in 1922. The experience of the SIS was one of the bases on which the ISO was created, and in the early decades, many Swedes had cycled through the ISO's head offices. Intrigued by this connection, Marco had even spent an afternoon googling the history of the SIS, which first suggested a sordid relationship to wartime Nazi propaganda. He quickly discovered that he was reading about two agencies, the Swedish Standards Institute and the short-lived State Information Board, both of which had the same initials in Swedish. This became a recurring joke in his story, because Marco himself had grown up in Sweden in exile in the 1980s. One of Marco's many nicknames is "the Swede," which we used to tease him for his excessive attention to detail. "Of course it had to be the Swedes!" he exclaimed. "I feel like I'm in the middle of a vast conspiracy!"

We had a good laugh, but not without some uneasiness. Conspiracy, among our group of friends in Paraguay, was as much a coded denunciation of political extremes as it was among liberals in North America. But we all knew exactly what he was talking about. Every time any of us began to investigate some mundane regulatory apparatus we encountered connections multiplying too quickly for us to keep track of them. Worse still, our sense that we were on the verge of being able to fully describe the nefarious networks kept increasing, but our understanding at this scale never settled on stable explanations. Careful as we were to give people in our story the benefit of the doubt, powerful villains nonetheless always seemed to be lurking just beyond the frame. During the Lugo's time in office, we had tried to remain skeptical of the dozens of rumors of plots to overthrow him, only to find that at least one—and probably several others—were accurate. A certain amount of skepticism seemed entirely appropriate.

It was around then that Alejandra noticed a police truck driving slowly down the driveway toward the house. We were in a peculiarly isolated place, a luxurious cottage, with a pool, a trellis heavy with passion fruit, and stunning views of one of Stroessner's favorite vacation spots. The cottage belonged to a wealthy friend who let us borrow it when I visited Paraguay, to take a little research retreat away from the noise of Asunción. We all looked forward to these weekends; although we worked through most of the day, these were the times when everyone was most comfortable, most able to be themselves, to vent their frustrations, questions, sometimes tears, securely. The property covered several hectares, so that one had to wander far from the main road, and through two gates, to get onto the property. And there was this beige pickup truck, coasting slowly across the lawn, a creeping reminder that in Paraguay the state may be absent, or present, but the police are rarely far away.

As the reigning Paraguayan male of the house, Marco walked out to speak to them. The cops never got out of their car but chatted with him about how nice a day it was, how pretty the property looked. They asked where the owner was and accepted his explanation. They then casually asked if he could contribute for gas. The gas contribution is a familiar idiom in Paraguay, and it would be flippant to say that it is only a way of collecting bribes or running a protection racket. Patrol cars sit idle all over rural Paraguay waiting for someone to put gas in them, and local police stations have very meager budgets. It comes almost naturally, then, to suggest that if people want the police to do their job, they need to find a way to fill the tank. Over time, the gas contribution becomes an ongoing relationship between the police and local property owners, with its own set of parameters and performances. So it's not always clear what kind of transaction is in play when the police ask for gas money, but the request always plays on both the desire for and the threat of a coherent state, able to mete out both standardized and unpredictable violence.[9]

When the police car turned around and drove slowly back up the drive, Marco walked back to the house calmly, but shaken. He had not contributed gas money, not knowing the relationship that the house's owner had already established with the local police, and not wanting to confuse the matter. But the disturbance had not been resolved and hung over the rest of our weekend retreat. It made it seem likely that the man who owned this house probably made these contributions regularly, quietly. If he didn't, then the arrival of the police that day at the house could have been construed as a kind of threat, and as a sign that something had changed, that a new sort of agency was being asserted in the relationship between police, thieves, and cottages in this area. If he did, then it was still an awkward reminder of just how much even our ability to do research was conditioned by the tacit relationship between knowledge, property, and violence.

## TOTALITARIANISM, NEOLIBERALISM, ANTHROPOCENE

In his influential book on conspiracy theories in the Cold War US, Timothy Melley argued that conspiracy theory was a product of what he called "agency panic," a response to the increasing complexity of social life and the decentering of the liberal subject. "The recent surge in conspiracy narratives . . . is better understood as a response to the sense that, to quote one cultural critic, 'our specialness—our humanness—has been taking it on the chin a lot lately.' It stems largely from a sense of *diminished human agency*, a feeling that individuals cannot effect meaningful social action and, in extreme cases, may not be able to control their own behavior."[10] For Melley, this was primarily due to the way that large-scale social organizations (governments, corporations, international agencies) acted in ways that didn't quite line up with the story of individual freedom that lay at the analytic heart of liberal social thought.

While there is a long tradition of using the term "conspiracy" to denounce unreasonable or paranoid analysis, there are good reasons why it is hard to get away from it in social theory. Conspiracy theory is an iteration of what Paul Ricoeur once called the "hermeneutics of suspicion," an interpretive tradition that included Marx, Freud, and Nietzsche, thinkers who actually began with the assumption of a hidden agency lurking below surface phenomena.[11] Thus, as George Marcus explains, when we try to explain away conspiracy theories by making reference to political economic conditions, or deep cognitive structures, we are not so much revealing their true meaning as we are replacing one conspiracy theory with another.[12]

Our day of agency panic at the cottage showed that our own analysis couldn't help but move through a repertoire of at least three conspiracies that are inescapable in Paraguay. The first is the oldest: Cold War dissidents experienced the Stroessner regime as an insidious apparatus that might at any moment infiltrate the most intimate recesses of everyday life.[13] In this frame, the regime was marked by three figures: the *pyrague* or "hairy foot" spy, the bodies of the disappeared, and the fabulous wealth of regime cronies. All had an uncanny absent-presence that mirrored that of the dictatorship itself. Anybody could be a pyrague or not, just as any disappeared person might still be alive, hiding, in exile, or being tortured in the notorious "technical department" of the Asunción police. So too were the riches that Stroessner and his closest friends seemed constantly to be amassing through theft, or through the discovery of buried treasure, or because international donors kept offering them "loans." The Stroessner regime, and both its internal and external relations, were known through rumor. When the regime fell, and police archives were discovered, it turned out that a lot of those rumors were true, and as the Colorado Party maintained control of most of the state apparatus, the conspiratorial frame for understanding Paraguayan politics remained relevant.[14]

But then just at the moment when Stronismo began to fall apart in 1989, a second kind of agency panic set in, as globalization took hold and Paraguay was opened to new forms of international plunder. One of the great contradictions that faced everyone on the left in Paraguay in the 1990s was the sense that while their politics had been forged as a critique of Stroessner's police state and controlled economy, they were equally anxious about what came after, the erosion of state power by neoliberal reforms. It suddenly became clear that there were aspects of the regime—in particular the promise that government stability could secure, and eventually expand, some form of welfare—that were now at risk. Just as the Cold War dissidents were succeeding in chipping the state apparatus away from the Colorado Party, international actors like the World Bank, IADB, and the US Embassy were conspiring to transfer Paraguayan wealth to multinationals like Monsanto, Cargill, and ADM and to a new migrant elite.[15] As elsewhere, the historic realignment and rescaling of government that occurred after the end of the Cold War led to a resurgent uncertainty about who controlled the complex web of governmental arrangements that enabled the flow of riches out of the country. The nostalgia for authoritarian figures like Stroessner, captured so effectively by Nicanor, was one effect of the neoliberal moment.

As the neoliberal conspiracy began to congeal around soybeans in the early 2000s, Paraguayans found a third reason to panic. If the agential locus of governmental power was hard to spot, now even the objects of government were becoming newly animate. Were soybeans things to be manipulated, or were they actors with their own interests? Were they merely emanations of capital, or neoliberalism, or international extractivism, or were they something more monstrous besides? The panic of genetic modification was perhaps the first version of this to center on the beans themselves as agents of impending ecocide, a comforting story, in some ways, that at least one form of environmental collapse had an easily locatable culprit. But after Silvino Talavera's death, soy's agency also became far more complicated than its genetics. Was it possible, for instance, that when the Nicanor government abandoned its own ban on Roundup Ready soy, claiming that it had no choice, it was not simply corruption or cynicism speaking, but an acknowledgment that soy had, by 2004, become a political actor itself, giant but indistinct and every bit as insidious as Stroessner's spies?

Anthropocenic conspiracies are more than human, and because of that they complicate older conspiracies from which they are born. Carbon, to name just the most obvious example, turns out not to be merely a resource or a waste product but an actor in its own right that has been shaping government all along.[16] The soy of "la soja mata" created a similar sort of problem. The slogan allowed activists to name an object, a target for regulatory intervention. But that object and the regulatory instruments that were invoked to deal with it turned out to be far more lively than they initially seemed and completely entangled in one another. If activists involved in that project were to accomplish any of their goals, they would not only have to figure out how to appropriate the evanescent state from the dictator's old party, they would also have to figure out how to turn soybeans into manageable objects once more using only the tools accreted through past conspiracies.

And so let us end there for now, with conspiracy as the final character in this book, an epistemological trickster that shadows the absent presence of all the other characters. Soy is always a conspiracy, because even if it is not in your tofu, it's probably in the vinaigrette, in the "ethically farmed" salmon, in the formaldehyde-free pressboard, and it's gotten there through the contrivances of Swedish industrialists and international development money and the repression of communists and Brasiguaio farmers and American pigs, and neoliberalism. And all state projects are conspiratorial, because every time the promises of regulatory stability, social justice, or welfare seem to become possible, they conjure some new version of the very violence for which they were supposed to be a remedy.

# PART II  AN EXPERIMENT IN GOVERNMENT

My friend Jazmín was working the election tables the night that Fernando Lugo became president-elect of Paraguay. As the results began to emerge, she walked, jubilant, incredulous, and more than a bit fearful, down the Plaza de la Democracia. Jazmín had grown up among communists, human rights lawyers, and a growing group of middle-class technocrats who had believed since Stroessner's ouster that they could someday rebuild the country. Nineteen years later, Stroessner's Colorado Party remained in power, using the state bureaucracy as an electoral machine. The likelihood of winning this election had seemed remote, and she still wondered if their victory might be nullified with violence. The Plaza, a huge park that sits between the Congress Building and the police's Central Command, had been the site of a military massacre of student demonstrators only ten years previously.[1] "You know how I knew we had won?" she said to me, months later. "I was walking in front of the police station, where the police were lined up watching the square, and I could see some of them crying. Then I knew. Their world had fallen apart. I'll never forget that sight."

In retrospect, one can point to at least three unrelated conditions that made Lugo's victory possible outside of the growing conflict over soy, and each of them also gives a sense of the problems that sat in wait for him. The first condition was the sweeping political shift occurring throughout South America that some have called the left turn or the pink tide.[2] Leftist governments included moderate social democrats like Brazil's Luiz Inácio Lula da Silva and Argentina's Cristina Kirchner, as well as comparatively radical socialists, like Venezuela's Hugo Chávez and Bolivia's Evo Morales. These four leaders in particular had commanding support of their electorate, and after decades of Cold War dictatorships followed by austerity measures in the 1990s, the shift to the left in these countries had created a regional political ambience in which it now seemed possible to get behind dreams of social reform.

The second condition was the person of Lugo himself. A defrocked rural bishop from the contentious department of San Pedro, Lugo was a highly unusual candidate. His clerical past in the tradition of liberation theology gave him an undeniable populist appeal, and his outsider status made it seem plausible he might curb corruption. Lugo had spent his life building support among campesino organizations. But because Lugo was not campesino, he also appealed to new democrats, that group of urban professionals like Silvia González and Miguel Lovera scattered throughout the NGO sector: socialists, transparency reformers, human rights advocates, environmentalists, students, feminists, and LGBTQ organizers.

Lugo was able to bring these constituencies together along with a coalition of small leftist parties in a movement called Tekojoja. The movement was named after a campesino colony that had been attacked by soy farmers during an attempted eviction, and one of the top campesino leaders in Lugo's group of rural advisors came from there. But if for many rural activists Tekojoja represented, as they called it, a *trinchera*, a trench in the struggle to stop the soybean frontier, the name was also conveniently anodyne. Guarani for "living together in harmony," the word *tekojoja* itself could be taken to mean something more abstract like social welfare or justice. This also made it possible for Tekojoja to form a further alliance with the Liberal Party. Ideologically vacuous, the Liberals were a well-established clientelist machine that had served as the counterweight and mirror image of the Colorados since the nineteenth century. In return for their support, Lugo offered them some of his largest patronage plums, including the positions of vice president and minister of agriculture.

The third condition for Lugo's victory was internal conflict in the Colorado Party itself. For two decades, the Colorados had won every general election by crushing margins.[3] Since the constitution prevented presidents from running for more than one term, the party held nomination primaries which were often more fractious than the elections themselves. In 2007, the party split during one such primary, when the losing candidate refused to endorse the nominee, releasing his faction of the party to "vote their conscience." This was a deci-sive blow to the Colorado candidate: a sizable number of Colorados said at the time that though their allegiances lay with the party to which they had be-longed since birth, their conscience was with Lugo.

So Lugo won the general election, stunning the country and almost all in-ternational observers, including me, and became the first non-Colorado presi-dent in sixty-one years. And yet his odd path to victory also meant that his actual power in the executive was severely restricted. Lugo's close allies won al-most no representation in Congress (only three Senate and two congressional seats). The Colorado Party remained firmly in control of the judiciary and the bureaucracy, which it had built up over three generations. Even in the execu-tive, Liberals monopolized high-ranking political appointments.

But though Jazmín, a brilliant political strategist and a tireless organizer, understood all of these conditions better than most, the day of the election was something else entirely, a pure moment of rupture in which a whole new future suddenly seemed possible. For the first time in history, the police state was crying, and the apparatus that it had controlled for so long was now at the disposal of a completely different state project. Within a few months she would be working in a midlevel bureaucratic job in the Ministry of Education. And like so many others who entered government on the hopeful winds of Lugo's vic-tory, she was about to find out not just how mundane the work of governance is, but also how unruly regulatory instruments can be.

This section of the book is not about Jazmín in particular, but about people like her, who were appointed to work in SENAVE with Miguel Lovera. It was these functionaries who saw their role as shoring up the trench against the soy frontier, to protect campesinos from its excesses and to make space for a different agribiopolitical assemblage to thrive. And as the most contentious governmental experiment within the sprawling proyecto de estado attempted by Lugo's coalition, it is perhaps not surprising that it was also central to the way it fell apart.

# CHAPTER SEVEN

# Capturing the Civil Service

L ike so many new democrats living in Asunción, Miguel Lovera saw
the defeat of the Colorados as a historic victory of progressive politics,
and when Lugo called him to take over SENAVE, he was more than
happy to oblige. Curious, dynamic, brilliant, Lovera epitomized the kind of
manager I would meet throughout Lugo's government, who saw themselves
embarked on a grand experiment to reshape their country's future. He was
not a member of the Tekojoja Party, although many of his top advisors were,
and he didn't see himself as responding to party interests. Instead he viewed
the state in structural terms, as an apparatus that had been built up to promote the interests of both the dictatorship and what he consistently referred
to as "agribusiness" rather than "soja." That state model had its roots in the
late nineteenth century, and, he as he put it, "[It's] not going to change with
Lugo, or with ten Lugos. It's only going to change when we have a society
that decides once and for all to change." But he did feel that he could have
an effect on the small piece of which he had been put in charge. He told me,
SENAVE "was an institution that directly . . . served one sector, agribusiness.
It's that simple. And, well, that's what is going to change."

But what precisely was this thing he was going to try to change? Lovera's
office was on the thirteenth floor of an ugly double office tower in downtown

Asunción called Edificio Planeta, a building that, when I first walked in the door, confronted me with an image of the state at its most pathetic. Here, the government of Paraguay looked like nothing more than a very great number of people sitting at tiny desks between moldy cubicle walls, walking the hallways with cell phones, drinking mate or coffee, and waiting for the elevator. Waiting on the dilapidated red couch outside of the executive secretary's office on the thirteenth floor, often for hours at a time, I had trouble wrapping my head around the scale of what the people inside were doing. It was one thing, while sitting in a squatter camp, or an academic classroom, or at an angry NGO meeting, to denounce the state as the ideological projection of power relations, as the nexus between objective truth and police violence. But in the confined spaces where governance actually happened, the whole enterprise seemed excruciatingly boring, and highly unlikely to be successful. Somehow, it was these folks, with their daily anxieties about jobs, clients, and broken printers, laughing together about last night's television shows or yelling at their maids over the phone, their desks piled high with papers, pictures of their children, and thermoses, who struck fear and loathing into the hearts of activists at some points, and hopes for a new kind of society at others.

Most of those who entered Lugo's government assumed that this condition was not a natural state for the civil service, but rather a product of decades of one-party rule, and one of their goals was to reform it. The Colorados had maintained power through the masterful use of clientelism, which meant that the primary mechanism for distributing state services, resources, and civil service positions was by awarding them to clients of powerful patrons within the Colorado Party.[1] For many new democrats, combating clientelism was an end in itself, part of the sluggish transition to democracy that had been underway since 1989. For others, clientelism was bad primarily because it was an impediment to carrying out other projects. If the idea was to treat an agency like SENAVE as a regulatory instrument to affect the distribution of soy, then not only was this instrument extremely complex, most of its parts seemed superfluous or counterproductive, structural accretions of past agendas, interests, and controversies. All of Lugo's appointments encountered some version of this problem, but in SENAVE it was particularly acute, because those accretions had been to the mutual benefit of two of Lugo's most ardent foes: the Colorado Party and the soy lobby. And so, as we embark on the short story of the Government of Beans, we need to start far away from those beans, in the office and hallways of

Edificio Planeta, where activists learned to bend the enemy's tools to their devices.

## PAYROLLS AND FREEZERS

The clientelist structure of the Colorado Party dates back to the decades after the War of the Triple Alliance (1865–1870), when Asunción's fractious elite families resolved themselves into two parties: the Asociación Nacional Republicana (or Colorados, after their signature red scarves) and Partido Liberal (known as the Liberals, and traditionally wearing blue). For the first half of the twentieth century, the Liberals held power.[2] The Colorados took control in a 1947 civil war. The Colorados centralized the state through an extensive hierarchical system of *seccionales*, party offices that doled out patronage and provided surveillance for the regime. By the 1960s, the party effectively controlled all public service employment. Though it did not receive the same sort of scholarly attention as the PRI in Mexico, or the Peronists in Argentina, Stroessner's Colorados were a shining example of what came to be called "machine politics."[3] Even as the dictatorship collapsed in the late 1980s and gave way to regular democratic elections, it was this machine that kept the party in power by ensuring that the civil service, and the many goods at its disposal, continued to respond to Colorado interests.

In regulatory agencies like SENAVE, this top-down model of clientelism was complemented by a bottom-up system of bribery and embezzlement, where front-line functionaries collected sums from those seeking an agency's services and then passed some of the amounts collected up the patronage hierarchy.[4] One of the clearest signs of this activity appeared routinely in the year preceding any election, when the heads of key agencies were switched out for known political operatives with no expertise in the role to which they were assigned. So if civil service positions were one of the most important forms of patronage, they were also the medium for other patronage, as client networks within the civil service would both collect and distribute bribes and gifts.

One of the effects of democratization in the 1990s was that with Stroessner out of the way, the Colorados fractured into several competing currents, each following different men in vying for control of different parts of the patronage system. Internal conflict transformed the system into what Gustavo

Setrini calls "pluralistic clientelism," characterized by fluidity and competition in the channels of patronage rewards.[5] According to Paraguay's civil service law, functionaries couldn't be fired, which meant that appointments created a more or less durable foothold for different client networks, but with every change at the top of the bureaucracy, new clients would be installed throughout the hierarchy to offset the influence of old clients. Movement of patrons multiplied patronage appointments. During the 1990s, when structural adjustment was making most governments in the region trim their civil service, Paraguay's expanded by close to 50 percent.[6]

To be fair, the Paraguayan state was still small by most regional standards. But what public sector employment had been created by attempts to improve state services had become remarkably inefficient, with legions of government workers doing almost no actual work.[7] These employees were referred to as *planilleros*, because they showed up in the payroll (*la planilla*) but not at the office.[8] So common was this practice that every few years a reform would find thousands of government employees who had no office at all, or who supposedly worked many different jobs in different parts of the country simultaneously. Added to this was another category of employees who did no work, not because they didn't want to, but because their bosses didn't trust them. Legally barred from firing employees, political bosses resorted to moving the untrustworthy to *el freezer*, a civil service no-man's-land in which people continued to receive a salary but were effectively stripped of any duties, power, or access to information. The Ministry of Finance maintained two whole buildings for unwanted employees who showed up at work to receive a salary but had nothing to do. Still, nonworking functionaries were only the most extreme cases. The normal condition of the civil servant was to work at a job that consisted, in part, of a perpetual struggle to maintain intraparty alliances.

The fact that this was normal isn't the same as saying that everyone thought the system was legal or good. For instance, among bureaucrats I knew, the question "Who is your *patrón*?" was considered slightly forward and was often a way of teasing fellow workers. The question "For whom is he or she collecting [*recaudando*]?" was always whispered behind people's backs. But very few people were in a position to imagine a way of changing these systemic practices. Normalcy is key to any clientelist system: on top of being the only viable way to access state resources, it becomes so ingrained in people's social and familial lives that it is virtually impossible to imagine oneself outside of it.[9] It even makes it hard for anticlientelism to express itself in terms that aren't, to some degree, clientelist.

But this also gets us to one of the trickiest aspects of assessing clientelism. Just like its close cousin, corruption, in the era of democratic reform, clientelism isn't just an analytic description of a particular set of relations, but an accusation that one political group makes against another.[10] And so whether a given set of relationships appears clientelistic or not depends in large part on the position of the accuser. Many of the new democrats in Lugo's entourage had spent their lives accusing Colorado bureaucrats of clientelism from outside the state apparatus, as journalists, social scientists, and development consultants. The stakes, and the layered meanings of these accusations, would necessarily change as the same people moved into government positions themselves and began to compete for control.

## GEOGRAPHIES OF TRUST

To get to the thirteenth floor of Edificio Planeta, one had to ride up one of two very small elevators, usually packed with other employees, but once there, one entered a different world, set momentarily apart from the rest of the institution. The offices were slightly larger, the air conditioning a bit more effective, and the heavy wood furniture gave proceedings there a sense of gravitas that was hard to find among the tiny particle board desks that filled most of the rest of the building. But even on my first day there, the comparative luxury of these offices only underscored the degree to which the people who worked there felt garrisoned and isolated. Lovera trusted almost no one in the institution. He had brought five confidants with him into the executive suite, including Silvia González and a public relations manager named Inés Franceschelli, whom we will soon come to know much better. These were the only people in whom he had complete *confianza* (trust). But there were plenty of others whom he wasn't sure of yet. On Lugo's instruction, Lovera had appointed two people to upper management positions from within the ranks of Tekojoja, and he'd hired a handful of lawyers and technicians whom he knew from graduate school. So even in his office and boardroom, he was always on guard, describing the walls as thin, and carefully watching the errand runners who milled about the hallway.

The language of confianza was everywhere in the bureaucracy, and it always operated on at least two different registers. The first was formal: the law of the civil service called all discretionary appointments *cargos de confianza*, and was very clear about the limits of such appointments to the very top positions in state agencies.[11] Underneath this was a more informal use of confianza that was simply a way of talking about workplace alliances. Everyone, regardless of where they were placed in the institution, needed to know who their people were, their *gente de confianza*. Among upper management, of course, these two definitions often overlapped, as people used "cargos de confianza" to describe tasks they could only ask trusted allies to carry out, and used their limited ability to hire people arbitrarily as a way of cementing these alliances. Lugo's finance minister even described this as a codified system among upper management. "We used 'stoplight' criteria," he said. "Every vice minister had a color code for her personnel. Red were the incorrigibles in whom you could not trust. Green were the people of change, and yellow depended on the circumstances."[12] Although I never heard anyone else put it quite so boldly, this basic arrangement was true across Lugo's government: the "people of change" were allies of the government's program.

In demarcating a hazy zone between official political appointments and unofficial bureaucratic alliances, confianza was, in other words, the language of clientelism. Correspondingly, confianza also came with a ready set of clientelist tools for dealing with the untrustworthy. Chief among these was the freezer. Lugo's appointees weren't quite as brazen in their freezing practices as Colorados before them, and Lugo's minister for the civil service was an outspoken opponent of the practice, but its use was still widespread.[13] Managers sent untrustworthy employees to posts with little responsibility and even placed them in isolated offices, nooks and crannies in ministry basements and quiet hallways to which they could move their desks and where their phone and internet access were limited. At least three of the regulatory agencies I got to know used such nakedly clientelist tools to combat clientelism.

Since most of Lugo's appointees were new to their jobs, the criteria they used for sorting the trustworthy from the untrustworthy were often based on very little information about people. This meant that some of the implicit criteria of trust operated through prejudice. For instance, Lovera was clear, from the beginning, that there was a geography of trust that corresponded not to the people themselves, but to the kinds of posts they occupied. Like most Paraguayan bureaucracies, SENAVE was bifurcated into administrative and technical sections, with different pay structures, appointment procedures, and unions. For Lovera, the biggest problems lay on the administrative side of the institution: "Look, we have 432 employees. Of those, 150 are technicians who work in agriculture-related activities. After that, there are twenty in the legal and financial administration. The rest should be our army for inspections and for administrative support. But at least two hundred of these administrators were hired as part of the Colorado regime's clientelist practices. And that's our straitjacket. Because these are civil servants, and the rigid labor rights make them more untouchable than nobility."

As a general rule, Lovera had more confidence in his technicians than his administrators. The former, after all, required some sort of independent credential—a degree in agronomy, chemistry, or biology, and often a further certification to become an inspector or licensor. This meant that all of these positions were to some degree based on the person's merits, rather than simply family or party relations. By contrast, all but the very top administrative positions required no credentials at all and, as a result, employees here were more obviously hired for their loyalty to a previous boss. Lovera's head of human resources told me frankly that she didn't know what most of them did with their days beyond plotting to overthrow them.

Lovera's offhand joke about nobility, though, is very telling. On the one hand, it indexes a normative history of bureaucratic reform, of the rise of meritocracy in the civil service out of aristocracy.[14] On the other hand, it sarcastically inverts the class position of the majority of the people Lovera wished he could fire, uneducated, low-ranking employees with little social status either inside or outside of the institution. Part of why technicians at least appeared more trustworthy had to do with shared cultural capital. Like new democrats, the urban professionals who staffed most of Asunción's leftist NGOs, educated technicians, spoke the same language of professionalism and competence, of dress and comportment, and tended to share a commitment to at least the Weberian aesthetic of office life. They were far easier to relate to than the unqualified secretaries, chauffeurs, and paper-pushers whose very presence made the politicization of the civil service so obvious. So while technically trained civil servants may have entered their posts through a suspect patrón, they seemed more trustworthy because they appeared to share the values of reformers. More than anything, what they shared was class.

This brings us to one of the primary functions of traditional clientelism and one of the greatest difficulties that Lovera (and civil servants in Lugo's government generally) encountered as they sought to reform the system. All political movements need to find a way to build class alliances between wealthy supporters, professional administrators, and the popular bases that vote for them. In Paraguay this also included bridging the cultural and class divides between urban and rural, and between Spanish and Guarani. The Colorado Party (and to a lesser extent the Liberals) were experts at forging these asymmetrical connections through patron-client relationships.

Lugo's presidency, by contrast, was based on a wholly different sort of alliance between the Spanish-speaking urban professional left and the

Guarani-speaking rural and peri-urban poor, which was held together primarily by Lugo's persona and a vague promise of social welfare. That sort of electoral alliance didn't translate well into the everyday pragmatics of building trust within state institutions. Instead, the new practices of trusting technicians over administrators produced a kind of "meritocratic clientelism" that created horizontal, rather than vertical, alliances, principally between urban professionals.[15] Lugo's victory created an unprecedented boom in public-sector jobs for new democrats and other members of the middle-class Left. A large group of people who knew each other through their work in NGOs and the arts now moved together into government jobs. Many admitted that their only real reason for having a job was that they were friends with someone, and most were wryly open about having found, or lost, a patrón in Lugo's coalition. But because these relationships were more horizontal than traditional clientelism, they were less good for distributing the immediate spoils of electoral victory to the poorer and more rural parts of the country.

This is a common enough phenomenon in countries moving from a clientelist system to a professionalized civil service.[16] Structurally, the project to reform the civil service tends to turn government employment into a site for the reproduction of the middle class.[17] But Lugo's coalition was far too weak to support the inevitable strain that this caused, and the professional middle class was simply too small a constituency to build lasting political community in the Government of Beans. As Lovera's small group of confidants was to discover, the hardest bridge to forge was that between the urban and the rural. They all came from urban professional backgrounds, and many of them could barely speak Guarani. This didn't matter in trying to conduct business with other professionals, since Spanish competency is the primary cultural requisite for joining the middle class in Asunción. Yet all other alliance building in Paraguayan politics, alongside most appeals to the rural poor, was conducted in Guarani. Not being able to speak it was a sign not just of a cultural separation from the majority of the institution's employees, it was also a separation from the victims of the soy boom.

THE RETURN OF THE RURAL

We're now in a position to understand a further structural danger that lay in wait for Lovera at SENAVE. During his two years as president of the institution, Lovera was under constant attack from Colorado and Liberal bureaucrats who plotted to have him removed and replaced by one of their own.

But these were the battles that Lovera was expecting, and he fought back, finding ways to demobilize many employees, and exposing bribery and embezzlement practices among several of his middle managers, inspectors, and lawyers. What he was less ready for was a corruption scandal that arose from among his supposed allies within Lugo's coalition.

That story centered on a man I'll refer to as Darío, a political operative whom Lovera had appointed to a top administrative post at the request of Lugo.[18] He was supposed to be one of Lovera's strongest political allies in the institution, but from the moment I entered his office for the five-minute interview he allowed me, I could tell that he came from a very different social and political position, if only because he was obviously suspicious of my presence. Because he was part of the administrative branch, Darío's position gave him access to those hundreds of bureaucrats that Lovera didn't trust, and to teams of Colorado brokers whom he suspected of being experienced bribe takers. Lovera began to suspect that Darío was taking advantage of this when he realized that files on job vacancies and candidates were being hidden from him: Darío seemed to be constructing his own network of confidants within the administrative branch. This discovery dovetailed with hard-to-substantiate rumors about "suitcases of cash" making their way upward in the institution toward Darío's office from the countryside.

The immediate problem for Lovera was that Darío was protected by the head of the Tekojoja Party, Sixto Pereira, who was also one of the most influential men in Lugo's inner circle. Pereira was the first campesino leader to be elected to the Senate from outside of the main party structures, and he was by far Lugo's most important rural ally.[19] For some time already, tensions had begun to surface between Lugo's new democratic supporters and Pereira, who was widely accused of using state programs as a way of doling out patronage to his campesino supporters.[20]

But of course it is hardly surprising that when part of Lugo's coalition became tied up in a clientelism scandal, it centered on his rural constituency. As a form of accusation, the discourse of clientelism has always tended to be used by educated urbanites against the rural poor. The blame for this might begin with anthropology, which began to use the term "clientelism" to describe rural cultures in Spain and Latin America in the 1950s.[21] These early studies of rural social structure focused on the importance of *compadrazgo* (coparenthood) to rural Catholic communities, offering a structure whereby peasants of different class status could form ongoing bonds of hierarchical reciprocity. Paraguayan campesinos even made an important appearance in this literature, in Elman and Helen Service's ethnography of a Paraguayan village:

> Typical peasant attitudes are those we associate with Europe before the spread of the "protestant" or "capitalist" ethic. . . . We never discovered any sentiment among the peasants that hard work and intelligent management or enterprise could achieve other than a small and ephemeral reward. . . . The conception that economic improvement can be achieved only through the aid or influence of a *patrón* is very prevalent, in spite of the fact that for many years there have been no agricultural haciendas. The most usual response from a peasant who is queried about his economic and technological difficulties is not that he needs a steel plow, better seed or a yoke of oxen, but that he needs a good *patrón* who will help him.[22]

These sorts of descriptions of rural culture were picked up in the 1960s by political scientists as ways to describe political networks in modernizing countries.[23] Even urban studies in this early literature argued that urban clientelism was a transplant brought by rural migrants into rapidly industrializing centers like Buenos Aires and Mexico City. In the developmentalist frame favored by these scholars, clientelism remained a vestige of premodernism.[24]

Today, scholarship on clientelism has become more nuanced, with most acknowledging that its pervasiveness is less a holdover than an integral part of democratic apparatuses.[25] But in Paraguay, urban professionals still blamed clientelism, and the many political evils they associated with it, on the tenaciousness of rural ignorance. Try as they might to build alliances with rural supporters, new democrats in Lugo's coalition were tacitly suspicious of campesino tactics. In other words, although they might be sympathetic to the plight of victims of the soy frontier, they were part of the same geography of distrust that made it so easy for the courts to dismiss the voices of Silvino Talavera's relatives. Whether Pereira was really on the take, or whether the suspicion around him was merely a product of new democratic anxieties, is beside the point. The accusation was a symptom of the weakness of Lugo's coalition.

Lovera eventually fired Darío and several other people around him involved in the scheme, and in doing so he contributed to a growing rift in Lugo's coalition that was ultimately its undoing. We'll get to that in a couple of chapters. But for now let's consider the task at hand, from the thirteenth floor of SENAVE, as Lovera and his band of social-justice technicians and environmentalists tried to capture the institution away from the Soy State and to put it to use as a protector of rural welfare. The hive of bored and sometimes conniving Liberal and Colorado clients who filled SENAVE offices were only the most obvious of Lovera's obstacles in building the Government of Beans. Cutting across it was also a simmering distrust of the very people whom that government most hoped to serve. And all this could be seen even in the insipid office block of Edificio Planeta, baking in the diesel fumes of downtown Asunción, a hundred kilometers from the nearest soybean.

# CHAPTER EIGHT

# Citizen Participation

The first time I visited SENAVE's main laboratory complex, the director complained to me that the head office was totally unresponsive to her needs. With a wry smile and a cock of her head, she said, "El estado no pasa Calle Última." This refrain, "The state doesn't reach past Calle Última," which refers to the ring road that separates Asunción's downtown from its suburbs (literally the "Last Road"), is one of the most common ways of criticizing the centralized state in Paraguay. Here it was particularly ironic: the SENAVE laboratories are not far beyond Calle Última, only a few kilometers from Edificio Planeta, in the suburb of San Lorenzo. But she was only the first of many high-ranking civil servants to tell me that the state was absent even in the government offices in which they worked.

If the country-city divide appeared to be one of cultural politics inside Edificio Planeta, a few kilometers away it was starkly infrastructural. The reference to Calle Última pointed to a very real problem for functionaries who didn't work downtown. Asunción's recent, rapid growth had created a snarl of traffic from dawn to dusk, and it wasn't unusual for it to take two hours to get downtown from San Lorenzo.[1] The lab director complained that she had spent whole workdays stuck in traffic trying to get to meetings downtown, only to find they'd been rescheduled by the time she arrived.

The simple transfer of documents or samples from one office to another could take days. But if the head of the laboratory division of SENAVE felt that the state was distant, one can imagine what it felt like to live by the soy fields, several hundred kilometers from San Lorenzo. In the countryside, and particularly for campesinos who were still waiting for the state to deliver on promises of land redistribution, health care, or sanitary services, Calle Última was a bitter dividing line beyond which most functionaries rarely ventured.

Much farther from Edificio Planeta, stationed on the outskirts of an advancing sea of beans, Gerardo ran one of SENAVE's sleepy outposts, a small regional office of the decentralized branch on the outskirts of one of Paraguay's many crossroads towns. Gerardo was a certified SENAVE inspector, comfortable working in Spanish, Guarani, and Portuguese, and his family ties to the Liberal Party had secured him his post in 2009, when the Liberals controlled the agency. He was a people person and an able agronomist, and he quite liked his job, which offered him a comfortable salary and a degree of independence. But far from the bustle of Asunción, Gerardo often worked completely alone for weeks at a time, as other staff, from the cleaner to the person hired to help with manual labor, rarely received their paychecks and so rarely showed up to work, except to move the three goats tethered outside the office window.

Gerardo was single-handedly responsible for covering an area of close to six thousand square kilometers, including some of the most coveted soy-growing territory in the country. He received dozens of requests for service per week, everything from multinationals needing him to certify their silos, to angry campesino groups denouncing their neighbors for pesticide violations. But a single inspection often required him to spend the entire day in his pickup truck, and he had to spend at least one day a week driving into Asunción to deliver paperwork or to attend training sessions. Any complicated case requiring more than one inspector or, worse, a lawyer, would have to be organized days in advance to allow someone time to drive out from Asunción. With that sort of workload, it was to be expected that inspectors like him would have to pick and choose which calls to answer, between those that offered coffee in a nice air-conditioned front office, and those where he would be met with committees of campesinos carrying machetes, mad at the neighboring sojeros, and equally mad at the state for having ignored all of their calls to that point. There were sometimes bribes involved, Gerardo once admitted to me, but the incentive structures of the Soy State didn't need bribes to work.

Distant as he was from the machinations in Edificio Planeta, Gerardo's comfortable work life was completely transformed the day Miguel Lovera became his boss. In July 2010, he received a call from Lovera's planning director, Inés Franceschelli, to tell him about a new inspection initiative they were about to start in his area. She called it the Citizen Participation Unit, and that week it required Gerardo to drive his truck into the city, pick up a larger-than-usual group of people, and take them to visit campesino and indigenous communities affected by pesticide drift in his territory. For the next week, and then regularly thereafter, Gerardo would act as the inspector and driver for the group. He was highly skeptical of this initiative, and believed that both Lovera and, perhaps especially, Franceschelli were a bit overzealous and unrealistic. But he was affable and, particularly when called from the head office, didn't overtly question what he was being asked to do. What he couldn't know at the time was that he was about to be dragged into one of the Government of Beans's most audacious institutional experiments. The Citizen Participation Unit was an attempt to forge a new kind of relationship between the regulator and the rural poor that would serve as an alternative to clientelism.

## DECENTRALIZATION

Centralized bureaucracy is a common feature of many Latin American countries. Capital cities were formed first as colonial outposts and later as power centers by groups of elite settlers. When these colonies declared independence from Spain in the early nineteenth century, many adopted a republican model of government based on Napoleonic France.[2] But centralization only really came to be seen as a problem in the 1980s, as development experts began to worry about their complicity with authoritarian regimes and to look for more local forms of development assistance.[3] Decentralization became a key part of the developmental tool kit, and a component of the new, postauthoritarian constitutions that many countries in the region passed at the end of the Cold War.[4] As part of this trend, Paraguay's 1992 constitution boldly (if somewhat ambiguously) promised to become a "unitary decentralized state" by promoting autonomous departmental and municipal councils with their own revenue streams and powers.[5] Despite this, a comparative analysis of decentralization in Latin America in 1999 found that Paraguay's reform had been the least effective of the many attempts throughout the region.[6] As we've seen, SENAVE was a case in point, an explicit attempt to decentralize the Ministry of Agriculture by making many of its offices more independent. Nonetheless, it had replicated the spatial tradition, concentrating almost all of its personnel in a single building in downtown Asunción.

Six rural offices like Gerardo's and three stations at the main border crossings were the extent of SENAVE's ground presence in the countryside. Far from being considered the front line of the institution, the decentralized offices were treated as backwaters and used as bureaucratic freezers. As Franceschelli herself put it in 2010:

> The regional offices were empty shells. They were storage facilities for functionaries. The functionary had some problem—you didn't want them to be seen or they were good for nothing—you threw them in the regional office. . . . They don't even have a system for receiving requests for services, still today. So, for example, you say, "I have ten or a thousand or ten thousand hectares (it doesn't matter), and I want to produce seeds," you have to come all the way to Asunción to request your seed producer registry. It's insane.

This centralization was one of the most pernicious problems that Lovera and Franceschelli believed they needed to address when they took over SENAVE. So in keeping with the urgency of the work in those early days, they hatched the Citizen Participation Unit as a novel way to get more people into the countryside to respond directly to complaints. The unit began with two teams, each one outfitted with two pickup trucks, whose job it was to travel to the countryside and follow up on *denuncias*, complaints made by citizens about producers. Franceschelli described it this way:

> First, the idea is to put the voice of citizens into the institution, to open a new, official entry channel. That is, if a denuncia enters via the unit, the institution is there to respond. Nobody can ignore it. It allows us to bypass the papers that get lost at the front desk, that are lost on desks of the technical directors, etc. . . . So on the one hand it's to deal with denuncias . . . to put citizens inside the institution. And it also allows us to put the institution among the citizens, the nonproducers.

Because they were thinking big, the unit quickly became much more than a rapid-response team, growing into a node that articulated multiple state services with rural communities. All of Paraguay's state institutions suffered from the same centralization problem, but because SENAVE was built to service the agribusiness sector and had a comparatively large budget at its disposal, it was in a privileged position to change this. SENAVE had a lot more pickup trucks at its disposal than, for instance, the Secretariat of the Environment, the Forestry Institute, the Ministry of Education, or even the National Indigenous Institute (INDI). And many of the problems in the communities affected by the soy boom were not just about pesticides. So when a denuncia came in that involved things outside of SENAVE's technical jurisdiction, like water contamination, deforestation, or putting students or indigenous communities at risk, the Citizen Participation Unit could now invite representatives of those institutions to accompany them on their inspections.

The Citizen Participation Unit was therefore a wide-ranging agribiopolitical proposal, using complaints about pesticide drift as an opportunity to articulate the full promise of rural welfare at specific points of conflict. Nor was the proposal limited to the notion of articulated service delivery from Asunción; it also mobilized a novel understanding of citizenship that would increase its reach.

> We've created [the unit] to be an office of articulation, with other institutions and organizations. So although anyone can approach us, for us to move the machinery of state presence, we ask that there please be a sponsoring organization that is our local reference, so that citizens can be organized, because it's very difficult to intervene when a community has very disparate interests. So that's what we took as our working principle.

The plan was to avoid responding to individuals with problems and instead to encourage citizens to organize their problems together into aggregate denuncias.

The Citizen Participation Unit was therefore designed to get around some of the problems of institutional centralization by creating the conditions for groups of bureaucrats to meet simultaneously with groups of citizens in the countryside. And yet in at least one respect the work-around also reinforced the problem: the unit was still run out of the Edificio Planeta, and its insistence on putting together teams of Asunción-based functionaries for trips to the countryside exacerbated the many difficulties the government pickup trucks always encountered as they tried to pass Calle Última. To be fair, it's hard to imagine them doing it differently: the geography of government, and the geography of trust, made it almost impossible to immediately outsource radical new projects to anyone already stationed outside of Asunción. But the irony was not lost on people like Gerardo, who found it vaguely absurd that "more decentralization" meant, for him, more driving in and out of the capital.

## MOBILIZING THE STATE IN PICKUP TRUCKS

The Citizen Participation Unit occupied a room with stained acoustic tile on the seventh floor of Edificio Planeta. But if the room was dingy, the people hired to coordinate the unit entered their jobs with unusual levels of enthusiasm and gusto. Even by the standards of Lugo's government, the members of the unit were an odd assortment of functionaries. Because they were mainly going to work with campesinos and indigenous groups, fluency in Guarani was a prerequisite, as well as a comfort (as campesinos often say of urbanites who are willing to move to the countryside) with getting one's trousers dirty. In other words, it required a certain commitment to breaking the usual social distance between functionaries and the rural poor, to facilitating the sorts of trust that were so difficult to achieve between most urban professionals and campesinos. Most of the staff hired to do this job had been frontline activists before, drawn from alternative farm movements, radical church groups, and leftist media organizations, and most were members of the Tekojoja Party, hired by a well-placed patrón whom Inés had trusted to form the team.

All of this set them apart from the older functionaries, like Gerardo, with whom they had to work. Unit members approached their work as a vocation rather than a job, more an extension of their activism than an attempt to carry out a state function and get a salary. They were willing to work longer hours, and they tended to get impatient with the routine squabbles over bureaucratic procedures that consumed so many of their more experienced coworkers. Nor did they dress the part of the state functionary, showing up to work in jeans, checkered shirts, and hiking shoes rather than the suits and pressed polyester of the office staff.

But if the Citizen Participation Unit wanted to set up a parallel institution within SENAVE, they soon found out how difficult it would be. It's one thing to notice the fleet of unused pickup trucks in the various parking lots belonging to the institution and to create a new bureaucratic channel for responding to complaints. But it is quite another to find a way to mobilize those trucks to reach the complaints. The trucks were appendages of a much larger network of material and bureaucratic relations that also needed to be mobilized for the trucks to leave the parking lot. And that network was full of detours and bottlenecks within which competing agendas also played, including other back channels that weren't so openly declared. A recurring example of this centered on the endless difficulties in approving per diem payments and gas vouchers, which were processed by a single office on the administrative side of the institution. Functionaries were given a per diem for food and other expenses incurred while traveling, but in principle these needed to be approved and delivered (usually as an envelope of cash) before the teams left Asunción. These requests almost always encountered delays, either because they were returned for information missing on the forms, or because they were simply "lost."

Lovera's team soon discovered that the problems went further than this in SENAVE, because gas vouchers and per diem requests were also a favorite medium for small-scale embezzlement. This involved petty examples, like the fact that many high-level state employees were known to take dubious business trips to Buenos Aires whenever they could to take advantage of high per diem allocations for Argentina.[7] And it involved much more intricate ones, like the systematic replication of per diem requests by administrative directors collecting money for their political bosses. With all of the delays in approving per diems, functionaries knew they were unlikely to be paid retroactively, and were therefore reticent to leave Asunción until they had managed to get their envelopes. A pickup truck carrying five functionaries had to clear five separate per diem requests and one gas voucher before it could move. For the Citizen Participation Unit, which imagined that it could respond quickly to rural complaints by filling pickup trucks with people from multiple state institutions (each with their own internal bureaucracy for processing per diems), this was a constant headache.

The problem with per diems in turn exacerbated the tension between keen newcomers and older civil servants. At the beginning, many activists in the Citizen Participation Unit believed that their work was too important to suspend for lack of per diems or other *trabas* (hurdles) that the bureaucracy might put in their path, and they occasionally left town without the requisite envelopes.[8] When Gerardo first met members of the unit, he dismissed their enthusiasm with a knowing smile: "They'll change, if they last." But as elsewhere, the distinction between functionaries who insisted on cashing in their per diems and those who barreled ahead regardless was also morally charged. Unit newcomers tended to look down their noses at the old timers, the certified inspectors, the lawyers, and the drivers on whom they depended, for lacking work ethic, dedication to the regulatory project, or even a sense of patriotic duty. And it was no surprise, then, that on top of all of the structural barriers the institution placed on the unit's work, many of their coworkers also dragged their feet when called to action, as subtle retaliation for the condescension that they rightly detected.

## BEYOND CALLE ÚLTIMA

After Franceschelli told me about the Citizen Participation Unit, she suggested I join one of the pickup trucks, leaving the next day. She put me in touch with a unit leader I'll call Amada, a one-time radical farm organizer who now led one of the units on weekly expeditions out beyond Calle Última. It took about five phone conversations to set up our meeting—Amada was always on the move, her cell phone cutting in and out, and her fast, colloquial Spanish, mixed with Guaraní slang, at times was hard for me to follow. I was more than a little intimidated by this person with whom I was going to spend the next week. But like so many people in the Government of Beans, her willingness to have me along—the only variable of consequence to her was space in the truck—signaled a whole new way of being a bureaucrat from the one I was used to.

Gerardo, who had driven into the city from his regional office the night before, picked me up at 4 a.m. several blocks from my friend's house (if you want to pass Calle Última, you have to do so long before rush hour). I squeezed into the back of the truck's cab on the side where the door didn't open, and tried to introduce myself in the blackness to everyone present, as the first of many gourds of hot mate made the rounds. We would be in the truck for almost seven hours before we reached our first stop, several kilometers northeast of the city of Curuguaty, where a small community of indigenous Avá Guaraní were complaining about pesticides being sprayed around their school. We spent the next three days visiting community centers and schools with similar complaints, staying the night in a dormitory at Curuguaty's community radio station, a frequent stopover for activists.

It wasn't until later that night, as we all sat around a table debriefing, that I took stock of our unlikely group. There were two pickup trucks, each led by one of the members of the Citizen Participation Unit. My truck was led by Amada, the fast-talking activist from Tekojoja, the other by Serena, a soft-spoken nun who had left her convent to better foment social change. Each truck also had an inspector: Gerardo, the laid-back Liberal, and Cézar, a hardened old (and therefore Colorado) agronomist, who had been one of SENAVE's first certified inspectors. There were also two lawyers, the only two people in the trucks who spoke no Guarani: Camelia, a wealthy Liberal with designs on public office, and Alejandra, appointed by Silvia González, who complained all day about getting burrs in her pants. There was Larisa, an inspector in training with no clear affiliation, Jorge, a young Liberal driver, and a Canadian anthropologist scribbling in his notebook. And finally, there was Úrsula, a disgraced former director of INDI, who had been demoted when Lugo took office. Everyone knew she was Colorada but no one talked about it, or about the fact that for her, the truck was a freezer.

Everyone got along, bound by Paraguayans' seemingly endless capacity to stay awake, drink mate, and tease each other. But the tensions were never far below the surface, and there were three topics of conversation that brought this out most clearly. The first was soy itself. Amada and the other newcomers all talked about what they were doing as confronting la soja and sojeros, even though, in August, we didn't encounter a single soybean anywhere. Even as we passed Calle Última, in other words, the trucks had taken on the language of campesino resistance, and this clearly made the agronomists uncomfortable. They often corrected the conversation by reminding everyone that we weren't just talking about soy, but about agriculture in general. And when we talked about pesticides and genetic modification, the agronomists would often begin arguing that people's fears about these things were misplaced, before conceding that bad practices were still going on.

The second recurring conversation was about political affiliation and rank. A running joke was that everyone (except the humorless Úrsula) would at some point be called *pinche*, a deprecating term for a low-level employee. Given the fact that two newcomers, Amada and Serena, held rank over everyone else in the truck, there was more than a touch of bitterness to some of these references. In return, the Liberals, with Cézar joining in, would joke about the day when Lovera would finally get sacked, the implication being that Amada and Serena wouldn't be far behind him. Meanwhile everyone seemed uneasy about the recently announced Department of Internal Affairs set up to run anticorruption investigations within SENAVE. (Before Lovera's mandate was up, Cézar and Larisa would be caught taking bribes during one of these stings, and Camelia would even be shown on national television accepting bribes in front of hidden cameras.)

A third tension revolved around procedure and job description. For instance, as 3 p.m. approached, the inspectors would begin pointing out that the workday was almost over. Amada would invariably push people to work later, saying, "soy doesn't stop growing at 3 p.m.!" The difficulty of getting out on the road, of getting out past Calle Última, made her adamant that they do as many visits as they could before heading back to Asunción. The inspectors invariably won these arguments, pointing out that any inspection signed outside working hours would not be legally binding. But the daily return of the argument dramatized the degree to which the Government of Beans required a change in tempo, an increase of intensity against protocols that were out of phase with the temporality of soy.

As I bumped along, trying to keep up with the conversation and to help out when we got stuck in the mud, or lost for hours on some back road among a herd of cows, I found it tempting to think of our little group (including the anthropologist) as a microcosm of the Government of Beans. Perhaps, I thought, I was just falling into easy narrative tropes, as though the story of something as dull as regulation could only be told as a road-trip movie full of colorful characters with foreshadowing backstories. But there was something, the way that the trucks brought together a hackneyed version of the welfare state as an agribiopolitical response to a soy that wasn't even really there, that perfectly encapsulated so much of Lugo's experiment. And whether the trucks were a microcosm or a goofy aberration, the important point was that out beyond Calle Última, these ten road-weary emissaries of Edificio Planeta were the only representatives of the Government of Beans that many campesinos and indigenous complainants would ever see.

# CHAPTER NINE

# Regulation by Denunciation

O n my second morning with the Citizen Participation Unit, we woke in the small city of Curuguaty, only a few kilometers away from the place where, two years later, a massacre would bring an end to Lugo's government. An overnight mist had encased the trucks in ice, and most of us hadn't slept well in the unheated dormitory behind the Curuguaty radio station. Those who dared took frigid showers before we all headed down to the market to eat hot *picada* (a thin meat soup), and to buy hats and gloves at a store that specialized in one item: packing tape, used to hermetically seal bundles of marijuana before export to Brazil. It was a good reminder that there were other plants in the area defying regulation, other agribiopolitical assemblages whose relationship to soy complicated the knots of politics and violence that SENAVE claimed to govern.[1] We also picked up some logs of salami, loaves of white bread, and squeeze tubes of mayonnaise, which would suffice for lunch without eating into anyone's per diem envelopes. Then we headed out in search of our first denuncia.

Two hours later, we got lost somewhere on the dirt roads north of Curuguaty, trying to find a colony called Karajakái. This part of Canindeyú was full of old land-reform colonies, settlements sprawled out along straight roads with a house every hundred meters, roads of frozen red mud that all started to look the same. We were looking for a store run by a campesino group that had called in a denuncia of their sojero neighbor, and we had promised to be there by 9 a.m. Even though Karajakái was a large colony, covering over ten thousand hectares and at least five thousand residents, Gerardo couldn't find it. Finally, after asking our way a dozen times, facing down suspicion about our trucks and some loud suggestions from members of our own team that we should just skip it and go on to our 11 o'clock appointment, we found the store—really an unmarked warehouse—at a nondescript crossroads. We were over two hours late.

Karajakái is a pseudonym, and though it corresponds to a real place, I've taken some liberties with the details to conceal the identity of those who hosted me there. In this book, I treat it as exemplary of dozens of colonies and denuncias I encountered over the following three years, usually with a couple of people who were in that original convoy.[2] None of these colonies was the same. But after a few days of this I started to see a pattern, in both the content and form of the denuncias and our response. In fact, as we pulled up to the community store that morning, I saw Gerardo brace himself and even give a little eye roll before opening the truck door and stepping into the encounter. At the time I read it as cynicism, but after a few days I began to brace myself as well, for the confusion, the anger, and the predictability of what was to follow.

## DENUNCIATION AND RESPONSE

A delegation of men and women, about forty in all, was waiting for us in the yard in front of the store, and because we were late they were fighting for shade under a couple of small mangos whose leaves had been depleted by winter. The ten of us took some time to unpack ourselves from the trucks, and our hosts, in turn, began to form a circle, watching and waiting for us to set foot on the property. Several of them were holding machetes or thick wooden clubs. I don't think any of us believed we were in physical danger, but just the afternoon before, arriving two hours late to a similar crowd, we'd been yelled at for over an hour before we could extricate ourselves. It was after that encounter that Gerardo told me he preferred to let Amada make the first move, to enter the ring, to see how people were going to react. He would wait with the truck, knowing that sometimes one needs to prepare for retreat.

This time we did not encounter outright hostility, and soon we were all in the yard, doing a standard round of greetings. Every man in SENAVE's convoy walked around the inner circle, shaking the hand of every male resident. Local women stood either slightly back or remained seated. Amada's presence as our leader disrupted this somewhat, since she did the rounds as well, acting as a man would, but also extending her hand with a knowing smile to all of the women, and refusing to take it back until even the most reluctant shook it. I tried to follow her lead, but with less success, and didn't insist when I was confronted with nervous laughter. The other women from the truck didn't make the rounds at all but shook only the hands that were nearby as they took up positions on the periphery. When all of this was done, we moved into the dark warehouse and were offered chairs. Most of the local men sat on barrels or squatted around the edges, and most of the women disappeared entirely. After the bright sunshine outside, the windowless space was gloomy, probably built originally as a cotton depot rather than a meeting hall. Three men designated themselves as the spokespeople, with Santiago, the oldest of the three, taking the lead before a beat-up chalkboard.

I was expecting him to launch directly into the community's denuncias, but Santiago insisted, first, on telling us the history of Karajakái, and the complicated local tensions out of which their grievance arose. His story began by following the script of pioneer citizenship in northeastern Paraguay. Residents of the community had only been here since 1992. Until then most of them had been landless, living in and around the city of Santaní, and were members of a militant Marxist organization known as the Movimiento Campesino Paraguayo. The coup in 1989 had made land available to many such groups, after so many of Stroessner's cronies had their holdings expropriated. Karajakái was one of these, established on what had been a ten thousand–hectare holding of one of Stroessner's exiled compadres. Arriving not far from the crossroads where we now sat, these pioneers had begun to cut a colony out of the forest, building not only their own farms, but the schools, churches, and community stores that ensured some sort of institutional permanence.[3] The colony prospered, first on logging, and later on cotton and tobacco production, and grew very quickly for the first decade of its existence.

Like many such colonies, from the moment it was founded, Karajakái found itself in competition with two other groups making claims on nearby land. The first was a small group of indigenous Mby'a, currently about ten families, who had been living there since at least the early 1960s, and who named the place Ayvu Reko. Santiago was vague about how land had been divided between Karajakái and Ayvu Reko, but he claimed that their indigenous neighbors had had no formal land rights at the time of the expropriation. When Karajakái won the land, they had offered the Mby'a five hundred hectares of forest at the northern end of the parcel, and this piece passed into the ownership of INDI, the centralized administrator of all indigenous territories. The residents of Ayvu Reko used that small forest of hunting and gathering, as the rest of the land was slowly deforested by the Karajakái pioneers.

The second neighbor was a gigantic ranch farther north that, at the time they arrived, was still mostly forested. The ranch belonged to Ulysses Teixeira, a member of one of Paraguay's largest landholding families, from an early wave of Brazilian land speculation.[4] And yet relations between the ranch and the colony were fairly harmonious, in large part because Teixeira and one of his sons played by the rules of good patronage. The Teixeiras had provided jobs for many of the colonists and had built the local church and helped with the school. This sort of relationship had been a central part of land reform practice from the outset, even though it didn't figure in any government planning documents. In most new colonies, campesino families relied on nearby benefactors to help with infrastructure when the state proved too slow or unresponsive, and they were often key sources of employment. Teixeira had helped the colony prosper, and in return, colonists respected his property and didn't target it for occupation or expropriation.

From Santiago's point of view, their current problems started about five years back, when Teixeira had removed all of his cattle from the land and rented it out to a company called Nuevos Montes, a subsidiary of Agrofértil, a massive agricultural firm owned by Brazilians. As soon as Nuevos Montes moved in, they cut and burned down the remaining trees on the ranch and converted the pastures to soy fields. Somehow, in a way that no one quite understood, the five hundred hectares of land at the tip of Karajakái belonging to the Mby'a had also fallen into Nuevos Montes's control and been destroyed. Santiago believed that corrupt officials at INDI had negotiated the sale and taken advantage of the Mby'a residents. In a single year, 2005, the area had been completely cleared with bulldozers, the logs gathered into piles and burned. At Amada's prodding, Santiago and a few others talked about forests thick with animals that had disappeared in six months of flame and mechanical violence.

As dramatic as this story of forest destruction was, it seemed to belong to a different time. Campesinos had filed a denuncia about it at the time with the INDI, but they had never heard a response and had quickly given up. Their denuncia today was different: with the forest gone, the soy came right up to the road at the edge of the colony. In the summer, planes passed over daily, and the smell of pesticides was insufferable. According to Santiago, they had been complaining about the farm ever since the beans had moved in, first to INDI and INFONA (the agency responsible for forest management), but nothing had come of it. Later they had contacted SEAM, the Secretariat of the Environment. Our visit, they said, was the first time that they had received a serious response to any of these complaints. "The state," Santiago repeated, "is completely absent."

The list of denuncias was long, and the longer the meeting went on, the more difficult it became to listen to. There were the usual complaints about *agrotóxicos*. No one felt they had been sprayed directly, but residents frequently saw the planes pass over their houses and were afraid that they could be. "In the summer, they get up at 4 a.m. and start working, and they're out there spraying all day." Particularly along the road, the smell was constant during these seasons, and anyone passing the fields would have to deal with the stench and the headaches that came along with it. The assembled group talked of rashes, stomachaches, vomiting, diarrhea, fatigue, and general listlessness. They also claimed that their gardens were affected, particularly tobacco, which had wilted and turned white, and cassava, whose roots weren't "filling up" as before. Corn was stunted, and beans and oranges didn't look as healthy as usual. They'd completely given up on cotton only a few years earlier.

Residents of Karajakái had increasing trouble finding markets for their products, and they said this problem was also related to the soy. The products were deteriorating, and they received fewer visits from the trucks offering to bring them to market. No one liked to take the road to the nearest market any more on their own because it passed by the soy field, where they felt exposed not only to the spray but also to robbery. Meanwhile, the main roads heading south to the highway were in shambles, and every year during the soy harvest they became a thoroughfare for massive trucks leaving the farm at all hours of the day and night. The damage to the road sometimes made it unusable to anything but the heaviest trucks. The farm occasionally maintained parts of the road themselves, using graders to flatten out the worst parts at bottlenecks for their own trucks, but this was clearly a self-interested procedure. Worse still, the local water treatment system had broken down because the PVC pipes that had been laid under the roads in the 1990s by a World Bank–funded development project had been shattered by the heavy traffic. Two years ago most of the colony had returned to using their wells, which were contaminated with pesticides and made everyone sick.

Finally, closing the ranch down had led to fewer jobs for young men in the town, which had created discord not only between generations but between households. The ranch had not provided huge amounts of work, but there was a steady stream of requests for *changueros* (day laborers), and this, combined with market for logs, cotton, and tobacco, had generated the town's cash flow.[5] Now the soy farm offered only occasional jobs in the summer, giving more hours to fewer people, and those jobs were inflexible, meaning that men were in competition with each other for a handful of highly coveted positions. This made it hard to organize any kind of collective reaction to the farm because many of the young men were careful to keep their employment prospects open for the next season. Still, the jobs were risky. In one high-profile case, a young man had almost been killed mixing chemicals without the appropriate protective gear. He'd been rushed to a nearby hospital and never fully recovered from the injuries to his hands and lungs.

Stories like this last one hinted at conflicts between neighbors that I would later hear more about when talking to people on my own. Disagreements commonly occurred between the older men, who acted as spokespeople in these meetings, and women whose sons had at one point worked in soy. And it was around these stories that other stories would sometimes emerge as well, of children dying from terrible disease, of miscarriages, suicides, or of young people being stabbed at parties in the hot summer nights when money flowed unevenly through the colony.

Santiago's account, filled in by others in the room, took the form of a litany of quasi-events, many of which were not entirely coherent. But they were also very familiar, adding up not to a specific legal denunciation, but to a diagnosis of the life of abandonment in campesino colonies of the twenty-first century. It wasn't just the lack of government services, the difficulty finding markets for agrarian products, or the fights with neighbors, but the palpable sense that something had shifted that made all of these conditions harder to live with. And that something had come with soybeans, with the disappearance of the forests and of working relationship with the patrón, and with the smell of poisons in the air. Most of all, these changes made the promise of rural welfare more distant than it had seemed when they were cutting the colony themselves, when everything was moving in the right direction.

The denunciation of the soy farm was not here, nor anywhere else, a clearly bounded performance, and I always got the sense that it could go on indefinitely. In the early days of listening to these complaints I was usually highly attentive, straining for the moment when everything would come together and the crimes committed would become obvious. But denuncias, as a genre, were not formatted for criminal trials. The connection back to soy, or to the specific farms being denounced, was often stretched. And yet soy was always there, and it was equally hard to imagine how any of these stories was not about soy, squelching the pioneer aspirations that had brought people here less than two decades before. My own anxieties stemmed from the anticipation of response: how could this nostalgic desire for a better life, for a long-lost sense of future possibility, be translated into an application of pesticide laws?

Gerardo later told me that he never let the denuncias get started for this exact reason. But Amada encouraged them, allowing the stories to flow out with supportive nods and sighs, and the occasional question that prodded more responses. This one, in the dark warehouse at Karajakái, went on for close to two hours. Eventually, though, she would draw things to a close and begin a speech of her own, which I'll paraphrase here from the many iterations I heard. "*Bueno*," she would say,

> You have the constitutional right to live in a clean environment. The Colorados never respected this right, nor did they do anything to stop the sojeros, who are the biggest threat to the environment. Today, though, I'm here to tell you that we're changing the way that we're doing things at SENAVE. I know no one comes to listen to your denuncias, but we've just heard this and understood it. We know this is going on all over the country, and we're committed to doing what we can to change the situation.
>
> But there's really only so much we can do as SENAVE. We were created by a law called 2459/04, and our mandate is to regulate the use of pesticides according to law 3742/09. As you may know, that law is not very strict, because it was passed by Colorados in Congress. But our main weapon is a decree called 2048/04, which no one has ever respected.[6] Sojeros cannot do what they are doing, and even if the state has refused to regulate before—and we all know why—we are here to show you that this law can be applied. We're here to tell you that we can change this situation. The impunity is over!

But there is something we need from you. We're just a small group. Even within SENAVE or SEAM or Lugo's government, there is only a small group of us who feel this way and work this way. We need you to support us. And that means you need to keep making these denuncias. I will give you the number for SENAVE and my personal cell number [here she wrote it on the blackboard], which you can call to tell me if you're being sprayed or something else is going on that shouldn't be. You need to get to know the state, and the different agencies. You need to understand the difference between SEAM and SENAVE and INFONA, and you need to call the appropriate agency for the appropriate problem. But you also need to keep organized here. You all know that the state is nothing, we are nothing, Lugo is nothing without organized folks in the country who can denounce, and march, and demand when the time is right.

It was during these moments that I could most clearly see SENAVE's regulatory proposition at work as a form of response. It began with the performance of the denuncia, which conjured soy as a hyperobject, with all of its convolutions, its quasi-events, its widely distributed harms, and its multiple indirect ways of meting them out. In response, Amada offered a constitutional right and, behind it, the project to build a new kind of regulatory state, a new agribiopolitical future built by concerned citizen groups and activist bureaucrats.

## DENUNCIATION AND THE COMMUNAL CITIZEN

Lugo's government was not the only member of Latin America's left turn to experiment with regulation through denunciation. In their analysis of the transformation of health care under Brazil's Worker's Party (PT) government, João Biehl and Adriana Petryna described what they call the "judicialization of the right to health," in which patients became litigants, suing the state for the treatments that were their right under Brazil's constitution.[7] For Biehl and Petryna, the process was a symptom of a dysfunctional Brazilian health care system. But it was also an example of a fundamental tension between the universality of rights discourses and the uneven practicality of service delivery and regulation. They insisted that all rights are in fact struggles for jurisprudence, quoting an old interview with Gilles Deleuze:

Justice does not exist! Human Rights do not exist. What matters is jurisprudence. This is the invention of Law. . . . The challenge is to create and not to make Human Rights applicable. It is a matter of inventing juris-prudences so that, for each case, such and such thing could not have been possible.... It is not a matter of right of this or of that, but of situations that evolve ... to struggle for jurisprudence ... to create the right.[8]

Beyond this recognizable tension in the meaning of rights, though, the authors pointed to the peculiarity of Brazil's leftist government, an "activist state," in encouraging this process. Even as certain state actors worked to restrict access to expensive treatments that would, if universalized, become economically unsustainable, other activist functionaries colluded with the judicialization process to ensure the right to health of particular patients. Judicialization became a "parallel infrastructure in which various public and private health actors and sectors come into contact, face off, and enact one-by-one rescue missions."[9]

The emergence of the Government of Beans from the Silvino Talavera case contained much of the same logic. It was precisely through the judicial-ization of Silvino's death that soy had emerged as an object of concern, as a focus for widespread campesino anger. By seeing soy's violence as a bundle of individual cases, and encouraging as many of these toward legal action as possible, the Citizen Participation Unit could turn the small success of the Talavera case into something resembling the right to a clean environment, the right to health, the right to a modicum of state protection.

But Amada's speech also took us a lot further than this. Citing the incom-pleteness of a constitutionally promised right, she insisted that rights must be created through collusion between victims and certain state function-aries. By handing out her personal cell phone number, she began to build that parallel infrastructure, sabotaging an ineffective universal law that was stuck on paper in the capital, and replacing it with a new channel for de-nunciation and response. In the idiom of state absence, these rituals of de-nunciation and response became instantiations of a new, present state that was not simply a guarantor of rights, but a collective project of a new kind of citizen-subject responsible for building rural welfare through continuous denunciation.

More than chances to respond to particular denuncias, Amada saw these encounters as an opportunity to turn pioneer citizens into regulatory citi-zens. Unlike pioneer citizens, who built the state by carving it out of the forests and demanding land titles from the Institute for Rural Welfare (IBR), regulatory citizens would continually make the state present by participat-ing in the regulation of environment and health in the colonies they already lived in. Meetings like this one served a pedagogical role to help people understand the subtleties of environmental law and to better participate in this project. Back in the truck, she described this as a kind of Freirian *concientización*, whereby participants in a meeting would be invited to talk about their experiential reality and link it with available legal tools.[10] Linking reality to law also allowed her to link campesinos to functionaries and finally, as we'll see below, to invite them to participate in the practical aspects of regulation itself.

It's important to state here that the ideal participant was something slightly different from the individual rights bearer usually implied by the word "citizen." Amada rarely referred to these places as "colonias," the usual term to describe small pioneer settlements, but instead preferred *comunidades*, which implied a coherent, collective, political identity. What Amada really wanted to foster were collective subjects, composed of preexisting committees, peasant organizations, or, particularly in the case of indigenous villages, a whole community ideally represented by a chief.[11] The collective nature of this subject was essential, not only because it allowed the Citizen Participation Unit to reach more people and cover ground more quickly (as Franceschelli had told me when first describing the project) but because it was rarely possible to account for the harms of soybeans in terms of individual bodies. Instead, the victims of those harms were communal bodies, constructs of a romantic notion of collective rural life. Although SENAVE protected Paraguayans, it also protected collectives of Paraguayans, and through them an implied national way of life. In fact, as our trucks moved from one colony to another, from one denuncia to another, there was often an explicit discussion in the trucks, not about the health of the bodies we had seen, but about the health of the community we had visited, along with comments about the degree of Paraguayanness we had witnessed.

Some of the immediate effects of this are obvious: if harms were considered widely distributed, the community in its agentive capacity was rarely so diffuse. Amada commented constantly on the need for strong leadership among the organizations that they worked with, and despite her own critiques of this situation, in practice this usually meant working closely with influential middle-aged men. In meeting after meeting we encountered groups of such men, the leaders of local organizations, owners of cooperatives, indigenous leaders chosen by the INDI, and local school teachers who claimed to represent the victimhood of those who lived nearby and were able to narrate a range of complex local problems in a convincing manner. This led to a certain contradiction in practice. While Amada was a voluble feminist who teased male leaders for their machismo and did everything she could to encourage women's participation in our meetings, her model of decentralization and inclusion of the countryside did tend, at least in the short term, to amplify local patriarchal hierarchies by reaffirming male leaders as the conduit for state resources.

Moreover, the similarity of this sort of governmental decentralization to the Colorados' clientelist structure was not lost on anyone. Under the *seccional* system pioneered by the Colorados, the more effectively local strongmen consolidated their power, the more likely they were to acquire state services for their clients. In return, *seccionaleros* acted as the rural surveillance agents of the centralized state, the *pyrague* spies who fed information about dissidents and other enemies of the regime up through the Colorado Party. Amada's system of denunciation began with a very different strategy that ultimately had similar effects: by linking citizenship to victimhood on the soy frontier, she created a personalized snitch line that enrolled denunciants as agents of state surveillance. She presented this as a form of empowerment (*ñomombarete*) in which, by reporting their victimhood, the assumed victims became the surveillance arm of the portion of the state with which they were allied. It's not surprising that the main accusation lodged against her by others in our truck was that she was using her bureaucratic position to create political bases for the Tekojoja Party by recruiting voters through local strongmen.

As should by now be clear, none of this critique is meant to undermine the sincerity, and difficulty, of what Amada was trying to accomplish. Like all activists I met in rural Paraguay, Amada's work was successful only because she was pragmatic, taking the elements at hand and trying to move them forward. That necessarily meant taking remnants of the last version of rural welfare attempted under Stroessner and repurposing them to make them serve other ends. During that regime there was no distinction between state function and partisan ritual. If responding to soy meant making the state present, then there would necessarily be some political performance involved, and with it a lot of the trappings of clientelism.

## INSPECTION AND CITATION

Everything about the way our encounter with Karajakái was structured now affected how the inspection of Nuevos Montes played out. After quickly stuffing our mouths with salami, we bundled back into the trucks with three local men to head off to inspect the farm they were denouncing. Inspection of soy farms involved some sort of participation of the denunciants, in large part because it was the only way to acquire the intimate knowledge of roads, gates, and people's names necessary for finding our way around. But it was also useful for a second reason. Many people said during their denuncias that they had previously been visited by inspectors claiming to be from SENAVE or some other state agency. "But after we gave them our denuncia, they went to talk to the sojero, and *opa re'i*" (a popular Guarani expression meaning literally "it ended pointlessly"). The expression implied that the inspector had merely gone to the sojero to collect a bribe. So by asking campesinos to accompany them, Amada was also proving to them that she was acting in good faith.

It was almost a kilometer before we reached the field of Nuevos Montes, which was covered in winter wheat. Beyond a minimal gate, we drove another three kilometers through the wheat to a silo complex with a small office and dormitory, a chemical depot, an airstrip, and a hangar with two planes. As we approached the gate around the main office, two young men armed with shotguns met us at the gate and addressed us in Guarani-inflected Spanish. Amada convinced them to put their weapons down, joking that it would be ridiculous to shoot a woman as small as herself. A few minutes later, a much larger man emerged from the office wearing a white, button-down shirt. The manager, it turned out, was a genuine Brazilian, hired in Brazil by the Brazilian owners of the company, and he flew in on weekdays but maintained his home on the other side of the border. The only Paraguayans in the complex were the men with the guns; otherwise it felt like a little Brazilian oasis surrounded by wheat.

The manager began by trying to speak to us in heavily accented Spanish, a courtesy. He was annoyed about being inspected, but most annoyed at the company that we brought with us. "We know who these men are," he said, pointing to the campesinos who had guided us here. "What are they doing here? You do know that these people live nowhere near our fields, right? They're just local troublemakers. And right now they are trespassing." He allowed us to inspect his flight log, maps, and chemical depot while he tried to get his lawyer on the phone. But he became increasingly agitated with what he considered Amada's and Camelia's minor concerns: whether or not the planes passed over the local water source, why some of the pallets in the pesticide depot had both Roundup and 2,4-D on them, and whether or not they intended to plant a barrera viva along the southern edge of the property. He shifted to Portuguese as he got more frustrated—while Amada, a fluent speaker of Portuguese, continued talking to him in Spanish. Over his objections, she drew up a citation of noncompliance detailing a series of regulatory infractions, and Gerardo, acting as the official inspector, signed the form on behalf of SENAVE.[12]

When his lawyer finally answered his phone, the manager passed him to Camelia (our lawyer), and we all heard him yelling invectives in Portuguese, until she hung up and passed the phone back. We walked outside, back into the wind and the wheat, and the manager emerged again, now holding the phone in the air so we could hear his lawyer yelling at us. The guns were drawn again, and we beat a hasty retreat, piling back into the trucks as Gerardo let the coils warm on his diesel starter. On the way back, someone laughed and said, "That was nothing! At least they didn't have dogs like that farm last week!"

As we reached the road separating Nuevos Montes from Karajakái, we returned for a short debrief with those who had accompanied us. After some friendly banter about the encounter, Amada gave another quick speech that I would also come to know as routine:

> What we did there was issue them a citation for noncompliance with three regulations—fumigating near a water source, not keeping their flight log in order, and not planting a barrera viva. I've got the carbon copy here. It gets passed up to the legal aid office, who will verify that I filled out the form properly. They will then issue a formal complaint that gives the farmer two months to begin complying with the regulation. After that, SENAVE will come back for a follow-up inspection, and, if they fail that, the lawyers can issue an administrative indictment. And if they fail a third inspection, they can be fined.

Here, as in most versions of this speech, Amada had to follow up by explaining how the protocols worked. An administrative indictment, she explained, was the equivalent of pressing criminal charges, but for matters that fell under the jurisdiction of administrative courts.[13] The strongest penalty they could ever issue was a fine, up to a maximum of five million guaraníes (about $1,000 US), but usually less for a first offense. And yes, it would take three visits over the course of about a year before they could issue that fine. This was the protocol, and there was nothing they could do to break out of it.

There are two things to take from this final scene. First, these were always moments of reckoning, in which everyone present took stock of just how feeble regulatory instruments really were, even when the state was present to use them. When rendered in the technical language of regulatory proto-col, the grand confrontation was somehow tamed, an awkward performance of the illusion of authority.[14] Standing, that day, in front of a sea of wheat, with kilometers of road in either direction, and some of us still anxious to get off the open road lest Nuevos Montes had more serious means of retalia-tion, the administrative citation seemed unlikely to accomplish much.[15]

But the second thing to notice is that Amada did not avoid it, and instead insisted on bringing denunciants into the minutia of the process ahead. It might not work; it might end in nothing, "opa re'i," but there was a way it could work: there was a clear path for those carbon copies to take, unleash-ing specific bureaucratic responses along the way. Amada understood that to have any effect downstream, a certain care needed to be put into crafting the document, and that this care was at least as important as the actual of-fense being denounced. In effect, she was inviting regulatory citizens like Santiago to move beyond their Freirian denunciations, and to care for ar-cane bureaucracy. Campesino activists were well versed in this kind of doc-umentary work, primarily in the IBR, and Amada was giving them the tools to begin similar work in SENAVE.[16]

So while everyone there was skeptical that their denuncias, and the ci-tations they produced, would be successful in eliciting the kind of state response they hoped for, they also knew that they *might* accomplish some-thing. And therein lay the germ of the Government of Beans. As those cita-tions made their way back to Asunción, into the lawyers' offices at SENAVE, and as some of them elicited responses that came back to the countryside, the Government of Beans might eventually stitch together a parallel infra-structure, a new relationship between state and country. Like the decades of requests made by pioneer citizens to the IBR for expropriation, land titles, and a fair return on their cotton, each denunciation of a regulatory citizen against a sojero might eventually add up to something that looked like the right to live in a clean environment or even rural welfare writ large.

# CHAPTER TEN

# Citation, Sample, and Parallel States

P ickup trucks from SENAVE carried more than people back and forth across Calle Última. We've already encountered one of the other crucial things that rode in those trucks: citations, the carbon-copied forms produced in response to denuncias. Papers like these had a relatively clear path ahead of them once they got to the city, where they would be dropped off at SENAVE's legal office. And in this way, the material work of the Citizen Participation Unit resembled the work of previous generations of campesino activists who worked the pathways and protocols for the movement of legal documents in Asunción. But Amada was simultaneously trying to build other pathways through SENAVE, trying to create parallel infrastructures for the Government of Beans that took advantage of the wide range of agribiopolitical instruments that the agency housed. This was particularly true of SENAVE's laboratories in San Lorenzo, some of the best scientific infrastructure in the country. In addition to drawing up citations, therefore, the Citizen Participation Unit also collected samples that could be brought back to the lab for analysis.

It was clear from the beginning, however, that inspection teams had much less knowledge about how sampled materials worked in the institution than they had about citations and therefore little sense of how to care for those materials. During the first several months of visits to the countryside, no one even carried sterile containers. In Karajakái we collected a wilted tobacco leaf and shoved it into a backpack. A shriveled cassava branch ended up in a plastic bag that had previously held salami. As we walked onto the gigantic property of Nuevos Montes, we were directed to a water hole surrounded by wheat, so Amada asked if anyone had anything to take a sample with. Someone found a discarded 300 milliliter bottle of Fortín (a popular brand of cane alcohol) with the cap lying beside the road, and so we collected water in that.[1] The bottle, joined the next day by two 2 liter bottles that had held Nico (a national cola brand and castaway from our lunch) knocked around in the bed of the truck. Amada wrote down their provenance in a spiral notebook, but no one was clear about what would happen to them once they got back to town.

When I visited the lab myself, technicians scoffed about these samples, telling me that they'd been unable to do anything with them, and it's from them that I took the term "protocol" to describe the problem. Protocols are a kind of bureaucratic infrastructure, a recipe that facilitates the movement of semiotic artifacts like citations and samples, and structures their meaningfulness from one site to another. Put differently, protocols allow inspectors to anticipate the future of the traces they deliver to the next bureaucratic instance. The future journey of the citation was well known to Amada, who talked about it in her speeches with denunciants. Back in the head office, Lovera and González tried to make sure these legal systems were working well, that the citations were being received and handled according to protocol. Initially, no one was doing the equivalent work for samples, and so as they moved from one site to another they became meaningless. But the Citizen Participation Unit flooded the lab with samples anyway, and in so doing revealed another set of limits to the Government of Beans.

EVERYDAY LAB PROTOCOLS

Most of SENAVE's labs were housed in the small complex of well-appointed buildings set back from the main road in San Lorenzo just beyond Calle Última. Every week, paper bags holding crumpled leaves, samples of produce taken at border crossings, pesticide bottles taken from barges at the port, and dead insects plucked from pheromone traps would find their way to the reception desk just beyond the gate. From there, samples would be triaged into one of five different labs (chemical, microbiological, phytopathological, entomological, fertility) and worked over by the group of earnest, well-trained, and underpaid technicians, most of them recent graduates from the National University next door.

By far the most routinized work that happened in the lab involved the certification of phytosanitary materials. So, for example, anyone wishing to sell pesticides in Paraguay needed to have their product approved by SENAVE. They would send a sample of the product to the lab, which used a spectrometer to confirm that it contained the concentrations of chemicals advertised on label, and to verify that these fell within the standards established in the Codex Alimentarius. The Codex was not only a list of allowable chemical thresholds, it also came with a series of protocols indicating how the technician was supposed to use the spectrometer to produce the reading that made sense on the list. Once confirmed, SENAVE would issue a certificate for the product in question, allowing the vendor to put a SENAVE sticker on all containers of the substance sold within the country. In short, the sample entered the lab and was transformed into stickers that would allow other inspectors down the line to follow sticker-reading protocols of their own when inspecting trucks and farms.

This is where the lab looked most like a moisture meter, discussed in chapter 4, functioning as a market device whose role was to "inform" the materials in question. The laboratory, together with the protocol, acted as what Paul Kockelman calls a semiotic "sieve," sorting samples into bureaucratically recognizable categories that functioned as information further down the chain.[2] That is, by passing the material through the laboratory, chemical distributors were able to add value to their product by adding documents and connecting it to authorized bodies (SENAVE, FAO, the ISO). Although the Codex was nominally about food safety, most lab technicians (and agronomists in general) talked in the more neutral terms of consumer confidence. For example, farmers using 2,4-D wanted to be sure that what they were spraying on their fields was what it said on the bottle, while consumers of tomatoes wanted to know that they were not poisonous. For the most part, then, this kind of laboratory operation was uncontroversial. The protocols were rigid and easy to follow for someone with technical training, and most players in the chain of chemical importers, mixers, distributors, and consumers could see value in the operation. Even environmental critics, though they might find the regulations too lax, preferred to have chemicals certified rather than not.

The main problems that emerged around this sort of lab work had to do with volume: as the soy fields grew, the lab was not equipped to deal with increasing numbers of samples and became an infrastructural bottleneck. Not only did samples have to make their way to the lab, but until 2010 the lab had only one working spectrometer, which could only analyze two samples at a time. (When I was there, a much more advanced machine had been donated by the German Development Organization, GIZ, but no one knew how to calibrate it, and so it sat, shiny but unused, in the corner.) This meant that the lab caused certification delays, particularly as the volume and variety of chemicals being imported into the country increased. Delays and bottlenecks in turn created a market for queue-jumping techniques, from bribery (which everyone denied) to using political contacts to pressure the lab to treat certain samples faster than others (which everyone admitted occurred). A black market in agrochemicals continued to thrive, and this in turn fed the narrative that the problem with Paraguay's chemical market was a lack of regulation and a lack of information, rather than a problem of the sheer volume of toxins entering the country. And in this capacity, Lovera could be said to have been successful: SENAVE undertook several high-profile busts of unregulated chemical importers, and as a result the market became more standardized, with more phytosanitary materials becoming "informed" materials. During the same period, however, agrochemical imports into Paraguay quintupled in volume, and since the overwhelming effect of all this certification was to improve access to export markets, we can only assume that improving the laboratories also contributed to increasing the amount of soy planted in the country.[3]

The second primary role for the lab was what people referred to as "phytosanitary vigilance," one of the most basic, and bluntest, agribiopolitical instruments at any state's disposal: SENAVE was responsible for monitoring the entrance into the country of various kinds of plagues, primarily insects and other crop infections, and in so doing was supposed to turn the border itself into a phytosanitary barrier to protect national crops from foreign plant ailments. In principle, for instance, any truckload of oranges entering Paraguay from Argentina had to be inspected to make sure that it didn't contain any mold or caterpillars that might pose a threat to Paraguay's own fruit crop. Orange samples were to be extracted at border crossings and sent to the lab to be examined by an entomologist and phytopathologist to make sure that no unwanted visitors were arriving along with it. In practice this almost never happened. A large number of the fruit samples removed from trucks at the border were replaced in return for a bribe, while another portion went home with inspectors, where they were eaten or resold.[4] A small percentage did make it back to the lab in San Lorenzo, but by the time the inspections were accomplished, the trucks were already deep in national territory, and usually unloaded onto market tables. The entomologists I spoke to at SENAVE considered this sort of work a kind of detection and warning, but though they had found many new and problematic plant bugs over the years crawling around in their samples, not one had ever been denied entry into the country.

Although in principle both certification and vigilance activities involved the simple application of bureaucratic protocols, lab technicians made a fairly stark distinction between them. Certification work, in addition to being routinized and dull, produced no attachments for technicians, who seemed uninterested in the samples that came through the door. Regulatory qualifications remained stuck to the materials that the samples were supposed to represent, and lab technicians were more likely to tell me stories about their equipment, or with the difficulty getting the materials they needed to carry out tests (particularly solvents) than about any given test carried out. The laboratory produced stickers on bottles, seed bags, and crates of produce, which would be discarded with the bottles themselves. In other words, although they had been trained as scientists, the lab workers were producing not scientific knowledge but rather legal qualifications through a process that stopped the moment an inscription fit into a legal text. Certification protocols were about maintaining the legal infrastructure for the movement of goods, rather than discovery. As Bruno Latour has put it, "Law produces no new knowledge. . . . It has better things to do than to know: it maintains the fabric of imputations and obligations."[5] For young science graduates, the fabric of imputations and obligations was not generally what got them up in the morning.

By contrast, these technicians were keenest to talk about the results that emerged from trying, unsuccessfully, to prevent pests from entering the country. Indeed, the pointlessness of the activity seemed to make it more interesting, as though avowed futility offered more space for exploration and creativity. Even if the results of these operations were generally descriptive and taxonomic, they began with genuine puzzles, and the technicians took pride in their discoveries. The entomologists in particular kept track of the insects they had found, not just where they were but who had successfully identified them. A moth discovered in a bag of tomatoes might initially signal a property of the tomatoes, but eventually became detached from the tomatoes and set off its own string of references and put entomologists in contact with researchers at the university or at the crop research stations and the national Museum of Natural History. While there were routines and protocols to be followed, the acts of successive inscription with which the technicians were involved were different each time. Since their association with a particular product was basically meaningless, what mattered was the general knowledge created, the more durable inscription in the registry of Paraguay's known pests.[6] Here the legal protocols fell away, and technicians found themselves carrying out something more like basic science.

In other words, SENAVE's labs produced results according to a spectrum of practices, from legal to scientific, but which generally promoted two distinct agribiopolitical projects. On the one hand, they bolstered contractual compliance along the soy chain, thus helping to promote soybean exports. On the other, they produced the image of the national crop as a single population whose health could be described through a national registry of biological agents and, in principle, improved through border vigilance.

This is why the samples dropped off by the Citizen Participation Unit produced such problems for the labs. These samples fell into neither of these categories and required a wholly novel way of thinking the relationship between law and science. Two technicians spoke to me about their initial excitement at receiving water samples from the unit, since they challenged them to use their equipment to produce new kinds of results. They had the open-ended feel of scientific work, because they came without a clear set of obligations or a clear regulatory grid to which they were supposed to correspond. But they soon found out that the samples were freighted with all sorts of other obligations. Because they arrived as part of an implicit, often hazy, denunciation, these samples turned the labs into improvised forensic units. Only these obligations were not nearly as clear: here the law could not tell them how to find what it was asking them to find.

## WHO DECIDES IF WATER IS CONTAMINATED?

Six months into Lovera's term, a perfect case presented itself for testing the lab's responsiveness to this new kind of demand. In January 2011, Rubén Portillo, a young cotton farmer from a colony called Yerutí, fell violently ill after his neighbor fumigated his soy crops. Although he had no respite from the vomiting and diarrhea for almost a week, Portillo was reluctant to go to the hospital in Curuguaty because the community's only road access had been engulfed by soy. Reaching the hospital meant driving a horse cart almost twenty kilometers along a muddy track straight through soy fields that reeked of Roundup. By the end of the week, though, Portillo finally decided to make the trip with his sister at his side. He died shortly after reaching the hospital, and in the following days, twenty-two of his neighbors also fell ill and began showing up at the hospital with similar symptoms.[7]

A young, sympathetic doctor working the emergency ward that week decided to call in the case to the newly created Office of Epidemiological Vigilance in the Ministry of Public Health.[8] For functionaries on the receiving end of that call, there was more than a hint of the Silvino Talavera case in the details, and this looked like the first opportunity to mount a similar response. The doctor agreed to accompany SENAVE inspectors from the Citizen Participation Unit and lawyers from a human rights NGO back to Yerutí. What they found was an isolated land reform colony settled in 1991 in the middle of the forest. It was now what one newspaper described as "an oasis in the middle of a green desert. From there, whichever way you look, you see soy plants, a half meter high, extending to the horizon. Only occasionally does a solitary tree remain as testimony of the native landscape."[9] It rained during that first visit, and even SENAVE's $4 \times 4$ trucks got stuck in the muddy tracks between the beans trying to get back to the highway. Horrified, the inspectors mobilized local media, eventually convincing a local prosecutor to investigate a massive soy farm owned by Brazilian farmers that surrounded the southern tip of the colony where Portillo lived. The prosecutor sent a forensic expert to the field alongside SENAVE, and they took water samples from Portillo's well and from the creek that separated his fields from the soy.

According to staff at the lab, this was the first water sample to arrive there that was clean enough for them to work with, and the media attention, lawyers' scrutiny, and extra pressure from Edificio Planeta all meant that they put quite a bit of time into researching how to conduct their investigation. In the end, the laboratory reported that Portillo's well contained traces of three pesticides: endosulfan, aldrin, and lindane. The first two were barely present, below thresholds the lab considered worrisome. But the amount of lindane, a highly toxic organochlorine, was more difficult to discount. When I interviewed them about the case a year later, one of the lab technicians involved showed just how uneasy she was about this finding.

LAB TECHNICIAN: We found 0.03 micrograms per liter, and that was the limit set by the Codex Alimentarius, and that's the limit for food, but not for water. That's why in our report we told them we didn't have the bibliography. . . . It's simple when you're talking about vegetables. You go into the Codex page online, and if you want, for example, tomatoes, you get the maximum limit that they've now established—

because these change every now and then, right? So in that case it's really clear. We have to have less than 0.03, right? Because that's what's permitted. More than that, we need to sound the alarm. . . . But in the case of water and soil, it's difficult. We don't know what the permitted limits are.

ME: So the lawyers read it as though the limits were the same?

LAB TECHNICIAN: Yes, that was their legal interpretation. Because if you're not, or, well, it's complicated. Because the lawyer tells you that you are telling them that it's there! That was the thing in this case—that was from the interior, a sample from a well. And they also said that a man died from poisoning. But . . . they said it was the lindane that did it. At least, that's how they interpreted it, I think.

The technician struggled to explain how the lawyers came to this conclusion, but she was clear that the lab was not qualified to make such an interpretation because its protocols (its "bibliography") didn't work that way. That this was not ideologically driven is underscored by the fact that she didn't mention the most controversial aspect of the results: lindane was used not for soybeans but rather for killing lice, and though it had long been banned in Paraguay, many campesino households still had old bottles of it kicking around.[10] The technician here chose not to dwell on this, but rather on the difficulty of interpretation in the absence of protocol. The lab director told me, echoing a common refrain from North American legal studies, that the lab had fallen victim to the "CSI effect," where people had unrealistic expectations of their capacity to generate truth outside of established legal frameworks.[11]

What surprised the technicians most, however, was that even when they did manage to produce results, the results counted only if they confirmed what the lawyers wanted them to say. A subtle translation had happened: although the tests looked and felt like science in the lab, they were not producing scientific facts but legal judgments, and the enthusiastic science students had been turned into the research assistants of lawyers. In other words, forensic demands like this reversed the lab's normal relationship to law. For technicians, protocols like the Codex provided the infrastructure for the production of informed materials. But the forensic request asked the lab to create raw material that might or might not be used in the construction of a prosecutorial argument. This may be one reason the Citizen Participation Unit was a bit cavalier in its sample collection, since they knew that law would trump technical results in the end. Where lab results were inconclusive, or where the infrastructure (either legal or scientific) in the lab was insufficient to answer the direct questions being posed, the lawyers went ahead with an interpretation anyway, disregarding the advice of the technicians. At other times they completely discounted the laboratory results since they didn't help them in constructing their case.

## SHOESTRING PROTOCOLS

The Portillo case later floundered and never went to trial, probably because, like so many other denuncias made during those years, it was not robust enough to be sustained through Lugo's ouster.[12] But this case was one of those moments when the lawyers, lab technicians, and field inspectors were working at their best together. Most of the time, they barely worked at all, and the samples dropped off by the unit went nowhere. After a few attempts at analyzing the contents of our Fortín and Nico bottles, the lab simply stopped processing them. Yes, the spectrometer could detect some of the compounds they were looking for, but they couldn't interpret the results given how dirty the samples were. And everything else about the institutional protocol militated against getting a useful reading. Part of this was a jurisdictional issue: SEAM, not SENAVE, was responsible for water contamination. But SEAM had no labs at all. So the water samples were technically being delivered by SENAVE inspectors to SENAVE labs on behalf of SEAM, to create a reading that no one was sure how to interpret because they didn't have the protocols necessary to do so.

Here we see why the protocol, one kind of regulatory layer that mediates between rules and the real world, is so important: like the citation form, which anticipates the future interpretive situation in which the traces of an inspection will have to be coherent, the samples needed to have been collected according to protocols that anticipated the interpretive context of the laboratory. In the absence of such protocols, inspectors and lab technicians would have to work even harder to create the protocols together. And yet in this case, the technicians and the inspectors from the unit distrusted each other. Technicians told me they were willing to look for methodologies and protocols that they could use, and eventually they did develop a protocol for water samples. But they did not feel that the Citizen Participation Unit collecting the samples was meeting them halfway. The water samples were often not big enough (a liter was the minimum requirement), and reused containers made it almost impossible to get a clean reading. The Fortín bottles suggested to lab technicians that the unit didn't respect the work they did or, odder still, that they didn't even particularly care about the readings that they produced.

Judging by some of the chitchat I heard in the trucks, the technicians may have had a point: Amada, for one, was highly skeptical the labs would ever produce a useful result for the Government of Beans, and she focused instead on taking samples as a political performance in the countryside. But this may have had less to do with personal prejudices than with a pragmatic assessment of just how challenging it would be to build the parallel infrastructures needed to fully connect the laboratory into the parallel state she was building.

As a result, the Government of Beans never really got to the point of producing its own laboratory protocols, of creating that middle layer of bureaucratic infrastructure that might have endured beyond the coup. Most of what they did remained at the level of the gesture, the performance of a state that might be but still wasn't quite. But it is important to remember that these gestures were far from hollow. Everything that the unit brought back to Asunción had the potential to generate all kinds of disruption in the Soy State and, through the accumulation of denuncias, contribute to creating new bureaucratic infrastructures. That potential, latent in everything the unit did, was likely the main reason that the Government of Beans had to be stopped in its tracks.

# CHAPTER ELEVEN

# Measurement as Tactical Sovereignty

One day, Amada and the Citizen Participation Unit answered the denuncia of a local school teacher who claimed that a sojero I'll call Alcides was spraying his soy within drifting distance of his school. After a visit to the school, and a long sermon from the teacher, we found that Alcides's thirty-hectare farm was in fact several hundred meters away. He was the kind of front-line soy colonist whom we visited a lot in western Canindeyú, far from the Brazilian border. His farm was small, and he was likely up to his neck in debt. It was hard to see, from the field behind the school, how this one farm, in a whole area full of farms, could be a particular problem. The teacher, meanwhile, was obviously a locally influential figure with a grudge. But the drive had been long, and Amada wanted to accomplish something, so we set out to find a violation. There was no barrera viva anywhere, but the soy was set well back from the road, behind Alcides's own humble wooden shack and a small sheep pasture. Eyeballing the distance, Amada decided it was likely less than one hundred meters from the road and could therefore be cited for a buffer violation.

Alcides was standing on his porch butchering a lamb when we walked up. His arms, and much of his front down to his high rubber boots, were covered in blood. Unlike Paraguayan campesinos, who would have extended their right elbow for a handshake, Alcides gestured to the blood on his hands and declined to touch anyone. From the moment he saw the teacher, he visibly struggled to stay calm, and three young children ducked for cover while a woman emerged from the shack and stood silently beside him. Assuming we would question his right to own property in this area, he calmly explained, through a thick Portuguese accent, that he was actually a Paraguayan citizen. He had been born in Santa Rita and had moved here less than a decade ago to buy his own land. Amada eventually cut him short and told him his ownership wasn't in question. Instead, SENAVE was there to measure the space between the road and the soy to make sure he complied with the one hundred meter buffer regulation.

At that, Alcides flew into an expletive-filled rant in Spanish and Portuguese that I can only paraphrase here:

> This is total bullshit and you know it. This law doesn't make any sense, and if I complied I'd have to sell my farm—which is what this asshole wants from me because I'm Brasiguaio, right? But why are you harassing me? You can see I've got nothing! You should go to Alto Paraná, where the big guys are. In Santa Rita they have soy right up to the roads and houses, they have hundreds of thousands of hectares. But we know why you aren't there, don't we? Because they wouldn't listen to you. You couldn't do shit to them! You're fucking me now because you think you can, but you're nothing and you know it.

Amada asked Cézar (the Colorado inspector) to measure the space between the road and the soy, and he gruffly complied, likely happy to get away from the discomfort of the encounter. As one of the lawyers held the end of the tape down by the road, Cézar unfurled it past Alcides's house, through the sheep paddock and to the back fence. When he returned to our tense, silent group, he announced that the distance was 109 meters. Not willing to entirely back down, Amada drew up a citation report saying that Alcides still needed a barrera viva to protect his own house from pesticide drift. Alcides silently grabbed the paper in one bloody hand and spat on the ground.

No one had enjoyed the encounter (except perhaps the teacher). In the truck, Amada tried to reason that, as the state, they had to apply the regulations equally, to farms of any size and anywhere in Paraguayan territory. But Alcides's rant about Santa Rita had made everyone uncomfortable. Helpless before the inspectors and an emboldened local xenophobe, Alcides had used his association with soy and with Brazil to belittle the Paraguayan state in its guise as the Government of Beans, and to question the sovereignty of the inspectors as emissaries of that state. But he'd perhaps also revealed a deeper meaning behind the measuring tapes, as though they had less, ultimately, to do with pesticide drift than they did with the state's raw ability to conquer and control territory.

The encounter offered a new answer to a question that had been puzzling me since the beginning of my project. I knew why barreras vivas had become contentious among lobbyists in Asunción, but why were they so controversial on the ground? Why did the Government of Beans spend so much time trying to precisely measure their absence, and why did soy farmers take so much offense at the practice? When I asked campesino friends back in Carmelitas if they had ever been visited by SENAVE, many initially were dismissive. More than once the response was something like, "SENAVE? Aren't they the people who measure stuff?" A few months previously, a local campesino leader had called some of them to a meeting with SENAVE, which had turned out to be fairly standard: *funcionarios* had arrived in a SENAVE pickup and listened to a long list of grievances about a local sojero. They followed this up by wandering around the community, rolling out a long tape measure and writing down the distances between crops and houses, rivers, roads, schools, and churches, and then they'd given a speech about the lack of barreras vivas and written up some papers. And then they had left, and "opa re'i": nothing had happened.

If that was the standard experience of these encounters, then why did campesino organizations keep calling Amada? Why was SENAVE pouring resources into it, and why did sojeros like Alcides get so angry about it? As the practice became more widespread, campesinos continued to request and participate in these mundane measurements, accompanying the inspectors, pointing out places of noncompliance with the regulations, holding the ends of tapes or cutting posts to serve as markers. Anticipating measurement, campesinos often announced distances in their denuncias. The Citizen Participation Unit, in other words, had partially succeeded in producing a citizen who read the landscape in regulatory terms. But like so many other things the unit did, even despite the existence of protocols, it was unclear to me that any of these measurements produced any regulatory results.

What Alcides made clear was that, mundane as it was, measurement was also a way of conjuring a far greater promise, and threat, of the Government of Beans. Measurement enacted the Government of Beans in relation to soy, a quintessential moment of "intra action," as Karen Barad calls it, when one agency interferes with another.[1] For Barad, measurement is causal, "the intra-active marking of one part of a phenomenon by another." All of the examples of measuring in this book, from the moisture meters and spectrometers to the tapes used on buffers and barriers, produced slightly different versions of soy and the state. When inspectors unfurled measuring tapes in response to a campesino denuncias, they were not so much threatening to limit the beans as they were threatening to change them by changing their relationships with other actors. While the moisture meters produced "informed beans" promoted by a Soy State, the tape measures produced something wholly different: potentially dangerous soja that needed to be contained by the Government of Beans. The former brought beans into closer relation with customs agents and overseas buyers; the latter brought them into relation with environmentalists, welfare advocates, and campesinos. And it did so in a particularly threatening way, far more than the collection of water samples or the reading of flight logs. Because unlike spectrometers and flight logs, measuring tapes had been a character in land struggles for decades.

### WHY BARRERAS VIVAS ARE LIKE LAND REFORM

Ask anyone for directions down one of the long, straight roads that make up smallholder colonies, and they will give you the answer in meters, often very precisely, as in, "Fulano's house is 1,800 meters past the school." Each one of these statements speaks to a history of hopeful young pioneers helping a surveyor, sent by the IBR, to measure their community. Colonists remember the surveyor's name decades later, and I know of several towns that were actually named after the person who surveyed them. Well into the twenty-first century, campesinos petitioned the state to measure their land, paid bribes to state surveyors to produce the maps, and enjoyed accompanying them around on their work, carrying their equipment, participating in its manual aspects, and keeping an eye on both their neighbors and on the visiting technicians.[2]

Of all the activities carried out by the IBR, measurement marked a critical inflection point, when the work of clearing, settling, and cultivating could be officialized as part of a national political project. Measurement by IBR surveyors didn't always produce land titles, but it did perform the promise of rural welfare and the complicity of the state with campesino aspirations. Measurement wrote these aspirations into the landscape, both in local memories and in the survey stakes that remained. Along with the measuring tapes, the theodolite (the optical instrument used by surveyors) required a certain amount of brush clearing, mowing, and even the destruction of gardens, as surveys cut lines of sight along the edges of property. That it was always local campesino men who carried out this work is not incidental: the project of hacking out lines with machetes and driving stakes into the earth was the central activity that made surveying a participatory, fun community exercise.

And though the long-term effects of surveying were uncertain for participants (it did not guarantee a land title), it did leave traces that helped campesinos further solidify their land claims. Most importantly, measurements produced government-issued temporary occupancy permits that reduced the threat of eviction during all-too-frequent police raids against squatters. Occupancy permits didn't always prevent evictions. But sometimes they did; sometimes even evidence of a survey, without the permit, was enough to wave the police off by sowing doubt about the legality of an eviction order. And this meant that a campesino plot informed by measurement (i.e., that had some sort of official paper attached to it) was mildly less likely to be the target of eviction than one that wasn't so informed. The more one requested visits from state functionaries and asked them to leave traces of those visits, the more solidly their claims became inscribed in chains of responses between campesinos, bureaucrats, and the police, and the more the promise of some eventual rural welfare seemed attainable. So while the relationship between the visits of functionaries, property rights, and the promise of rural welfare was always uncertain, at this more tactical level, the level of becoming involved in ever-unfolding relations of response, measurement was one of those practices that conjured the possibility of property rights.

Campesino measurement, like all ways of performing campesino sovereignty, did not just affirm the possibility of a progressive state; it also directly antagonized rural elites. In the original formulation of land reform, campesinos' property was created at the expense of *latifundios*, those large holdings with few people living on them. The fact that, at the beginning of the reform, so many hectares of forest were owned by absent companies made redistribution somewhat easier. But later, when less of this land was available, tensions around measurement arose between campesinos and ranchers who had also benefited from Stroessner's largesse. Questioning the legitimacy of old landholdings and staging land occupations were the primary ways that campesinos asserted their rights. By the time I started accompanying surveys in 2005, most of the land claims I was party to were requests for surveyors to measure "fiscal surpluses," that is, land that had been fenced off by ranchers in excess of what their property titles showed. For all intents and purposes, most claims about fiscal surpluses derived from a disagreement between local recollection of past surveys and the current positioning of a fence. But when campesinos claimed to have found a fiscal surplus, what they literally meant was: this land doesn't belong to the rancher or sojero, it belongs to the state, and because it belongs to the state, it belongs to us.

So as much as surveying was a practice that consolidated the state around campesino aspirations, it also ate at the edges of private property, claiming back territory for a campesino state project. It did this legally but also, much to the irritation of large owners, it did so literally, as groups of campesinos aiding a survey would often jump the fences along with the surveyors. Though routine, this gesture was illegal, and its illegality was clearly part of its power, like the occupation of disputed land, since it placed campesinos not only at the nexus of state and territory but also as exceptions to the law, and in some small way, therefore, as its authors.

The resonances between these surveying practices and the actions of SENAVE's Citizen Participation Unit should by now be clear. The unit, accompanied by campesinos carrying stakes and measuring tapes, also appeared around the edges of large properties, promising some form of welfare for campesinos who were rarely visited by state functionaries. In both cases, the act of measuring was at best an aspirational activity, and everyone understood the results to be uncertain. The IBR was terrible at converting surveys into actual property titles, just as SENAVE was terrible at converting citations into actual barreras vivas. In fact, there were reasons to think that, in many cases, campesinos would prefer not to have barreras vivas at all. (While they offered some respite from pesticide drift, they also blocked the view from houses, fields, schools, and roads, creating dangerous blind zones and capturing dust from passing cars. In some areas, barreras harbored snakes and rats, and provided perfect cover for motorcycle thieves). But this didn't diminish the value of the measurement itself as a gesture of sovereignty.[3]

The same was true of sojeros, whose anger about measurements was usually directed primarily at the campesinos accompanying SENAVE inspectors. It was bad enough that state representatives might demand to measure the contours of their properties—it was far more galling that their poorer neighbors showed up alongside them, jumping the fences along the edges of their fields. It drove them crazy in the same way to have campesinos present when inspectors read their log books, or even when they encountered them in the elevators at Edificio Planeta. If they had always been able to count on at least the tacit understanding that SENAVE was working in their interests, it now seemed plausible that SENAVE would start working in the interests of campesinos, and that the informing practices that were at the heart of export agriculture might suddenly start to work against them.

This tactical takeover of a piece of the state, and these small incursions onto specific plots of land, were something less than the proper capture of territory, and less than a rupture in the relations of governance, less than an agential cut that, once and for all, turned the Soy State into the Government of Beans. Instead, I think of them as practices of tactical sovereignty that insinuated themselves into the chain of responses between soy and the state, ever so slightly changing the potential futures of territory, bureaucracy, and even beans themselves. It played on the anxieties of sojeros not by clarifying the present, but by undermining the apparent direction of the future. All of the most dangerous moments of experimental governance under Lugo were like this. They gathered strands from the past and wove them into the bureaucracy of the Soy State in a novel way so as to (potentially) shift its course.

## TACTICAL SOVEREIGNTY

About a kilometer outside of Karajakái, the Citizen Participation Unit has gathered to assess a field of wheat on a cold August morning. We're an odd bunch. There are the recently appointed members of the Government of Beans, epitomized by Amada, who is looking out for any sign of contamination or even risk of contamination. There are the veteran inspectors, Cézar and Gerardo, who know plants and chemicals and how to move in a bureaucracy, and the lawyers, who give weight to the papers. There's a Canadian anthropologist and Úrsula, the representative of INDI, who is supposed to help liaise with indigenous communities in the area. And there are three campesinos from Karajakái, including Santiago, who helped guide us here. They are sharpening sticks and attaching discarded plastic bags to the ends, improvising flags that will mark off distances. Everyone is tense, but amicable, and when Amada calls a huddle around her clipboard, the discussion begins in good faith.

We are standing on a major road heading west toward the next colony, and we've come far enough from Karajakái itself that we can't see any houses. On one side of the road is a steep muddy bank about a meter high, with a scrubby hedge of low orange trees along the top of it. Santiago, our main campesino guide, says that's where Ayvu Reko, the Mby'a village is, just beyond the oranges. On the other side is wheat as far as the eye can see, a small fraction of the field belonging to Nuevos Montes. When we first came within sight of the wheat, Amada and I both had to catch our breath. Only five years previously, this was all forest, teeming with wildlife, but after a few months of bulldozing and burning, it was gone. And here we are now, a gaggle of well-meaning state representatives, in two pickup trucks, promising to do something about something.

The conversation ahead is going to be uncomfortable and everyone knows it, since they've been in this position before. Amada has brought out her clipboard, and now the clipboard demands a response.[4] Or rather, it demands several responses, but only one of them really matters. It asks whether or not we are standing on a *camino vecinal* (a neighborhood road) and, by extension, whether or not the soy field (as we're all calling it even though it's wheat) needs to be bordered by a barrera viva.

AMADA: The question is, are we on a camino vecinal?[5]

SANTIAGO: Of course!

CÉZAR: No. It has to be a camino vecinal *poblado* [an inhabited neighborhood road] for it to count.

[Gerardo nods in agreement.]

AMADA: [Decree] 2408/04 says "caminos vecinales, poblados," with a comma. This changes the meaning to "neighborhood roads and towns."[6]

CÉZAR: But that's just a mistake. They fixed it in [Law] 3742/09, and they took out the comma.

AMADA: But we're supposed to use 2408 to interpret 3742, not the other way around. And there's a comma. Anyway, even in 3742 it doesn't make sense. Article 68A says that you need a barrera between a crop and an *asentamiento humano* [human settlement]. Why bother putting in a stipulation about roads at all if the only roads that matter are already covered by 68A?

Everyone is quiet for a bit, having had this argument before. The laws are poorly written, the protocol is muddy, and there's no way to resolve this basic problem while standing on a road.[7] It's cold, and everyone wants to move on. But a lot is at play here.

**GERARDO:** If any road that someone might walk down is a camino vecinal, why didn't they just call it a *camino público*?

**AMADA:** That's what they should have done.

**SANTIAGO:** We use this road every day, by foot, by bike. It's how we get to the market. And it's how everyone gets to the agronomy school in the next town.

Another pause, and that seems to do it. But the form demands a response. Is this a camino vecinal or not? Is the company required to plant a barrera viva or not?

**AMADA:** That kid in Itapúa was killed on a road exactly like this. He was nowhere near houses, but he had to get to school and back on a road exactly like this. This is what the barrera viva is for!

Cézar takes a deep breath but doesn't answer. Later, at the garage, where we've gone to replace a filter on one of the trucks, he'll tell me that Silvino Talavera died from malnutrition, not pesticide poisoning.

**GERARDO:** Look, they couldn't have meant this when they wrote the law. This side of the property is at least five kilometers long. It's not reasonable to expect a farmer to plant a barrera that's that long. It's too costly.

Gerardo's evocation of economic common sense reveals the stakes of this seemingly petty argument. The misplaced comma has been in the text of these laws for six years already. But Gerardo and others have filled the form out without hesitation, interpreting the strange syntax by starting from the assumption that a law could not exist that wasn't reasonable for the sojero. That common sense, wherever it comes from (from training in agronomy, from a feeling of camaraderie with farmers, or from a culture of service in SENAVE), has reproduced itself through rote regulatory practice (we are talking, after all, about the routine checking—or in this case not check-ing—of a box on a carbon-copied form) to become protocol. It's not that the older inspectors are being disingenuous, or that they are in anybody's pocket. They may very well be, but the point is that whether or not they are, the effect is precisely the same, at least until someone interrupts the com-monsensical box-checking habit. It isn't lost on anybody in this argument that the box, as yet unchecked, now indexes thousands of similar boxes in the SENAVE archives, the accumulated documentation of every time a SE-NAVE inspector has decided that a road like this is not a camino vecinal. In so doing, they've maintained the cozy relationship between the regulator and the industry rather than interceding on behalf of the victims of pesticide exposure.

This is Amada's whole point. It is the Soy State that doesn't think this is a camino vecinal. She wants to have these conversations because she wants to make visible the tacit alliance behind this interpretation. And she wants to be able to cut through it by bringing another past into the conversation, displacing the putative common sense of the regulators and putting a dead boy in its place, daring Cézar and Gerardo to choose the former over the latter. The event of Silvino's death is reiterated again, and with it the disruption of common sense that hovers around the form. What makes the mundane little form suddenly so dangerous is that it has become impossible to fill it out without making a crucial distinction that decides whether this past will operate in the future. There are two options: either it is or it is not a camino vecinal. If it is, then the future welfare of the residents of Karajakái trumps, if only momentarily, the economic interests of Nuevos Montes, and the Government of Beans gains a bit of ground within this regulatory tangle. If not, we just walk away, and it is as though we have never been here. It is the form that brings the moment to this crucial point of inflection, and Amada makes this clear by gesturing to the form constantly. But the form, itself a vestige of past bureaucratic arguments, now structures the way the current dispute unfolds in a setting that the form makers didn't fully anticipate.

Of course Amada checks the box, and the road dividing Karajakái and the soy field suddenly becomes a camino vecinal. Amada, holding the pen at this moment, is able to harness a minor bureaucratic ambiguity, bending the road toward a new kind of future, one in which the legal department at SENAVE might be able to fine Nuevos Montes, and one in which the SENAVE archives might begin to fill with interpretive traces of Silvino Talavera rather than the common sense of sojeros. A tiny act of tactical sovereignty has just been performed along one of Paraguay's new borders, an act that would not have been possible if the regulation were clear, or if there was no distance between the empirical road and the legal fiction of the camino vecinal. Santiago, now holding three sharpened sticks, is getting ready to step into the wheat, to participate in the sovereign act of measurement that the form now endorses.

Veena Das argues that it is in part "the illegibility of the state, the unreadability of its rules and regulations that makes room for the arbitrary, *exceptional*, decisions that characterize state power."[8] This doesn't just occur out on the territorial margins, but is a pervasive feature of law.[9] A bishop in the presidency, a pendulum swing in regional politics, an environmentalist in charge of phytosanitary regulation, a dead child along the Brazilian border, an unlikely middle-aged woman in a pickup truck on a deserted road following the denuncias of a well-organized campesino organization, and suddenly the conditions for interpreting Paraguayan law, so long controlled by an economic common sense, seem to be up for grabs. The state may never be fully present, or the Government of Beans as such may never precisely exist; after all, they've barely begun to imagine the protocols they will need to create to make that happen. But in this moment of tactical sovereignty, when judgment can still favor Silvino's ghost rather than sojeros, Amada performs a tiny bureaucratic insurrection, vibrating with possibility.

## ARBITRARY BODIES

Then, just as quickly, the moment passed. After Amada left her mark in the box, the Citizen Participation Unit dissipated, and Amada stood alone at the side of the road. The two lawyers went back to the truck to warm their hands. The inspectors wandered off, slowly unrolling the tape measure into the wheat, marking off the five-meter mark for the barrera, with its little plastic-bag flags thrashing furiously in the wind. Then, gently telling Santiago he couldn't go any further, the two inspectors kept walking, as agreed, to the one hundred meter spot, so far from the road that they almost disappeared into the wheat. They were merely doing what Amada had asked them, planting little flags, but they were so small, so far out of hearing range, that they seemed both insignificant and, potentially, treacherous. When Amada turned around, even Úrsula had vanished, scrambling into the brush toward an unseen Mby'a hut, perhaps making sure people got their stories straight before Amada arrived.

This is always what it felt like to be part of Lugo's government: whatever tactical sovereignty seemed possible, it was always fragile, always beset by other projects. And at times like this one, that fragility looked like genuine vulnerability. Amada, channeling Lovera, channeling Lugo, deciding the undecidable, conjured the possibility of the Government of Beans. But that possibility would only ever stick if those around her took the decision seriously. And on this level, the Lugo government always struggled to prove that it had the capacity to remain, to shepherd documents like the citation form up through the protocols that awaited them in the legal offices, and into the archives where it would be joined by other citations. Tactical sovereignty needed to be reiterated, and for that to happen, specific bodies needed to remain in place. Standing out there on a nearly deserted road, it was obvious how easy it would be to move those bodies from where they stood.

If, for Das, sovereignty lies in the space between the illegibility of law and the exceptional capacity to decide, for Hansen and Stepputat it lies in the space between the sublime aura of the state and the profane, bare life of the ruler's body.[10] In Paraguay, as in much of Latin America, the figure of the strongman was not just a metaphor but a literal comment on the body of the leader or dictator. One of Stroessner's promises to Paraguayans was that his body was immovable, that he had a "heart of steel" and could endure, and not only his physical health but his reputed appetites for sex and violence were part of the mythology of the dictatorship.[11] But the ruler's body is not the only body through which sovereignty operates. This is true even at the most mundane level of the activist bureaucrat, whose interpretation of the law depends on her being by that road, physically present with the clipboard and pen.

A week later, Amada confided to me that she was struggling with a rare chronic condition that kept her constantly fatigued and occasionally sent her body into crisis, requiring months of rest and visits to doctors in Europe. Amada's power, the kind of charismatic aura that is hard to place materially, was always shadowed by her own corporeal frailty. Although she never made the connection aloud, as she told me this it was hard not to think of Fernando Lugo himself, who'd recently been diagnosed with non-Hodgkin's lymphoma, a cancer associated with pesticide exposure. Lugo's chemotherapy became a drama that connected his frail body to the constant media chatter about the frailness of his unlikely political coalition. More than that, he fit into a regional story on the Latin American left that centered on the increasingly frail body of Fidel Castro, who had relinquished the Cuban presidency to his brother, now overseeing the slow dissipation of communism.[12] Three months later, Néstor Kirchner (ex-president of Argentina and husband of the sitting president) would die suddenly of a heart attack, and the following year, both Brazil's president Luiz Inácio Lula da Silva and Venezuela's Hugo Chavez, the two standard bearers for different versions of the Latin American left, would go through their own very public bouts with cancer. (Chavez eventually succumbed, while Lula survived, only to later be thrown in jail during the right-wing wave that would overtake Brazil.)[13] The coincidence of all of these illnesses predictably became the subject of rumors about CIA agents carrying syringes. They also made clear how much Latin America's left turn was dependent on the personalist politics of a small group of leaders.

Paraguay's version of this predictably centered on the ever-looming possibility of rural violence. Lugo's frailty was mirrored by another play of sovereignty and bodies brewing in Paraguay's northeast, where a band of extremist renegades from the campesino movement had begun to use kidnapping as a way of gathering resources and drumming up support. Lugo had inherited the problem from Nicanor, whose presidency was tested early, in 2004, when members of a Marxist party called Patria Libre had kidnapped and murdered the daughter of another ex-president, Raúl Cubas. That event had come around to find Lugo. Its leadership in prison, members of Patria Libre had reformed in the north and announced their reemergence under the new name Ejército del Pueblo Paraguayo (EPP), or the Paraguayan People's Army, only weeks before Lugo was elected. In the official line, they were a radical group with ties to Colombia's FARC guerrillas, though in the first years it was more common to hear the opinion that they didn't exist at all and were instead an elaborate ruse to justify militarizing the countryside.[14] True or not, the stories of the EPP at the time signaled a new kind of state project that would compete with Lugo from the rural left, not through legal protocols and sample taking but through armed struggle. Their populist tactics of demanding that soy farmers stop fumigating their crops, or forcing ranchers, by way of ransom, to butcher and distribute parts of their herds to nearby families, left Lugo with a brutal conundrum. To attack them too forcefully risked alienating many of his supporters. Not responding meant exposing himself to accusations that he quietly supported the guerrilla movement. After the EPP kidnapped two ranchers in the first year of his presidency, Lugo erred in the former direction, branding the group as terrorists and promising to hunt them down, eventually assassinating several of its leaders. In response, EPP members took to attacking isolated police stations and killed several policemen over the next two years.

The story of the EPP was a side story to the Government of Beans, as was the rise of increasingly organized marijuana production and drug smuggling across the same northern provinces. But in the moments when EPP members surfaced, either in videos with their captives or as corpses following shoot-outs with police, they served to refocus the national discussion of sovereignty on the ways that state projects are always tied, in the final instance, to violence. It was around these more corporeal encounters that the limits of tactical sovereignty would be tested and ultimately proven too feeble to withstand the backlash from the Soy State. The legitimacy of the Government of Beans would turn on Lugo's ability to control violence, to strike an impossible balance between killing and protecting life. The Government of Beans could not rely on regulation alone, benignly promoting life and welfare by telling farmers to plant elephant grass; it also had to figure out the less tactical, more brutal expressions of sovereignty, and in this, perhaps to its credit, it was never particularly adept. Ultimately it would be precisely this inability to effectively control state violence, or even to provide a stable narrative frame for it when it erupted, that ended the Government of Beans.

# CHAPTER TWELVE

# A Massacre Where the Army Used to Be

A case of contentious measurement made national headlines in the final months of the Government of Beans. It was November 2011, when Lugo issued a decree regulating the Law of Border Security.[1] The law banned the sale, to foreign nationals, of land within fifty kilometers of the border, and revived an old piece of legislation removed by Stroessner in 1963.[2] It had been debated for years under the González Macchi administration, and finally passed in those busy early months of 2004 after Nicanor took power. There had been a brief uproar around the law's passage at the time, especially among Brazilian immigrants in the eastern border region who worried that they might lose their farms. But it died down after a quick amendment clarified that the ban was not retroactive and that Paraguay didn't intend to expropriate any land in Alto Paraná or Itapúa. It also died down because, like the ban on planting GMOs and the original barrera viva law, it was simply not enforced.

Like so many controversies that happened during Lugo's tenuous presidency, the kerfuffle over border security began with an executive decree that sought only to implement an article of existing law. Lugo's decree empowered the Military Geographical Department to begin a measurement of the fifty-kilometer line, a necessary precursor to enforcing the ban.

When surveyors showed up on a property belonging to one of the most powerful landowners in the country, Tranquilino Favero, they stepped too far. Instead of calling in political favors, Favero called reporters from the newspaper ABC *Color*, who drove out and intercepted military survey-ors while they were placing stakes. The surveyors were accompanied by a lawyer from the IBR and, tellingly, a delegation of landless campesinos from a large organization known as the Liga Nacional de Carperos, who appeared in pictures carrying shovels, stakes, and measuring tapes.

The momentary configuration of the Government of Beans in this day of measuring was an irresistible performance for all sides, as it clearly demonstrated the antagonism between soy farmers and the Government of Beans. Here were landless campesinos, empowered not only by the IBR but by the presidency and the military, walking into the middle of a soy field. When they were caught, the UGP called the measurers "invaders of private property," using the term normally reserved for condemning squatters. But here the invader was the state itself. Upping the rhetorical ante, and in clear recognition of the stakes of calling the state an invader, nearby sojeros were reported as saying that such invasions would inevi-tably lead to "civil war."[3]

The lawyer, the head of the IBR, and the general in charge of surveys were forced to apologize after having clearly pushed tactical sovereignty just a bit too far.[4] All attempts to measure the fifty-kilometer buffer from the border were suspended immediately. The fiasco over measurement of Favero's farm was perhaps the clearest vindication of what Alcides had told us a year be-fore: that they might measure his farm, but try to measure something deep in Alto Paraná, and they would discover that theirs was not the only state project operating, nor the only one capable of deploying violence to achieve its ends. And this was only one of any number of signs that the Government of Beans was reaching its final limits.

## THE UNRAVELING OF SENAVE

Back at Edificio Planeta, other tensions were beginning to be felt as well. The three main political parties (the Colorados, Liberals, and Lugo's coali-tion, with Tekojoja at the center) were preparing for the 2013 general elec-tions. It was early in the electoral cycle, but the parties were scrambling to respond to the emergence of a likely savior for the Colorado Party, a to-bacco magnate and financier named Horacio Cartes. Cartes was not a career politician; instead, his main claims to fame were his involvement in contraband cigarette trade and his conviction in 1989 for embezzling 35 million dollars from Paraguay's Central Bank.[5] His candidacy for the general election was buoyed by his great wealth and, like Lugo, his status as a political outsider. Liberals, who hoped to use their position in Lugo's 2008 coalition to bolster their own chances in the 2013 election, were busily gathering whatever state resources they could. Tekojoja was straining to find Lugo's successor, while others in the party (including many working for SENAVE's Citizen Participation Unit) were fortifying client networks.

Financially, the election was one rationale for why Darío, whom we met back in chapter 7, had developed an embezzlement operation inside SENAVE. When Lovera discovered the operation, he fired Darío along with a number of his accomplices. But Darío had not gone easily. A large number of older civil servants, including all of the members of SINTRA, a union linked to Horacio Cartes's wing of the Colorado Party, had sided with Darío and other fired SENAVE bureaucrats.[6] The union had been trying to undermine Lovera by accusing him of corruption, and now they used the sacking of Darío's network as evidence that Lovera was only protecting his own racket.[7]

In addition to or perhaps because of this, SENAVE was also experiencing unexpected budget pressures. Because of the difficulty in figuring out who was up to what and where the money was going, Inés Franceschelli had decided to put the Citizen Participation Unit on hold for the remaining months of 2011.

> We had to stop all those visits to campesino communities for three months. Can you believe that by August they had burned through the budget for per diems and gas for the entire year? And here we were; we still had to supervise planting, and certify the soy leaving the country. Those are technical responsibilities—it's true they're not social projects, but they're technical responsibilities that we had to comply with by law. I mean, whether we like it or not, soy is still 23 percent of GDP, so you can't put on a mask and say, "This doesn't exist."

At the moment of most intense crisis, these "social projects" had to be suspended. For that brief period, it again became clear that the core of the agency's work was providing services for the soy export chain. In this quote, even Franceschelli seems to have conflated the technical with the common-sensical economics of the Soy State; the social project of the Government of Beans had become expendable.

Meanwhile, infighting within the Tekojoja Party led to increasing rifts between key members of Lugo's administration, and a growing sense that the party would enter the next election divided into rural and urban fragments, competing against each other.[8] "From then on," Franceschelli told me, "from October or November 2011 until the coup, Lugo didn't answer Lovera's calls and didn't receive him. There, inside the government, we were all alone, doing what we could, what we believed in. And so of course the right took advantage of that situation." Things had gotten progressively worse from there, and everyone sensed that they might be entering the final phase of their experiment. Sensing that they would lose their bid to reform pesticide legislation once more, Lovera, Franceschelli, and Silvia González met one night at the office over a bottle of wine and decided to write up an executive resolution that regulated SENAVE inspectors, changing the definitions of "barrera viva" and "franja de securidad" once more.[9] The new regulation was called Resolución 660, and with a new budget year opened, they'd sent the Citizen Participation Unit back into the countryside to apply the new standards. This drew the ire of the UGP and ABC *Color*, and many of the older inspectors simply refused to enforce the new rules. By late May, the SINTRA union had begun a daily picket in front of Edificio Planeta, and Franceschelli had moved to Human Resources to try to get a handle on the endless labor disputes that destabilized the institution.

And then in June, three more things happened in quick succession that made Lovera and his allies think they were about to be thrown out. The first was a campaign by produce importers who blocked a border bridge in protest of tighter controls over their merchandise. It just so happened that border control had been revamped, creating a bilateral Integrated Control Area between Argentina and Paraguay, located on the Argentine side of the border. In the middle of the protests by truckers, one of Lovera's only trusted border agents had stopped a truckload of unwashed potatoes from entering the country.[10] After repeatedly trying to bribe the inspector to let them through, truckers had surrounded the agent's office, effectively holding him captive. The standoff had only been resolved with help from the Argentine embassy and, according to Franceschelli, the mobilization of Argentine troops.

The second event was the imposition of a thirty-day soy moratorium between the June harvest and the planting season starting in July. Ironically, the moratorium was a phytosanitary measure meant to control the spread of rust, a fungus that had recently become a problem for soybean growers throughout Paraguay. Rust dies off quickly if it doesn't have any soy to live on, and the moratorium is the best way to control it. Few farmers kept soy in the ground during this period, but enough of them did every year to allow rust to keep reproducing through the winter months. The moratorium, which affected a few farmers for the benefit of the many, was a quintessential Soy State measure, an agribiopolitical move to protect the soy crop from infection. But it was too convenient: the UGP used it against Lovera, calling it a "soy ban" and threatening to block roads with tractors unless it was lifted.[11]

The third was the collapse of a pilot project to test water quality. Franceschelli's brainchild, the study was an attempt to establish a new protocol for testing water in partnership with the Ministry of Public Health and CONAMURI. The idea was to improve communications between SENAVE's labs and field-workers, campesinos, and health professionals. During the pilot, inspectors were supposed to take samples in six pesticide hot spots, first in June, the off-season, then in September, during spraying season. And yet even this simple task had run into obstructions, and they only managed to take two sets of samples before the project became impossible to carry out. As Franceschelli recounted:

> On that project, I was receiving threats. "Oh you met with that bitch Perla again." And the laboratory people who weren't on our side would go out to take samples on the wrong day, or they'd go without the right containers. These things made you realize that . . . there was an enormous boycott. We had that all the time in SENAVE from the countryside. When there were resolutions, when the president of SENAVE made a decision—I have no idea why the hell it was like this—his own people would put it on the shelf and wouldn't tell anyone. We always had that. But in those days it was getting very aggressive, very threatening. And we could see they were generating conditions in the press, basically ABC.[12]

In the years after the coup, I heard similar stories of unraveling from other agencies, in the Ministry of Culture and Education, in the Secretariat of the Environment, the public television station, and across any number of NGOs and organizations working closely with the government. Unable to know exactly what was going on, Lugo's top functionaries kept turning to the newspapers to get wind of the plots being hatched against them. Conspiracy theories abounded, alongside speculation about new coalitions, double agents, and unseen alliances. Of course many of these turned out to be true, but none were as spectacular or as gruesome as what actually happened.

On June 15, 2012, Lovera called his most trusted advisors to his board-room to figure out a strategy to deal with the most recent sign of a campaign against him. From June 8 to 12, ABC *Color* had printed a series it called "Twelve Reasons to Fire Lovera," outlining the UGP's arguments.[13] According to Franceschelli, "We were trying to figure out what was going on, and we were making decisions. Because we thought in the previous two weeks of June, we said, 'They're going to fire us. They're coming for us and they're coming for our heads.' . . . We didn't think they were coming for the government itself." That's when everyone at the table began receiving texts that "a campesino" had been shot and killed in the district of Curuguaty. Only a few hours later, it would be clear that a massive confrontation had occurred, killing eleven campesinos and six police officers. From that point on, no one in the room thought that Lovera was the target anymore. Whoever the plotters were, they were after the president.

## THE MASSACRE OF CURUGUATY

The way it all ended, in a pointless rural massacre and a bloodless coup in Asunción a week later, was so sudden, so easy, that it gave people reason to imagine that a deep conspiracy underlay the whole thing. For several years afterward, the most prominent leftist slogan about the event was a question, "Que pasó en Curuguaty?" (What happened in Curuguaty?), and the most important organizing tool was a website by the same name.[14] In my own retelling, I draw primarily on the excellent, detailed analysis put out the following year by CODEHUPY, a Paraguayan human rights NGO.[15] But it too has a particular frame, a particular way of making agential cuts, appropriate to the courtroom in which many of the same lawyers would be battling for years. The CODEHUPY report takes a legal approach, trying to ascertain exactly who did what to whom and why, and in the end never reaches far beyond stories of individual culpability, of particular fingers on particular triggers. But it is just as easy to believe what one very well-placed soy farmer told me much later: "I don't really know what happened, if anyone ordered for the trigger to be pulled, but I doubt it. There were lots of plans in place for how to get rid of Lugo. All they needed was an opportunity." And so as I retell it, the Massacre of Curuguaty is a story of conjuncture, of how the tangle of increasingly tense relations that made up the Government of Beans finally fell apart.

This thread of the story begins on Finca 30, a piece of land originally registered in the nineteenth century to La Industria Paraguaya, the consortium of British financiers and Colorado politicians who at one point owned 2.6 million hectares of land.[16] Along with the rest of the land in that area, Finca 30 was slowly broken up during the land reform of the 1960s. It was the sort of parcel that could easily have been redistributed, could have become dotted with campesino colonies, like Karajakái and Yerutí, neither of which were far away. But instead of serving the pioneer citizens of the land reform, it served two other kinds of sovereignty projects. In 1967, a two thousand hectare piece was given to the armed forces for a military base. And in 1969, a fifty thousand hectare piece adjoining the base was sold to a company called Campos Morombi, part of another consortium owned by an influential Colorado senator named Blas N. Riquelme.[17]

Unlike many of Stroessner's old friends, Riquelme had managed to hold on to his land after the 1989 coup, adapting to the political winds in order to defend his property. Meanwhile, the military base, still mostly forest, had declined over the decades. In 1985, a surveyor reported that the boundary posts marking the line between the base and Riquelme's property had disappeared and that at least three hundred hectares seemed to have been eaten up by the ranch.[18] A decade later, a campesino organization from Curuguaty tried to occupy what remained of the base's land. The military kicked them off, but in 1999, it abandoned the base altogether, and the land came to be known to would-be colonizers as Marina Kue—literally "the place where the army used to be."

Different campesino organizations continued to eye the land. Activating the standard script of pioneer citizenship, they petitioned the IBR to have the land expropriated from the army while they contemplated further occupations. One of these petitions happened in 2004, the year that soy began to arrive in the area. In it, the would-be settlers reported that workers from Riquelme's ranch had suddenly begun to cut down the remaining forest in Marina Kue, and that it needed to be expropriated before the ranch took it over completely. In response, Riquelme filed a usucaption claim, stating that since it had been using the land for years, it now effectively belonged to his ranch.[19]

Thus began an eight-year legal struggle between Riquelme and the IBR to interpret the edges of an old property title amid the detritus of the dictatorship: a reviled old patrón and the ghost of a faded military. The story, in stereotypical fashion, was punctuated by the arbitrary repression of campesinos and dubious legal arguments that could only be resolved through executive decision. And all these tensions were now increasing as soybeans encroached along the eastern edge of the property. And as usual, the IBR would not have supported the campesino claim had it not been for intense pressure from local organizations. A new leader named Vidal Vega emerged during this wave, leading an occupation of the area, which was promptly evicted. In 2008, just after Lugo's election, Vega led another occupation, an act of tactical sovereignty testing just how weakened the Colorados had become. They were again evicted. Then in January 2012, just as the pressure was rising on the Government of Beans, Vega's group entered the ranch for a third time, set up camp, and refused to leave. This time they had better logistical support from the Liga Nacional de Carperos, whom we last saw carrying shovels for the military surveyors in Alto Paraná.

But then on June 15, for reasons that remain unclear, the minister of the interior, Carlos Filizzola, decided to move on the camp at Marina Kue with a huge, well-armed police force, including snipers positioned in trees around the camp.[20] When everyone was in place, the lead police officer and one representative from the community met in a field not far from the tents and huts that made up the occupation. The heated exchange lasted only minutes and quickly devolved into a bloody shooting match that left seventeen people dead, including the two negotiators.

It was this news that interrupted the meeting of Lovera's directors at SENAVE, appearing simultaneously on everyone's phones, just as it appeared on the phone of anyone with any proximity to Lugo's government or to the campesino movement. The bottom had fallen out of the Government of Beans.

In a sharp critique of the police actions that day, two of Paraguay's foremost human rights lawyers argued that the state had failed the test of legitimacy in its use of violence, and thereby stopped acting like a state.[21] Not only had the government shown itself incapable of meting out legitimate violence, it had used illegitimate violence against its own allies. Several campesino organizations began planning a massive national march against Lugo's government for its betrayal of the rural poor.[22] Liberals and Colorados, for their part, began planning impeachment, and by the time it was clear they meant it, it was too late for campesinos to change their stance. They debated simply transforming the march into a pro-Lugo demonstration. But their hesitation was decisive. Within five days, Congress had impeached Lugo on the charge of failing to carry out his office. Two days later, the Senate held a brief hearing, which Lugo refused to attend, for fear of violence. No one presented evidence for or against the president's removal, but the vote was decisive, and on the afternoon of June 22, Lugo was removed from office, leaving Federico Franco, the Liberal vice president, to assume his place.[23]

So ended the Government of Beans, pathetically, probably accidentally, killing its own supporters on a piece of land claimed by a grotesque old friend of General Stroessner's. But if the event proved just how debilitated Lugo's government was, it also put to rest the notion that the state was absent in the countryside. It's never been clear where the seemingly arbitrary violence at Marina Kue came from, or to what, precisely, it was a response. But the apparatus that mobilized around it was terrifyingly efficient in retaking control of regulatory agencies, police, and the national territory. In the years ahead, Paraguay's judiciary held an absurd and protracted criminal trial for campesino survivors of the massacre but refused to press charges against any of the police or the officials who had organized the raid. The veil of obscurity that hung over the entire procedure marked the inability of the attorney's office to even consider what illegitimate state violence might look like. The Government of Beans had to go, but the apparatus of police violence remained, to support the Soy State once more.[24]

As Horacio Cartes lumbered toward victory in the 2013 presidential elections, there were early signs of the Soy State reasserting itself. Only days after Lugo was removed from office, Gerardo (the inspector who had worked with the Citizen Participation Unit) got a call from the new president of SENAVE, telling him to ignore any regulations or directives that Lovera had put in place, including Resolution 660, with its definition of caminos vecinales and barreras vivas. "They didn't bother getting rid of it, I don't think," he told me. "They just told us to ignore it." The new president of SENAVE personally apologized to several sojero groups for the actions of the institution under Lovera. Within a few months, the minister of agriculture had also unilaterally approved four new varieties of genetically modified seed that were still undergoing regulatory testing. Out where the state was said to be absent, the repercussions were far scarier. In the climate of violence that followed the massacre of Curuguaty, six campesino leaders, including Vidal Vega, were assassinated by unidentified attackers in Canindeyú and San Pedro.[25]

But the most impressive sign came in December 2013, when protesters began confronting soy farmers in Canindeyú for not planting barreras vivas along a road not far from Marina Kue, Karajakái, and Yeruti.[26] In response, Cartes deployed special forces to guard the crops, flanking the fields where tractors were spraying. Where the law said that dense vegetation should stand to keep the pesticides in, there were now riot police keeping protesters out. The Government of Beans's awkward attempts to use the state to hold back soy were now simply inverted. In the line of police, the Soy State presented itself in its starkest form. Campesinos, neither pioneers nor regulators nor really subjects of rights at all, were now the foreign element from which soy needed to be protected.

## THE INVERSION OF DENUNCIATION

For those who orchestrated it, Lugo's removal was an impeachment, perfectly legal in the Paraguayan Constitution. For everyone else, the week of violence and political intrigue that took down the government amounted to a coup. In the years since, it has come to be called something in between, a *golpe parlamentario*, or parliamentary coup. Later, when similar procedures were used to topple Brazilian president Dilma Rousseff, some journalists even called it a *golpe a la Paraguaia*, as though something about the messy unraveling of Latin America's left turn had taken on a distinctly Paraguayan flavor.[27] But beyond the judicial intrigue, the end of the short-lived left turn in Paraguay was the end of an attempt to revive the promise of rural welfare by placing the lives and well-being of the poor above the imperatives of soy production.

The next Monday, carrying her last box of belongings out of Edificio Planeta, Franceschelli was in the tiny elevator going down from the thirteenth floor, and got squished in next to a large man she didn't recognize. Without looking at her, he began to yell: "Well if it isn't the fucking commies, and the whore who gave birth to them. We're going to rip them open. You thought you were going to boss us around—we're going to fuck you with an eight-battery flashlight. . . . We'll make those grimy, miserable disgusting sons of bitches cry for the next ten years." One of the other women in the elevator chimed in as well before they reached the ground floor and all got out. Franceschelli rode the elevator to the basement alone and left by another door, shaking.

> The whole feeling was that they were going to put everything to the sword [*entraron al degüello*]. . . . They took archives, all the archives from the Citizen Participation Unit, and made them disappear. They burned them. Well, they had a barbecue; before that they burned all the file boxes with all the files from all the meetings with campesinos, all the

inspections, the list of schools—they burned everything. It no longer existed in the nation-state. . . . We know the instruction was that nothing should remain. This we know, from the UGP, from Franco, nothing and no one was supposed to stay. They swept everything. Everything we had built, the whole state was reset to zero, or, of course, less than zero.

Because the Government of Beans was unable to build the protocols that would turn denuncias into robust regulatory responses, the denuncias were all that was left, and they were easy to destroy. Consider the water testing project, an attempt to build the kind of protocol that might eventually convert all those denuncias into a clear portrait of the social, epidemiological, and ecological problem of soy monocropping. The project would hardly have been conclusive, but it was Franceschelli's final attempt to generate something more than disparate complaints, an infrastructure that might outlast her time in office. The water testing project never collected its samples, the protocol became moot, and Franceschelli couldn't even figure out exactly why. Were the laboratory workers incompetent or obstructionist? Did they really resent having to work with local peasant groups? Were they just political adversaries waiting Lovera out? Or were they connected to a larger conspiracy that finally played itself out in Marina Kue on the bodies of campesinos?

Whatever the case, water contamination remained indistinct, a pile of denuncias, but not something solid enough to rupture the commonsense that kept the Soy State working. They remained quasi-responses to quasi-events, like all the rashes and headaches and malformed babies and shriveled cassava leaves, the diarrhea, hot winds, fetid smells, broken water systems, drying wells, bodies along roads, all piled up as denuncias, some moving toward an administrative indictment, even a fine, others bound to get thrown out or lost along the way. Soy itself, like all good conspiracies, never came into focus as a thing. And because it was created in response, the Government of Beans remained similarly unfocused.

But it's also clear that Franceschelli wasn't the only one to believe that a pile of denuncias, as it grew, was not inconsequential. There's an amazing and productive slippage in her account that gets right to the nub of what may—or may not—have been at stake in the coup against Lugo. The day that SENAVE staff burned the archives of the Citizen Participation Unit, she says, they erased the state. Of course for Franceschelli this is intensely personal, and the conflation of the archives of her social project with the state itself is reflective of her positioning in the whole affair.[28] The archive became a convenient metonym for countless similar processes happening across Lu-go's government that were slowly sedimenting other ways of governing. The growing pile of denuncias, still so small it could be hauled out in boxes and burned before a barbecue, were the chrysalis of some other possibility, of an alternate agribiopolitical arrangement that gathered the welfare promises of the past and set them against the proliferation of soybeans. Fragile and con-tradictory as they might have been, someone still felt the need to burn them.

Burning archives does not, of course, destroy all of the remnants of an experiment. But the act, like other acts of violence meant to reassert the Soy State in the wake of the coup, did put an end to a particular agribiopo-litical project. For years afterward campesino organizations and their urban supporters, the frayed remainders of Lugo's coalition, struggled to imagine starting again. In 2019, when I visited many of these communities again, most told me frankly, and fatally, "Soy won." To the extent that they were still involved in a struggle to change agriculture, it was on different terms, with different enemies, but nothing quite as easily articulated as "La soja mata," which had slowly faded from use. In the long shadow of the coup, the questions at hand seemed somewhat different. As the Government of Beans faded behind other, more immediate struggles, it became part of a longer story of the rise of the phytosanitary state and its central role in fortifying the Anthropocene's still-spreading monocrops.

# PART III | AGRIBIOPOLITICS

Joel Filártiga met Sofía and me in his high-rise condo in downtown Asunción. The apartment was generic for professionals of his generation, comfortable if a bit overstuffed with furniture. But the walls were unmistakably his, covered with framed line drawings, most of them portraits of his children, others allegorical, in the stark magic realist style popular among radicals in the 1970s. A shrine to his son, murdered by Stroessner's police, occupied a good portion of the sitting room. His daughter saw us into his bedroom, where he sat in a wheelchair by the window, and he began talking as though we'd been there a while already. I scrambled to turn on my recorder, and this is the first thing that it captured:

> I suffered through a lot of repression here for my fight against pesticides. When I was studying medicine I had a daughter with spina bifida and meningocele. My second daughter. Meningocele, spina bifida, and hydrocephaly. All because of DDT. . . . That was in 1954. There was a national campaign against malaria, and the insecticide they used was DDT. There was a great army of fumigators. They would fumigate all of the houses in the country. But at the same time those fumigators were [he paused, looking for the right word]. . . . They gave reports to the minister of the interior for

the dictatorship. Because they checked all the houses in the country, they'd look for a paper, and take it and keep it. . . . I was living here in the city. And my wife was pregnant. And two or three days after we knew about the pregnancy she was fumigated. Fumigated the plates, the kitchen, everything. They said that you could just wash it with water and it wasn't poisonous.

Sofía and I hadn't had a clear plan for this interview, in part because we thought we knew his life story. Filártiga was one of the most famous living men in Paraguay, a flamboyant mainstay of the left, who wrote anti-imperialist diatribes online, and whose long white beard could be spotted easily at demonstrations in downtown Asunción. He even signed his emails, with some justification, "the living legend." But we had contacted him primarily because his name continually came up in interviews with epidemiologists and health care professionals on the front lines of the soy frontier. Just like referring to pesticides as "agrotóxicos" or saying "sojeros" instead of "productores," dropping Filártiga's name was a way of indexing a political position, adherence to a tradition of radical medicine that long predated soy. So we didn't know quite what to expect. But what he offered us was nothing short of a reframing of the agribiopolitical present, and a new way of understanding the depth and contradictions of the Government of Beans.

Filártiga's memory, and his way of relating events, tended to run into and over itself, and it was hard to keep up with details of the story, though luckily some of it is published elsewhere.[1] Like many children of Colorado elites, he had been Stroessner's godchild, and his family went to Stroessner's infamous birthday parties. As a young man, though, he'd become increasingly critical of the regime.[2] After medical school, he had run a clinic he named the Clinic of Hope in the town of Ybycu'í and, according to legend, almost never charged his patients for consultation. It was there, in the mid-1950s, that he began to see the effects of new pesticides entering the country.

Folidol appeared in the 1960s, and they were still using DDT for lice. Then there was lindane. And then gammaxene and other organochlorides. Endrin from Shell. They used that for ants. And there were a lot more birth defects. . . . I started to see pregnant women with a huge pregnancy, always the result of anencephaly—no brain. A huge child, with a giant body full of water. And when I did the delivery I would get covered in water. It would burst like a bomb and a dead child would be born without a brain. I must have had seven cases of that. During cotton planting they used Folidol. That started in 1960 already, 1970. In 1976 they killed my son.[3]

This was how he told stories, shifting effortlessly from Folidol to murder, from the epidemiological effects of toxins to deeply personal persecution.

With the invocation of his son's murder, we entered familiar territory, the story that made Filártiga famous. In March 1976, Joelito Filártiga was tortured to death by Stroessner's police, during a period of acute repression known in Paraguay as Pascua Dolorosa.[4] The repression targeted rural organizations and church groups thought to be involved with a nascent guerrilla group called the Organización Político-Militar (OPM), of which Filártiga was rumored to be a member. Over the subsequent five years, Filártiga managed to get the case tried as a violation of human rights, and eventually won over ten million dollars in punitive damages in a New York second-circuit court.[5] The case was the first of its kind, and an important precedent in international law, important enough that a movie was even made about it starring Anthony Hopkins as Filártiga.[6] In the standard telling of this story, it was Filártiga's political activities, his international profile, and his dealings with known members of the OPM that made him a target of the secret police.[7] He had already been to jail several times when his son was killed.

The trauma of Pascua Dolorosa runs deep among activists of his generation, and I was not surprised to hear him invoke it almost as a storytelling reflex in talking about the dictatorship. So initially I just let him talk, assuming we had taken a tangent from pesticides. But the second time it came up, it became clear that this version of the story, so rarely recounted publicly, was also seamless, and followed its own narrative logic. If the standard story is that Joelito was killed because of Filártiga's communist sympathies, this is in part because the legal framing, so successful in court, boiled it down to a question of freedom of expression, of human rights in the face of totalitarianism. But alongside this usual version is an equally valid one in which Joelito was killed because his father criticized the Green Revolution—that is, not for being a communist but for being a doctor.

KREGG: And is that why they attacked your son?

FILÁRTIGA: For denouncing this work. . . . My professor and I did research on Folidol for three years. And when we finished the book, I guess they were listening to my phone. When we finished the book, they arrived at my house, took the book, and took me and tortured me. They told me I was against the country's progress, against industrialization.

The book in question was destroyed. The other author, also tortured, fled into exile. And some time later—I never managed to get the dates as straight as

I would have liked—they killed Joelito. Filártiga would go on to become an even more brazen militant against the regime, a champion of human rights, and an increasingly outspoken opponent of the use of agricultural pesticides, protected now by his international fame.

The details don't matter so much as the way that Filártiga's retelling of the last seventy years wove together plants and pesticides, sovereignty, torture, and the dangers of medical knowledge. In his recollections, there was very little distinction between Stroessner's Paraguay and the democracy that followed, and only technical differences between DDT, Folidol, and Roundup, or between the cotton boom and the soy boom. In this story the IBR was not just the vehicle for an unfulfilled promise of rural welfare, it was also the purveyor of pesticides that killed babies. As horrified as he was by soybeans, he saw them only as one episode in the decades-long ecocidal warfare of the Green Revolution. The through line was a rancorous morality tale about what it takes to live, about the contrast between those forces that promote life, reproduction, and vitality, and those that kill it.

There are many ways to pick up this story, and I've relied heavily in this book on excellent histories of the Green Revolution that show how the cumulative destructiveness of agriculture in the twentieth century follows from the imperatives of global capital. Raj Patel's masterfully concise article, "The Long Green Revolution," offers a particularly insightful guide.[8] Patel's project, to write a *longue durée* history of capitalist agriculture, shows just how much the second half of the twentieth century follows from the destructive logic of colonialism, industrial capitalism, and the development of nation-states. But what struck me most about Filártiga's story was the way that it pulled out another genealogy of the Green Revolution that is more latent in the critical literature, but which at least partially explains why an agency like SENAVE should become the front line in a struggle over the future of the food system: phytosanitary politics has always been about using state violence to organize the relationship between life and death.[9]

I have until this point used the word "agribiopolitics" as a way of talking about regulatory assemblages and to contrast the Soy State with the Government of Beans. But here I want to focus on another aspect of agribiopolitics, about how it organizes the health and welfare of communities of people and plants. In this final section, I present the Government of Beans as only one episode within a longer genealogy that highlights other connections among monocrops, barreras vivas, and the rural welfare projects of the 1960s and 1970s that circulated in Lugo's government. It's a story that complicates not only how we read soy's violence and the halting government responses, but how we read the Anthropocene generally. It also widens the field of historical detritus that is available for new experiments in living collectively.

# CHAPTER THIRTEEN

# Plant Health and Human Health

T wo years after the coup against Lugo, soybeans set off a minor scandal at the Universidad Nacional de Asunción that briefly pitted the Faculty of Medicine against the Faculty of Agriculture.[1] Dr. José Luís Insfrán, a professor of clinical diagnosis, circulated a report which claimed that Paraguayan hospitals had seen a tripling of blood cancers in the previous fifteen years, especially non-Hodgkin's lymphoma.[2] The study itself was modest, and Insfrán insisted, with appropriate scientific restraint, that it could not reveal the cause of this dramatic increase. That said, most of these cases came from the countryside, and Insfrán believed that they were likely linked to an increase in the use of GMOs and the pesticides that go with them.[3] But modest as it was, Insfrán's study was one of the first of its kind in Paraguay, and therefore a crucial test of how the industry would react to opposition spoken in the language of epidemiology. The study immediately garnered media attention, particularly on left-wing blogs, but also in Paraguay's main newspapers. Insfrán was a soft-spoken doctor, and hardly a flag-bearer for an epidemiological revolution, but he was very quickly shoehorned into the familiar role of doctors and scientists who have tried to raise the alarm about pesticide use only to be publicly attacked by the industry and its supporters.[4]

The response was swift, and perhaps predictable, but what was most surprising was where it came from. It began with a letter, written by several students and professors in the Faculty of Agriculture, claiming that the study was irresponsible and overreached scientific norms. Then it took this one step further, asking the president of the university to prevent the study from being published, and to sanction its author.[5] The dean of the Faculty of Medicine chose not to act on this request, and Insfrán kept talking to the media, bolstered by a small but important support group that formed around him. In September of the following year, he was involved in hosting a major international conference called Scientific Controversies, which attempted to showcase uncertainties about GMOs.[6] It's telling, however, that the article never appeared in a scientific journal, and all that remains of the study are his interviews about it.[7]

At that point, the soy sector had been increasing its hold over the production of knowledge in Paraguay for well over a decade. Since the mid-1990s, the agronomy school had been beholden to private financing, particularly an agency called InBIO, which was funded from royalties paid to Monsanto for the use of their patented soybeans. Even when Lugo created a new public financing program, known as CONACYT, agronomy monopolized the grants that it offered, and the UGP had a strong presence on the funding board.[8] The critical doctors who did receive funding had their studies attacked in the press. In 2019, to give only one example, when one of Insfrán's colleagues, Stela Benítez, began to go public with findings about genetic damage to children exposed to pesticides, the UGP attempted to discredit her by publicizing how much of her research grant had been used on catering.[9]

These arguments between agricultural advancement and medical knowledge are echoes of Filártiga's persecution during the Cold War and symptoms of a deep-seated agribiopolitical arrangement that was installed during that period. In the Universidad Nacional de Asunción, an implicit balance of intellectual power kept the medical and agriculture faculties separate, just as the Ministry of Public Health and Social Welfare remained separate from the Ministry of Agriculture, and the World Health Organization remained separate from the Food and Agriculture Organization. In other words, at these different scales, the constellation of institutions concerned with agriculture and human health were kept apart and were often in conflict with each other. One took care of human population health, while the latter took care of the plants that powered national economic development.

The long-term conflict between agricultural and medical sciences was mostly evident in the paucity of epidemiological information about the soy boom. Hector Cristaldo, the spokesperson of the UGP, loved to trot out official poisoning statistics to counter accusations that soy was killing people. Since the Nicanor administration, the Ministry of Public Health and Social Welfare had kept running tallies of the numbers of cases of poisoning in the country, including those by pesticides. So, for instance, in 2010, the Department of Toxicology reported a total of 907 cases of intoxication, of which 183 were clearly related to pesticides.[10] Of these only three had resulted in death, and all were suicides. The way the numbers were organized in the report made it hard to glean much else about what went into them, and this served the soy argument well. What Cristaldo really liked to point out was that most cases of pesticide intoxication—almost 86 percent—were reported in Asunción and its suburbs. For Cristaldo this showed that whatever problems pesticides might be posing for human health in Paraguay had virtually nothing to do with soybeans.

There was, of course, another interpretation of these figures, of which people within the Ministry of Public Health were keenly aware: rather than reflecting actual exposure deaths, they reflected the flimsiness of the epidemiological reporting system in rural areas. To begin with, most people complaining of health problems resulting from pesticides never made it to a public clinic because there were so few of them in rural areas, and they charged fees for basic services. People who sought out medical help often ended up in private clinics that were prohibitively expensive, or in the care of spiritual and herbal healers who operated outside of the public health system altogether. Not only were the public clinics desperately understaffed, many of the doctors and nurses who worked there were skeptical of patients' claims to be suffering from pesticide exposure. They were therefore reluctant to note such claims on official forms, particularly in areas where municipal politics were beholden to sojeros.[11] In other words, Paraguayan epidemiology did not pass Calle Última, which meant that the closer one got to soy, the farther one got from the ability to say anything authoritative about the health effects of pesticides. For this reason, even though it was rarely explicit, Lugo's attempt to reform public health in Paraguay was actually closely linked to his government's response to soybeans.

Lugo's public health reform centered on two ambitious proposals: to make medical consultations free for all Paraguayans and to extend the system of care into underserved rural communities. The policy, and consequent changes to the Ministry of Public Health, would later be remembered as the project with the most immediate positive impact on rural welfare. Lugo's health minister, Esperanza Martínez, was a widely respected physician from the Tekojoja Party, and was the only minister under Lugo's government to implement major structural changes with little opposition from Congress.

Buoyed by the same reformist energy that produced the Citizen Participation Unit at SENAVE, Martínez began a project to build and staff the rural clinics that could now deliver these free services and extend them further. The new health centers led to a palpable increase of state presence and a steady flow of young nurses and doctors out of the capital and into rural areas. Martínez also reorganized rural health care around what she called "family health units," primarily nurses who trained rural women in preventative health measures, focusing on hygiene, diet, first aid, and basic health vigilance in the home. The plan followed a well-known urban-to-rural health delivery system popularized by Cuban doctors who had offered medical services throughout the region during the Cold War.[12] It was, in other words, a version of a socialist biopolitical project that sought to make the state present in rural areas by helping citizens to become responsible for their own health.[13]

The Family Health Unit program was similar in a lot of ways to SENAVE's Citizen Participation Unit. Not only did it attempt to bring centralized services out into the countryside, it also facilitated the flow of denuncias, as well as data and samples, back to Asunción. The epidemiology department developed a new version of a regulatory tool known as the Health Vigilance Protocol, which required health centers to report specific health incidents, including poisoning, to a central department known colloquially as Vigilancia.[14] Most people I met in public health believed that an effective combination of new healthy citizens and decentralized information gathering would change the way Paraguayans talked about pesticides. And yet the analogy to the Citizen Participation Unit also hints at the key problems that Vigilancia would be up against. Like SENAVE, it built a model of intervention based on punctual denunciations that was better for dealing with extreme events than with slow, toxic violence.

## TOXIC TRANSLATIONS

One of these clinics was built in Karajakái. On my first visit there with the Citizen Participation Unit, retold in chapter 9, we heard the usual denuncias about skin rashes, headaches, and diarrhea during spraying season. Campesino activists were very happy with the construction of the clinic, which they saw as one of the most positive of Lugo's accomplishments. They told us that their various denuncias of health problems related to agrotóxicos had been brought to the clinic and taken seriously, and that doctors assured them their cases were being reported back to Asunción. They clearly believed that these cumulative denuncias would eventually be available for putting together a case against Campos Nuevos and other soy farms in the area.

When I visited the clinic a year later with Sofía, however, I was given quite a different story. We were received by the doctor on duty, whom I'll call Lilian, a young woman who was immediately suspicious of us but who warmed up when I described the project. Although Lilian was not political herself, she said, she subscribed to Martínez's new vision of public health and described her own life in this isolated area as a kind of sacrifice to bring "abandoned people" into the national project. Even though aspects of her class bearing (her limited Guarani, her Asunceña accent, and the easy way in which she said she was "not political") made it clear that she was not of the place she was serving, like many young doctors I met scattered throughout the country, Lilian was sympathetic to the lives of the campesinos she served. Moreover, she was horrified by the scale of soy cultivation, and when I asked whether it was having an impact on people's health, she simply said, "How could it not be having an impact?"

But there were two reasons it was hard to turn this apparent truism into actionable data. In her two years there, she had managed to get proof that only one health complaint had anything to do with agrochemicals. In that case, an employee of a local farm had been poisoned while mixing chemicals without appropriate protective gear, and the owner of the farm had paid for his employee's treatment and given an unknown amount of money to the family to avoid a lawsuit.[15] None of the other cases reported to her, she said, were actually due to intoxication.

> We see a lot of people around here who have diarrhea or skin rashes who attribute that to the fumigations, and claim that their water is contaminated. In most cases the skin rashes turn out to be a fungus that is endemic to this area. We're in a swampy lowland, and there's just not much you can do about it, especially in the winter. And when the diarrhea came up in large numbers, well, we tested a whole bunch of wells, and we found not even traces of agrochemicals, but we did find E. coli in a lot of wells. The water table is very high here, so the wells are sometimes just a meter down. They easily get contaminated with bacteria.[16]

So the clinic did what good rural clinics do everywhere. It gave out antibiotics and pamphlets about hygiene for diarrhea and creams for fungus.

This didn't mean that there weren't any connections between fumigations and health problems. Lilian acknowledged, for instance, that many families were using their wells only because soy trucks had destroyed the piping that connected their houses to the local water tower. But spraying season was also E. coli season, and she couldn't ratify for her patients that the correlations they made between diarrhea and the smell of glyphosate were indications of causation. And so Lilian, sympathetic though she was, had never reported any of these cases to Vigilancia.

Lilian didn't believe that spraying soy was causing acute intoxications, but she was sure it caused cancer. The problem was that the kind of infrastructure required to generate this sort of proof was far outside of what a local doctor could access. The only way she participated in the production of epidemiological knowledge was through reporting acute health issues with clear, proximate causes. Epidemiology is forever chasing statistical correlations but is notoriously open to doubts about the causes of slow violence. Here this problem was exacerbated by the fact that because the specific system created to improve reporting of pesticide exposure was devised in an environment overdetermined by the Silvino Talavera case, which took acute exposures to be the most pressing effect of the soy frontier. The Government of Beans invariably imagined epidemiology as a practice of adding up events, rather than trying to describe the uneventful.

Lilian couldn't see any way around this problem. But when I asked her why she thought it was so intractable, she offered another layer of systemic diagnosis. Unfortunately, by the time we sat down to talk, the batteries had run out on my recorder, and I was madly scribbling notes as she spoke, so I didn't capture the exact wording of what she said next. But it was something along the lines of "Without the soy, nobody here would have a health clinic anyway." There were three major patróns of the community, she said, all sojeros, who spent their money on highly visible local charity causes, of which the two favorites were the clinic and the police station.

> Yes, the state built the clinic, and it pays our salaries. But everything else you see here, the lights, the new paint, the refrigerator, and most of the medicines, those are all donations from a local patrón. When I need to get some basic medicines because we've run out, if I go through the ministry's bureaucracy, I'll never get what I need. Sometimes I go

to Curuguaty myself and buy what I need out of my own pocket. Other times I'll put in a request with one of the producers, and they almost always help me out. And it's the same with the police. The state built the local police station and transferred the people here. But they never have money to put gas in their cars. The local producers just have a running tab with them. This way most people are quite grateful, personally, to the producers, for helping the community out. I can't really complain either.

Feeling abandoned by incompetent or underfunded administrators on the other side of Calle Última, she didn't mind turning to local patróns to help provide first aid to local residents. As she told us this, she even switched from calling them "sojeros" to the more neutral term "productores." She left unsaid whether this might affect the reports that she would submit to the Department of Epidemiology, but she made it clear that so long as she depended on the soy farmers for her equipment and supplies, she would be better furnished with painkillers, antibiotics, bandages, and household hygiene leaflets than with information about large-scale pesticide use, or appropriate sample jars for finding contamination.

One can read soy farmers' contributions cynically as a way of buying the consent of the local population. Adding the police to the story, one could also think of this as a classic form of hegemony, with producers deploying the consensual power of the clinic beside the repressive power of the police. Either way, much of the state-building going on in Karajakái was being done directly by soy producers themselves. If the state was present, even some key parts of the welfare state, it was not despite soy, it was because of it. This is the standard neo-extractivist paradox outlined by Eduardo Gudynas: most countries participating in the left turn were able to partially rebuild their decrepit welfare systems by promoting extractive industries with long-term negative environmental and health consequences.[17] In parts of rural Paraguay, the paradox was just a bit closer to the surface, because the extractive industry in question played such an outsized role in the promotion of the human suffering that the welfare state was supposed to alleviate. If Lilian's soy-sponsored family clinic arose in part as a package of reforms continuous with the barreras vivas that protected people from pesticides, they were also continuous with the line of riot police that protected soy from people.

Dr. Soy, whose story I told at the beginning of this book, believed firmly that soy would be a generator of well-being, equality, and population health. And yet somewhere along the line, agricultural development ceased to be interested in the systemic effects that new crop technologies might be having on human bodies. That change marked a powerful shift in agribiopolitical discourse, and a collapse of the analytic imagination surrounding human entanglements with other living things. Taking our analytic cue from Joel Filártiga, we can read this antagonism between agriculture and medicine within a longer agribiopolitical story that reassembles elements of the rise of monocrops with the emergence of a new conception of health and welfare during the Cold War.

From one perspective, the Green Revolution was a quintessential example of what Michel Foucault famously called "biopolitics." It began, in part, as the world's most ambitious public health project. One of the primary sources of funding was the Rockefeller Foundation, which had until then dedicated its efforts mostly to eradicating ringworm and yellow fever in Latin America. As Marcos Cueto shows, the foundation became disillusioned with the scale of its impact and came to see fighting hunger and poverty as a more fundamental way to improve human well-being.[18] By systematically focusing technical expertise on increasing food yields, early Green Revolutionaries believed they could end not only famine but poverty itself.

In Foucault's story, the rise of health clinics, dietary movements, new regimes of labor, and new mores about sexuality in the nineteenth century all put "life at the explicit center of political calculation," creating new forms of regulatory intervention in the biological processes of human populations.[19] For Foucault, if sovereignty in the classic sense was the capacity to "kill and let live," biopolitics marked the emergence of a new form of control organized around the state's ability to "make live or let die."[20] This biopolitical concern gave rise to epidemiology, eugenics, and public health in nineteenth-century Europe and eventually to the welfare state. In places like Paraguay, the story is easier to trace agriculturally: the Green Revolution and the land reform of the 1960s were organized around the principle of granting the necessities of life to campesinos and encouraging them to thrive across national territory. Martínez's reforms to the health care system and especially the expansion of rural clinics were extensions of land reform and attempts to foster this population so central to the nationalist imaginary.[21]

Saying that Paraguayan biopolitics was based in agriculture requires more than an extension of the Foucauldian framework: it forces us to ask why, for all of his sophistication about human health care, Foucault had little to say about plants. It's not that agriculture is entirely absent from the story. Foucault in fact began his lectures on the topic with the story of recurrent grain scarcity in eighteenth-century France, when the state had to intervene in the distribution of grains to avoid famine and urban revolt.[22] And yet even the story of grain scarcity prefigures a lack of interest in agriculture or plant life per se. For Foucault and most other commentators on this period, the main biopolitical techniques deployed to deal with famine were price controls to stabilize the swings of a newly liberalized market in grain.[23] Grain is already an abstraction in the story, a figure bearing very little relation to the stalks and roots of wheat, barley, and rye, and the fields in which they grew.

In fact the urbanization that made biopolitics necessary was dependent on a revolution not just in how food was distributed, but also in how crops were grown. It's in this early modern period that we see the emergence in Europe of the monocultures that would become a "defining mark of Anthropocene ecologies," including the new biological problems that shadowed them.[24] But these don't appear in Foucault's account or in much of the biopolitical canon that followed. Rarely do we read, for instance, that grain scarcity was often a consequence of crop failure due to black stem rot in wheat, and that this period also saw the emergence of the first phytosanitary measures to protect the expanding wheat fields on which cities depended.[25] By the late nineteenth century, the vulnerability of monocrops to invasive pests from other jurisdictions created a need for the first national quarantines against infected imports. This began with phylloxera (the aphid responsible for France's Great Wine Blight), and later the Colorado beetle, which ravaged Germany's potatoes. Soon, phytosanitary regulators were struggling to keep up with a dizzying number of biological agents that threatened desirable crop plants, while government geneticists sought to create plants that would produce higher yields in monocropping environments.[26] Following closely the discipline of public health, plant health regimes began by separating healthy populations from sick ones, then tried to maximize the healthy populations by developing pesticides and fertilizers that, like modern medicines, would promote certain organisms and suppress others.

Clearly part of the reason for this lacuna is that biopolitics is a product of the era and the place in which it was written, when human life was considered categorically different from other life processes. Despite genealogies that date this separation of humans from others in European thought to Descartes or Hobbes or even Aristotle, in biopolitics that separation is a lot more recent.[27] Roberto Esposito points out that term "biopolitics" was already in use in the 1920s, long before it became associated with Foucault. But the Swedish and German philosophers who used the word at the time meant something quite different by it: biopolitics was a way to describe the state, not as a regulator of life, but as a living entity itself, an aggregate of organisms with its own vital force.[28] That prewar meaning of biopolitics was connected to fascist state projects that sought to produce vigorous, superior humans, as well as the crops and animals that fed them.[29] Foucault's primary intervention, therefore, was not to name biopolitics but to effect an ontological separation between "bios" and "politics," which not only made the politicization of "bios" seem noteworthy and dangerous, but also made it a singularly human affair.

In Esposito's reading, this is because a generation of postwar philosophers needed to separate themselves from fascism. But the separation also occurred at a moment when food production was becoming delocalized, and Europe and the US were increasingly looking to the colonies and postcolonies to the south to invest in agriculture while their own countries focused on industrial production. As Jason Moore has so evocatively put it, Europe's postwar prosperity was made possible by a new phase of appropriation of natural resources, what he terms the production of "cheap nature," much of which was happening at a remove from the centers of capitalism.[30] It was these same centers, that, conveniently enough, had tasked themselves with producing a new analytics of life proper to the Cold War. If the eighteenth and nineteenth centuries had separated biopolitical and agrarian concerns by placing one in the city and the other in the country, the Cold War increasingly globalized this separation that built welfare states in the north while offering agricultural development schemes to states in the south.

From that point on it became increasingly easy in Euro-American social sciences to forget about the entanglements between human welfare and the lives of nonhumans, and thus to prop up a taboo against reducing humans to their biological relations. That separation was a cornerstone of progressive politics in the mid-twentieth century, part of the creation of categories like "gender" and "culture" that could be contrasted with the biologically reductive "sex" and "race." Diversity among human populations could be celebrated without contradicting their unity as a species. But it's also in this ethical space that biopolitics took on its least critical flavor, as many iterations of the term merely signaled the ethical questionability of a particular governmental arrangement because of its biologization of difference.[31] This taboo against analogizing human and other forms of life obviated, for instance, any serious critique of fascist agriculture. Only recently, with the rise of environmental humanities and multispecies ethnography, and a new appreciation for the environmental history of agriculture, has this separation begun to break down, giving rise to a truly agribiopolitical literature in which such a critique is possible.[32]

What I want to suggest here is that Foucault's biopolitics can be read as a Green Revolution theory, not in the sense that it has much to say about the Green Revolution, but rather the opposite. Foucault's apparent disinterest in the monumental life politics being promoted as a form of global welfarism was a symptom of the same analytic taboo that for decades made it hard for academics, particularly in the global north, to see vast increases in crop production as anything but an overall boon to human well-being. The simultaneous rise of an abstract, universalist notion of human welfare and of an aggressive new practice for maximizing plant life at a global scale were rarely talked about together except in instrumental terms. And yet the complex entanglement of these two phenomena was highly consequential for the history of countries like Paraguay, and for understanding the perverse echoes of midcentury agriculture that played out during the Government of Beans.

If the Cold War needed biopolitics to help combat fascism, then the Anthropocene needs agribiopolitics, new genealogies of life that seek to explain the increasing segregation between diverse communities of humans and increasingly uniform communities of plants. And it is clear that the emblematic stories that will bring such a genealogy to the surface will not come from places like France, but rather from the front lines of the Green Revolution, where the separation between agriculture and human welfare, between biology and politics, were never quite as clean as they might have seemed to Europeans in the 1960s.

# CHAPTER FOURTEEN

# A Philosophy of Life

T he most celebrated scientist in the history of Paraguay was, first and foremost, a botanist. Born and trained in Switzerland, Moisés Santiago Bertoni came to Paraguay in 1886 to establish an agrarian commune and research station he called simply Puerto Bertoni, on the bank of the Paraná River. But even as he dedicated his life primarily to plants, Bertoni's science was excessive. He published over five hundred books and articles on botany, but also on zoology, philosophy, ecology, geography, entomology, climatology, history, linguistics, and anthropology, most of them single-authored, cranked out on his own manual press. By some oral accounts, he was a high-ranking member of the international secret society of the Druids, and he looked the part, cultivating an image of bearded intellectual grandeur that won him the title of El Sabio (The Sage). His presence in Paraguay is everywhere: his descendants are scattered throughout the country's agronomy schools and offices, and his name graces any number of parks, libraries, foundations, and museums.[1]

But although his personality looms large in Paraguayan history, most scholars today have an ambivalent relationship with Bertoni's published work.[2] I interviewed a number of plant biologists and agronomists about his legacy, and all gave a sideways smirk, saying that there wasn't much value in the science itself. One of his grandsons, an accomplished botanist in his own right, turned the tables on me: "It depends on your perspective. [Moisés] will be more appreciated from the perspective of an anthropologist like you, or a linguist, but he'll be less valued, less appreciated, by a zoologist or a botanist."

Ironically, Paraguayan anthropologists expressed almost the mirror opposite opinion; their discipline had started distancing itself from Bertoni after his death. Miguel Chase-Sardi, the most prominent Paraguayan anthropologist of the postwar generation, is reported to have said, "Regardless of how rigorous a scientist he was in the Natural Sciences, in the Social Sciences he was overwhelmed by a romanticism that makes his studies useless for Paraguayan anthropology."[3] Bartomeu Melià, Paraguay's current doyen of Jesuit anthropology, put it even more starkly to me: "I think we need to prevent people who don't understand anthropology from reading Bertoni, because it's the bad parts that will stick with them, and they'll miss the good parts. If it's an anthropologist reading him, or more likely fighting with him, then they will find interesting things, especially in botany." In other words, while the experts I spoke to feel that his work has aged poorly in their own fields, something about his aura remains unchanged, so that anthropologists assume he was a good botanist, and vice versa.[4] But this is precisely the point: Bertoni's thought is problematic to specialists because his grand vision takes in plants and people together in a way that most disciplines have long ruled out of bounds.

In my reading, it's not possible to separate the bad parts of Bertoni from the good parts or the plants from the people because all are wrapped up in a unifying philosophy of life. His thought is explicitly agribiopolitical. Bertoni understood evolution, economics, religion, and war all to be related to each other as living processes. And from this he developed a great synthesis of crop breeding, racial science, and nationalism that profoundly affected how Paraguayans narrate their history. That synthesis is deeply problematic, but taking it seriously opens up lines of questioning about the welfare state and the soy boom that more comfortable analytic frames tend to obscure.

THE PARAGUAYAN RACE

Bertoni arrived on the Paraná sixteen years after the devastating War of the Triple Alliance, when Paraguay was still a barely coherent political entity. The country had lost much of its territory and as much as half of its population.[5]

Organized agricultural production had completely collapsed, and plantations of sugar, corn, rice, cotton, coffee, cassava, oranges, yerba mate, and tobacco that had thrived before the war had all been abandoned; "the almost complete nonexistence of a rural workforce meant that the countryside entered into total paralysis."[6] As we've seen, the war entrenched the centralization of the Paraguayan state in Asunción, which remained virtually disconnected from its territory. Ninety-five percent of Paraguay's land mass was still considered public land, but it was rapidly being sold to foreign investors to pay war debts.[7]

To be an intellectual in Paraguay at that time was to dream of the birth or rebirth of a nation. In the immediate postwar period, this social reimagining was dominated by the philosophical liberalism that thrived in Argentina.[8] To liberals of the time, responsibility for the war rested with Paraguay's dead president, Francisco Solano López, whom they regarded as an insane despot, and to the simple-minded loyalty of the peasants and indigenous people who had followed him into war. Liberals called this mix of bravery and stupidity "barbarism," a kind of racial cretinism that could be cured only by injecting European blood into Paraguay.[9] For the next six decades, particularly under Liberal Party rule from 1904 to 1936, this basic interpretation of the war, and the possibilities opened in its aftermath, remained the official view of Paraguayan nation building. Among this class, an abiding racist distrust of indigenous people and peasants made it difficult to imagine them as part of any serious nation-building effort.[10]

It was Bertoni who offered the most enduring counterargument to this liberal theory of Paraguayan inferiority, which he published in *La civilización guaraní*, an epic three-volume ethnoracial history of the indigenous inhabitants of the forests he had just claimed as his own.[11] Bertoni believed that, far from being savages, the Guarani had superior intelligence compared to most races, and that they had built a noble and virtuous pre-Columbian civilization that spread from Argentina to the Caribbean.[12] The great Guarani civilization, Bertoni argued, had been partially disrupted but not destroyed by the Spanish, who had mixed with Guarani nobility the heritable virtues of literacy and advanced technology, producing a yet superior mestizo race. Over almost thirteen hundred bombastic, rambling pages, Bertoni found geographical, linguistic, cultural, and craniological evidence for his theory. But his crowning proof was in his reinterpretation of the War of the Triple Alliance. Instead of evidence of barbarism, Bertoni said the war demonstrated the innate valor of Paraguayan troops in the face of brutal occupation.[13]

Bertoni was of course not the only thinker to counter liberalism with a theory of racial mixing in this period; instead, he was part of a continental struggle over how to understand postcolonial biology in Latin America. On one side were the dominant liberal eugenicists who believed that whiteness needed to be preserved from contamination with indigenous blood. On the other were those who believed that racial purity was the sign of a decaying, retrograde Old World, and who saw Latin America's hybrid races as the beginning of a new human experience that transcended Europe.[14] Most famous of these was Mexican philosopher José Vasconcelos, who believed that Latin America's mixed-race "mestizos" were destined to become a universal, "cosmic race."[15] And just as eugenics drew on agricultural analogies (like horse breeding), *mestizaje* often drew on hybrid plant-breeding techniques to make its point.[16] It had recently been discovered that crossing different lines of corn (a Latin American cultivar) could produce extraordinary improvements in productivity, an example that both Bertoni and Vasconcelos used to promote their ideas about Latin America's hybrid supremacy.

Writing screeds against liberal intellectuals in Asunción, Bertoni remained marginalized from Paraguayan political life. But this was all to change soon after his death, and following another war (this one against Bolivia, between 1932 and 1935). The grueling Chaco War was fought in Paraguay's western desert, in which troops on both sides were as frightened of "white death," or thirst, as they were of "red death."[17] Soldiers returning in 1935, most of them campesinos, claimed their victory was based on their racial, cultural, and linguistic heritage, ethnic traits that had long been despised by liberal elites in Asunción.[18] A new movement, led by generals from the Chaco War and their campesino soldiers, built this sense of racial grievance into an assault on the Paraguayan state, and in February 1936 they briefly took control of government. The February Revolution, as it was called, had clear fascist sympathies and quickly banned all political parties. They erased the official history of the War of the Triple Alliance and replaced it with Bertoni's version, even going so far as to dig up Solano López's corpse and move it to a massive mausoleum in the center of Asunción.[19]

The literal reading of Bertoni's racial nationalism soon faded, especially after World War II, when its overt fascist resonance made it again unpopular with Asunción's intellectual class.[20] Paraguay was not the only country to go through a reckoning with its own prewar racial mythology, but theirs was particularly fraught. Even though the country had eventually distanced itself from the Nazis toward the end of the war, it remained hospitable to Germans, Italians, Japanese, and Taiwanese refugees in the years after the war ended, and the highest levels of government remained in the power of unrenovated authoritarian populists.[21] But the dismissal of Bertoni after the war may also have resulted from the way that his understanding of the politics of agriculture no longer fit with the emergent consensus of the Green Revolution. Even as he remained a national hero, his bountiful philosophy of life, his refusal to draw hard lines between humans and other living things, had become awkwardly outmoded.

## AGRARIAN VITALISM

Shortly before his death, Bertoni had declared himself an adherent of a biological philosophy known as "vitalism," whose relationship to fascism tainted the legacy of many thinkers of his generation. In its most basic form, turn-of-the-century vitalism posited that all life processes were animated by a substance, or "vital force," that transcended the "physico-chemical" composition of matter and was therefore unavailable to empirical knowledge. It counted among its adherents both biologists such as Hans Driesch, and philosophers like Henri Bergson and Friedrich Nietzsche, to whom we will return. For each of these thinkers, vital force was a metaphysical premise that served to explain the peculiar relationship between organic matter and time, particularly its apparent tendency to grow and dissipate, to reiterate in a linear way without ever repeating itself.[22] Most vitalists of Bertoni's generation thought about life, and life force, as residing in single organisms. These arguments could then be mobilized by analogy to the evolutionary development of species (or races) and to collectives like nations, whose shared racial characteristics gave them similar profiles of strength. Fascism derives from precisely this sort of analogy, building ties between the apparent source of strength in the human body, the human species, and the nation-state. As Donna Jones argues, this element was even present in vitalist anticolonial movements like Négritude or Vasconcelos's cosmic race (which is the product of mixing but strives toward universal dominance).[23]

What made Bertoni's vitalism unusual was that it was less a theory of individual organisms than an ecological theory that saw organisms as part of heterogeneous systems. In fact, he had begun his botanical training as a disciple of Ernst Haeckel, one of vitalism's most formidable opponents. Haeckel had coined the term "ecology" as a way of understanding Darwinism, and explaining how the development of organisms and species was a fundamentally mechanical process.[24] Only later did Bertoni become frustrated with the mechanist explanation of life, because it didn't fully account for those irreducible forms of thought that continued through the generations, for the wild fertility of his forest gardens, for nations that survived impossible wars, or for his experience of a mystical resonance in what he called the "cathedral of nature."[25] Vital force evoked all of this, especially when he retained from Haeckel the abiding belief that life is always situated in dense relational webs. Ecology referred not to relations that could be reduced to mechanistic explanations, but to relations that added up to an excessive, awesome, vital profusion. This basic insight was so fundamental to Bertoni's understanding of life that he resisted moving to Asunción, insisting that his work and philosophy were only possible when he was surrounded by forest. For Bertoni, vital force was always based in mystery, in the proposition that because thinking is a form of life, there is an absolute epistemological limit to our capacity to know it.[26] At times his work is reminiscent of Georges Canguilhem, for whom life, like science, is composed of generative errors.[27] At others he is merely in a state of perpetual awe at the natural abundance around him.

This is in part where Bertoni departs from most of his contemporary mestizaje scholars. For humanists like Vasconcelos, the relationship between hybrid people and hybrid corn, for example, remained largely analogical. For Bertoni it was literal, but only the beginning: where it became interesting was in examining the relationships not between races, but between species. Vitality always came from assemblages of living beings.

The best-known example of this is from one of his last and most enduring books, *El algodón y el algodonero* (Cotton and the cotton grower). Cotton had been grown in Paraguay since long before the arrival of the Spanish, and there had been a thriving national industry before the war.[28] By the time Bertoni arrived, commercial cotton had all but disappeared, though the native versions of the plants were still cultivated by indigenous Guarani in the area. Bertoni experimented with the plant for years and finally produced his manual for cotton growing in 1927. The book is eminently practical, discussing the economic and ecological conditions of cotton cultivation and breeding, at the level of the farm and of the nation-state. It's also implicitly an anthropology of the Paraguayan farmer. But really it is a manifesto for a new kind of nation-state built around a relationship between a noble race and a noble plant. "The life of cotton," he wrote, "cannot be maintained with scattered and adventurous elements, with an expensive or demanding workforce, with flighty or mercenary personnel, and it cannot abide populations with disorganized customs, restless character or industrial habits. It

is a family cultivar and demands a family. It is a democratic plant, autonomous, requiring personal initiative, especially for agrarian colonists who
know how much their independence is worth. Paraguay can, and must, be a
cotton-producing nation."[29]

In this earnest agribiopolitical work, hybrid cotton and Paraguayan mestizos thrive together as companion species, responding to each other in the
aspiration to a new society. Paraguay is not merely a Guarani nation, but
a Guarani-and-cotton nation built of two life forms recovering from war.
Indeed, the ambiguity of the Spanish word *algodonero* captures the fusion
of his ideas: "algodonero" refers to both the plant and the farmer. Bertoni's
hope for an "algodonero country" was a nation-state imagined as a positive
relationship between people and plants that would thrive and occupy territory together.

## VITALISMS, NAZIS, AND NIETZSCHES

Outside of Paraguay, Bertoni was always a marginal intellectual figure, and
I've never seen him referred to in international debates about vitalism. But
the tension that I just described—between strength through purity and
strength through profusion—is apparent in much better-known figures, and
one of these, Friedrich Nietzsche, is worth dwelling on briefly. Although
they came from different intellectual backgrounds, and almost everything
about Bertoni's celebratory tone contrasts with Nietzsche's dark critical po-
lemics, they both adhered to the view that life was a creative, aleatory force
that can never be fully harnessed by rationality. For both, the mechanical
reading of evolution and the utilitarian approach to liberal politics were two
sides of the same mistake, overlooking the power and grandeur of life itself
in favor of imposed mediocrity.[30] As a result, both were deeply suspicious
of purist theories of race and of the state in its regulatory or policing mode.

But the philosophical resonance with Nietzsche also points to other,
denser intellectual entanglements. Bound up in the migration of Europeans to Latin America, Nietzsche himself had a connection with Paraguay
that also prefigured the country's convoluted relationship to Nazism. Nietzsche's only sibling, Elisabeth Förster, moved to Paraguay the same year as
Bertoni, 1886, and went about building a utopian commune of her own less
than three hundred kilometers away. Förster arrived with her husband, Bernhard Förster, and a handful of Saxon peasants, also intent on building a
new world out of the imagined tabula rasa of Paraguay's postwar destruc-

tion.[31] New Germany, as they called it, was a genetic experiment, based on the conviction that Old Germany's Jewish problem was so advanced that the Aryan race could not hope to thrive there. Their tiny colony of industrious blonds, living on a plot of land leased from the Paraguayan government at usurious rates, was supposed to build an Aryan stronghold free of Jewish contamination.

In frequent letters to Paraguay, Nietzsche begged his sister to return home, condemning Bernhard as an anti-Semitic caricature of what he called "slave morality."[32] For him, life was excessive, a force of constant striving to overcome itself, and everywhere dangerous, since its providence was so extreme as to be absurd, destructive, and ultimately self-annihilating.[33] But the primary problem this caused was not death itself, which after all was inevitable, but fear, which produced reactive, resentful institutions that tried to preserve life from corruption. In his own Germany, Nietzsche could already see this logic of resentment at work in the growing threat of anti-Semitism, and it was a great source of pain for him that his sister had devoted her life to precisely this project.

At first blush, then, Bertoni's vision of life, his love of the exuberance of nature, and his impatience with the petty squabbles of politicians in Asunción all qualify him as Nietzschean, and seem to make him the opposite of Förster's resentful caricature. But as Roberto Esposito points out, the difference between vitalist profusion and protection is never all that stable.[34] Esposito calls institutions aimed at purifying life "immunological," because they work by negating the threat of diversity. He uses the example of the vaccine, a medical intervention that is inherently immunological, establishing a protective bulwark against certain fearful infections. It can also be seen as a form of strengthening, precisely as the kind of additive practice that allows for the continuing expression of life's strength.[35] By extension, the public health institutions that support vaccination can be seen as stultifying modern interventions, prohibiting and requiring behaviors in the name of a highly sterile conception of humanity's living interspecies relationships. Or they can be seen as internal to life itself, as part of the process of self-overcoming necessary to thriving.

Life and death intermingle in peculiar ways in Nietzsche's philosophy, and, for her part, Elisabeth Förster knew how to exploit its ambivalence.[36] After the failure of New Germany, her husband's suicide, and Friedrich's mental decline, Elisabeth returned to Europe and took up her new calling, promoting her brother's philosophical legacy. Famously, in Elisabeth's reading, Friedrich himself became an anti-Semite, and his philosophy became resonant with Nazi immunology. Nietzsche may not have intended his work to be used in that way, but the destructiveness of his notion of life certainly made such a reading available.

Similarly, it was a logical necessity of Bertoni's view that living is also about dominance. His view of a vital nation is underwritten by war, and he once declared that "Force, Law and Life are essentially inseparable."[37] Like any good crop breeder, Bertoni had very little sentimental attachment to genetic lines that fail, and his love of mixing people and species was everywhere underwritten by a desire for strength and supremacy. His vision of crop improvement resonated strongly with contemporary agrarian science in Germany and Italy, where "blood and soil" were connected not only metaphorically but directly through government research. As Tiago Saraiva recounts, fascism across Europe was invested in the personification and improvement of national varieties of plants and animals not as proxies for race but as a part of it.[38] Mussolini saw improved wheat as soldiers, while the Nazis considered Colorado potato beetles an army that, by weakening national potato crops, weakened the Aryan race. It's no coincidence that Bertoni also imagined a nation's glorious rebirth around the humble yet sturdy stocks of an improved native plant, cotton.

Whether or not Bertoni ever came to see that resonance, it was easily visible to those who took up his work right after his death in 1929. Even Bertoni's eldest son, Guillermo Tell Bertoni, played a crucial role in promoting his agribiopolitical vision during Paraguay's most explicitly fascist period.[39] It was Tell who would become Paraguay's first minister of agriculture in 1936, when he was appointed by the February Revolution.[40] The Febreristas not only believed in Bertoni's racial theory but also adopted some of his agricultural vision, redistributing land to peasants whom they believed could reactivate the nation. And though they were thrown out by the Liberals after only sixteen months in power, sending Guillermo Tell and the rest of the party into exile, their impact on agrarian policy was as important as their impact on racial nationalism. The Liberals essentially adopted the Febrerista agrarian reform, passing it into law in only slightly modified form.[41]

Aware of this legacy, and cognizant of the fact that their country remained hospitable to Nazis even after the war, Paraguayan anthropologists and sociologists repudiated Bertoni in the 1950s and never turned back.[42] Theirs was a local manifestation of a growing taboo against thinking the social and biological together. After the discovery of DNA undermined the metaphysical premises of biological vitalism, even histories of biology and agronomy expunged from their origin stories the ambiguous traces of vitalist thought.[43] Vitalism was relegated to the spiritual and environmental fringes of European agriculture, where it created the early models of organic and biodynamic farming.[44] Meanwhile, vitalist critical thought was also sanitized. That which survived after the war (most notably in the works of Georges Canguilhem and Gilles Deleuze) became a strictly philosophical affair, which maintained some of the aleatory possibilities of vitalism while uncoupling it from literal biological thinking.[45] Even Foucault's biopolitics can be read in this way, as a vitalist theory that simply replaces the concept of "vital force" with "power" and obviates discussion of biological processes in favor "biological discourses."[46] To put it another way, the rise of Foucault, and the tradition he created, is the mirror opposite of the fall of thinkers like Moisés Bertoni, who are retrospectively seen as naive about the necessary separation between politics and life.

And yet Bertoni's peculiar position, as a botanist witnessing the prologue to the Green Revolution, reminds us that while it became increasingly difficult to talk about population health in terms of genetic heritage and strength, the same was not true of plant biology. The basic practice of creating stronger populations through selection and hybridization became the official motor of postwar agriculture. The analytic separation between humans and other creatures would make it easier to elevate the agricultural techniques associated with fascism to an incontestable ethical plane. Before long, wheat breeders would be winning Nobel Peace Prizes, even as wheat growing became increasingly destructive of other life forms. Bertoni's cotton nation would undergo a similar liberal sanitization and, along with the other great cultivars of the postwar period, would soon become a stronger force than Bertoni could ever have imagined.

# CHAPTER FIFTEEN

# Cotton, Welfare, and Genocide

Appropriately enough, the golden age of Paraguayan agrarian development belongs to another Bertoni, Moisés's grandson (and Guillermo Tell's nephew) Hernando. Hernando Bertoni was a soil scientist, first educated in his grandfather's agronomy school, and later part of the first generation of Paraguayan agronomists to train in the United States. He didn't leave any written accounts of his own understandings of agriculture, but the agronomists whom he mentored in the 1960s all spoke the Green Revolution language of fertility, genetics, yields, and national production. Moisés's spiritualism, and any trace of a vitalist understanding of plant growth, was completely absent from these accounts, as was any explicitly racial assessment of Paraguayan farmers. And yet it was Hernando, and the agronomists he recruited, who would also bring about a version of Moisés's cotton nation, weaving cotton plants and campesino politics together into a hugely successful life project. In the process, they built the state apparatus that would support Paraguay's first great monocrop.

Hernando was a product of the STICA technical training program that we briefly examined in chapter 1. Created in 1943 through the cooperation of the US government and the Rockefeller Foundation, STICA was one of the first major development initiatives that the US promoted in Latin America, and it underwrote crop improvement initiatives in the region for decades to come. As Paraguay's doorway to the Green Revolution, the STICA program included all of the agribiopolitical contradictions of that period. It grew out of the Rockefeller Foundation's projects to improve rural health and welfare by "feeding the world," but it was also about territory, security, and population, in Foucault's classic sense. As Nick Cullather puts it, the Green Revolution was an imperialist biopolitics, and its core operating "concepts of food supply and balance expressed a new consciousness of connections between the physical vitality of other countries—health, living standards, and agriculture—and the security of the United States."[1] The US offered Paraguay the STICA program explicitly to gain support against Germany and later against communists.[2] It also aimed to create new markets for US expertise and agrarian technologies, including the burgeoning fertilizer and pesticide industries that grew out of weapons manufacturing.[3] As part of this new imperial project, it provided aid money that would allow US-friendly dictatorships to flourish.

Under STICA, Hernando Bertoni and dozens of other Paraguayan agronomists traveled to the US and Mexico for further training, and came back to Paraguay to set up their own public research centers. The program they brought home with them was relatively simple: crop yields would be maximized through improved genetics, soil fertility, and pest suppression. The standard goal was for countries to reach self-sufficiency in certain key crops, an early version of food sovereignty, and to be able to produce for export thereafter. Wheat self-sufficiency was Paraguay's great Cold War scientific achievement.[4]

But while the wheat program beavered away at Paraguay's dependency on a tiny amount of imported wheat, most Paraguayans experienced Hernando's ministry through a completely different program: the smallholder cotton program. However he had arrived at it, Moisés's sense that there was a compatibility between Paraguayan mestizos and the humble cotton plant turned out to be prophetic.[5] Fifty years later, with some international resources and a centralized, authoritarian government, Hernando's cotton program fueled an economic and political reorganization of the country.[6] So successful was the synergy between campesino families and Moisés's "democratic plant," so rapidly did it bring consumer goods to the countryside and draw peasants into a state-centered development scheme that within two decades, Guarani-speaking farmers were not only economically dependent on cotton but also utterly vested in it as a symbol of personal and national identity.

Cotton farming depended on a massive, multilevel agrarian infrastructure. The Ministry of Agriculture experimented with seed varieties with the help of the French cotton institute, while the National Development Bank provided credit to a network of ginning and export companies. These companies then hired middlemen who provided smallholders with the seeds and pesticides they needed and bought the fiber back at the end of the year. Under Hernando's stewardship, the cotton crop grew thirtyfold. By the 1970s, Paraguay was posting the highest economic growth rate in the region,[7] and campesino colonists were busily hacking their way through the eastern forests in San Pedro, Caaguazú, and Caazapá, as well as parts of Canindeyú, Alto Paraná, and Itapúa as part of Stroessner's great March to the East. The Paraguayan nation, centralized on Asunción, was now radiating outward through colonies of campesino pioneers with their cotton and tobacco plants, establishing the farms that soy would come to threaten three decades later.

## THE AGE OF WHITE GOLD

When I began visiting these cotton colonies, they were already under threat, and there was always a sense of nostalgia in the way people talked about their cotton. I received my first glimpse of the true power the plant held over people in 2005, after landless campesinos living in Tekojoja were attacked by sojeros and police, an event that eventually inspired the name of Fernando Lugo's political party.[8] A group of fifty families had occupied ten plots of land in Tekojoja that had been sold illegally to sojeros. Occupants built small houses with gardens and cassava plants and prevented sojeros from entering the territory and planting soy. On three occasions, soy farmers convinced local police to raid the settlement and burn down the houses, and each time the occupants returned, rebuilding their houses out of the flimsy, charred remains and continuing to subsist on their cassava. The campesino strategy was to hang on long enough to build a homestead, and soy farmers were determined not to let that happen.

I met Vicente after the first of these evictions. He was living alone under a lean-to made of two donated pieces of corrugated tin roofing, and with a small group of young men had planted several hectares of cotton on one of the plots. It was a risky proposition. Disease, low prices, and drought had all assailed cotton in the previous two decades, and the crop failed as often as not. But this year a sympathetic local rancher had provided the seeds and fertilizer at a reduced cost, and it had seemed worth a try. Still, of all those who had planted, Vicente had wagered the most, planting a full twenty-one *liños*, or rows, with only a borrowed hoe. It was shortly before harvest, when the cotton bolls were at their heaviest, their white fiber about to emerge spectacularly from the seed head, that the second eviction occurred. After the police rounded the families up, the sojeros behind the eviction swept through the community, first burning down the houses and later that same day taking plows to all of the gardens, digging up the cotton and planting soy in its place.

The next day, as everyone surveyed the damage, I saw Vicente briefly on the road. Of all the victims of the attack, among families with four or five children who now found themselves without homes or gardens, it was Vicente, the bachelor trying to start from scratch, who was the most upset. He was drunk and had been crying, and over the next half hour ranted about how beautiful his cotton had been. The rest of my companions avoided engaging with him, so I got most of his attention, but between his poor Spanish, my poor Guarani, and his distress, I understood little of what he said. Eventually he got on his *cabaju piru* (skinny horse), a bicycle that he had used to escape the eviction and that was now his sole remaining possession, and rode slowly off through the deep sand that had overtaken the road. I never saw him again.

Vicente's powerful emotional connection to cotton was common in Paraguay for several generations because it was one of the most palpable links between young men's personal aspirations, their physical prowess, and their dreams of collective nationhood. During the one season when I participated in a relatively successful cotton harvest, the bolls blooming in the scorching February sun were met with anxiety and excitement. But that was only a faint echo of the excitement of the harvest from previous decades. Each year in late March, families would begin to assemble in the weeks of picking season. Children would leave school, and a festive mood would be palpable. The days were grueling, but often treated like a sport, as bodies became dark and wiry. Pickers would rise before dawn and pick for hours before eating breakfast in the shade of banana or mango trees, then, strapping banana leaves on their heads, could pick for a few more hours before the midday sun forced everyone to take a nap until late afternoon. Young boys (aged nine or ten) picking for the first time would learn, through the cuts on their fingers, the way that the shape of the cotton boll and the human hand fit each other, the way that fingers fit between the four open shards of the dried boll, revealing the fibers within. Speed was the goal, but it was preceded by sensuality, by learning to make the boll release its cotton with minimal resistance or friction.

That good fingers were suggestive of virility was not merely metaphorical—good fingers, which reached their peak in a man's teenage years and began to decline in his twenties, were also the fount of great wealth and rewards. Picking season was the season for buying clothes, school supplies, and provisions like barrels of cooking oil and pigs, the time to whitewash the house, take parents to the doctor, and to court lovers.[9] The sleepy commercial strips of Paraguay's small towns would suddenly come alive. In a good year the future would open up wide; the possibilities for a young man, or a family, or a town, or a country would suddenly seem limitless. The harvests sent young men farther out into the frontier to find new land and to plant more cotton, following the promise of the land reform and a kind of political adulthood, the pioneering citizen, that came from rooting oneself and one's plants in the national project. Even as agricultural development experts saw cotton only as one among many potential export crops, it's the love of cotton that evoked the powerful promise of state-backed welfare that once followed the plant.

And yet it's worth pausing (finally) to think about the polysemic term that most campesinos used to describe the settlements in which they lived: colonias. These were colonies of the Paraguayan state, trying to extend its sovereignty over the eastern frontier by building pioneer citizens, and they were, indirectly, colonies of US imperialism, fighting communism with agricultural aid. In the agribiopolitical sense, they were security and welfare projects built of the association of human and plant populations organized by a central state. Calling them colonies also highlights their violence and, more specifically, the way that this violence was distributed to exclude other ways of occupying that space. A campesino colony, or a field of beans, or even a project to improve food security or maintain biodiversity always contained a layered history of killing. As it occupied space, it suppressed other living assemblages, both actual and possible, as a necessity for thriving. What the word "colony" flags more than anything, then, is this movement, this project of expansion and propagation that necessarily came at the expense of other lives and life projects.

## AGRARIAN KILLING

To say that growing certain plants involves killing others is not to make an absolute moral judgment. Agriculture is all about intimate relationships between different organisms, relationships that necessarily involve death.

Harvesting, slaughtering, burning, cutting, plowing, poisoning, shooting, clearing, trapping, weeding, culling, selecting, are all forms of killing.[10] Even growing a leguminous cover crop between rows of organic corn and squash is a way of choking out undesirable organisms that are constantly trying to take over a garden. As Donna Haraway might put it, agrarian work is all about figuring out how to make certain combinations of companion species flourish at the expense of others.[11] And yet clearly there are different ways of organizing the work of killing, different agribiopolitical assemblages to be fostered. The Green Revolution of the mid-twentieth century, while it was a triumph in the fight against widespread hunger and in many places produced new forms of human thriving, was achieved by stealing land from some people and organisms and occupying them with high-yield mono-crops for the benefit of others. As Anna Tsing puts it, landscapes like this "kill off beings that are not recognized as assets," and they accomplish this through an intensification and specialization of the labor of killing through an increasingly distributed agricultural network.[12]

This logic pertained across the entire network of relations that made cot-ton monocrops possible. For instance, in the 1960s, the Paraguayan crop research center produced a new variety of cotton known as Reba-P279, which was so successful that it eventually covered more than half a million hectares of eastern Paraguay. Bred by crossing Cameroonian and American varieties, P279 was perfectly adapted to Paraguayan rainfall levels and also had particularly long fibers, which, because they were hand picked, tended to stay long, and therefore to command high prices in international mar-kets.[13] But even the process of developing such a variety involved a very spe-cialized form of killing. To produce P279, plant breeders in Paraguay spent seven years planting hundreds of lines of cotton crosses, submitting them to environmental pressures, and selecting the strongest individuals for repro-duction while killing off the vast majority of the plants that didn't present the desired traits.[14] These crop breeders worked alongside entomologists, mycologists, phytopathologists, and chemists whose work was about culti-vating insects, fungi, and plants that they deemed pathological in order to figure out how best to destroy them. They then sent extension workers out to teach small farmers the combination of nurturing and killing practices that allowed Reba-P279 to thrive over large areas.

It's notable, though, that when we think about Green Revolution agricul-ture, we rarely think about the form of killing going on in the greenhouses of crop research stations and those on the frontier as part of the same pro-cess. We tend to think of crop breeding as a sanitized procedure that merely produces a registered variety, giving farmers tools to improve their production and corporations a chance to assert intellectual property rights. But we don't focus on the way that breeding itself occurs in anticipation of being able to plant half a million hectares of the improved plants, and that it is not just unviable cotton that is being selected out of agriculture, but all the other plants, animals, and people that might otherwise occupy all that space. In other words, one killing practice is underwritten by others: crop breeding relies on the destruction of forest and the theft of land just as colonization depends on the ruthless culling that we call crop breeding.

The cotton frontier advanced at the expense of the subtropical biome known as the Atlantic forest, which once stretched from the Paraguay River all the way to coastal Brazil. In the early phases of this clearing, STICA not only trained crop breeders but helped to organize the construction of timber mills throughout the area destined for colonization, including a central hub in the city of Caaguazú (literally, Big Forest).[15] When colonists arrived, they cut roads into the forest and then cleared individual strips back from those roads, creating what observers of satellite images call the piano-key pattern of deforestation.[16] Cotton colonies were generally settled by an early wave of young men, most of whom would only stick around long enough to cut down the best wood and clear one or two hectares of a ten-hectare plot. Hardwoods would be sold to mills, while the rest of the brush would be burned in large clay ovens to make charcoal.[17] They would then sell the land or, rather, sell the improvements on the land, by which they meant the labor put into clearing it. In the early years of any colony, income from forest destruction was more significant than that from crops, and the smog of charcoal ovens hung thick over the long rust-colored roads. Once these improvements were sold to a second wave of pioneers, colonies would convert from logging sites to sites for cotton cultivation.

Smallholder cotton colonies were not the only motor of deforestation during this period, and perhaps not even the most violent; cattle ranching, and soon more extensive production of wheat, corn, sugarcane, and soy, were also cutting down forest in parallel. But the project of rural welfare that cotton production supported was part of a process of biological annihilation that by the 1990s was being recognized as one of the worst in the world. According to Peter Richards, as late as 1960 there were still 73,000 square kilometers of standing forest in Paraguay, but by 2000 this had been reduced to 12,000 square kilometers.[18] Implicit here is a staggering loss of biodiversity in those forests, which once teemed with the tapirs and anteaters and jaguars that are now all but extinct in the country. And yet at the time it went almost unnoticed, and reports on the environmental destruction wrought by the Green Revolution didn't begin to appear in Paraguay until the early 1990s, when the Cold War was over, Stroessner had been removed from office, and the Rio Earth Summit had focused international environmental pressure on the region.[19] That year, both of the country's main newspapers ran a series of stories on how the Atlantic forest was almost gone, and still being cut down at an astonishing rate.[20]

## AGRIBIOPOLITICS AND GENOCIDE

There was one exception to this lack of notice, however: another form of colonial killing that did indeed cause a lot of intense international pressure but that was not recognized as part of the Green Revolution at all. In 1973, long before anyone was concerned about the loss of forests, an international campaign revealed Paraguay as the site of an ongoing genocide of the Aché Guarani, a large group of hunter-gatherers who lived throughout two of the most coveted cotton areas of the country.[21] The Aché had been hunted in Paraguay for decades, long considered the most "primitive" indigenous people on the eastern side of the Paraguay River. But as the cotton and cattle frontiers expanded, and their forests diminished, the violence perpetrated against them intensified. By the time news reports began to appear, Aché territory had been so drastically reduced that the last remaining groups were being rounded up and confined to reservations. The Department of Native Affairs assigned a famously brutal military commander, along with New Tribes Missionaries to oversee the reservations and deal with the "Aché problem."[22]

The international campaign to expose this process as a genocide was led initially by German anthropologist Mark Münzel, who demanded that the Stroessner government be tried at the International Criminal Court.[23] Münzel's account of what was going on in the Atlantic forest, and several of those that followed, compiled colonial atrocities, from disease and starvation to an active market in Aché slaves, torture, rape, Indian-hunting, and trophy killing.[24] But by invoking the word "genocide," Münzel insisted that something was going on beyond the slow violence of agrarian transition. A genocide is an event, a crime that cleaves the past from the future, and, in the postwar global political system, one that required international response.

As the campaign to save the Aché advanced, preeminent human rights lawyers, anthropologists, and genocide scholars weighed in.[25] Even Elie

Wiesel, one of Auschwitz's most famous survivors, lent his name to the case, comparing the plight of the Aché directly to that of German Jews in World War II. "Until now," he wrote,

> I always forbade myself to compare the Holocaust of European Judaism to events which are foreign to it. Auschwitz was something else, and more, than the Vietnam War; the Warsaw ghetto had no relation of substance with Harlem. . . . The universe of concentration camps, by its dimensions and its design, lies outside, if not beyond, history. Its vocabulary belongs to it alone. . . . And yet I read the stories of the suffering and death of the Aché tribe in Paraguay and recognize familiar signs.[26]

For Wiesel, the taboo against relating the Aché experience to the Holocaust was broken less by a formal similarity than by the smell of an old foe: "Is it pure chance that this is happening in Paraguay? Josef Mengele, the exterminating angel of Birkenau, lives there peacefully as an honored guest. Other Nazi potentates have also found refuge there. To what extent do they collaborate with their protectors? How happy they must be to be able to place their talent and experience in the interest of another Final Solution."[27] There is no evidence that any of Paraguay's many guest Nazis were directly involved in organized efforts to kill Indians. But Wiesel was certainly not wrong to detect kinship between Nazi life philosophy and the potent brew created by Paraguayan nationalism and the Green Revolution.

And yet the discussion of the genocide of the Aché remained confined by the awkward humanism of the postwar, especially in North America and Europe, presaged here by Wiesel's own discomfort about comparison. The primary academic effect of the campaign to save the Aché was a cringeworthy debate about whether "genocide" was the right word for the violence in question. The primary objection came from US anthropologists who argued that the violence did not technically constitute genocide since it was not organized by a state with the specific intent to erase a particular group.[28] Instead, they argued that the plight of the Aché was unexceptional, similar to many indigenous societies disrupted by agricultural advancement and peasant frontiers throughout Latin America.[29] In other words, at least from this particular northern perspective, mass killing didn't count as genocide, as an event worthy of international legal attention, if the primary reason behind it was agricultural. The death of the Aché did not qualify as genocide, for the same reason that so many settler-colonial states don't recognize the violence that they continually commit against indigenous people: because of a failure of the biopolitical imagination to understand the slow-burning, more-than-human horrors of these processes.[30]

In Paraguay, as in much of Latin America, social scientists were much less reluctant to use the word "genocide" to describe these processes.[31] But the awkward work of purifying the word shows just how much intellectual labor went into holding the killing of humans and the killing of trees apart in those places where the Cold War's intellectual and ethical infrastructures were being created. Genocide is, of course, a biopolitical concept, a crime defined as the purposeful eradication of a particular form of human life, and the maintenance of this definition had important stakes for the postwar liberal world order. The killing of the Aché was, by contrast, agribiopolitical, carried out primarily with agricultural intent, but also entangled, however messily, with racism, brutality, sexual violence, and the pleasures of annihilation. It is hard to locate the line between state intent and the various international forces that protected Stroessner and drove the Green Revolution, just as it is hard to disentangle the specific racism against the Aché from the overall thrust of agricultural violence. What's stunning about the international literature on this period is the degree to which these two instances of killing remained analytically separate from each other: the death of trees and fauna were environmental problems, while genocide was purely a human rights problem.

Even in the most unexpected of places, such as international campaigns against genocide, the Green Revolution got a pass, excused from debates about the worst forms of human killing while its continuities with fascist biology were conveniently forgotten. This is the same intellectual climate, of course, that produced Foucault's idea of biopolitics, leaving agriculture out of the question. Yet when we think of all of these processes through an agribiopolitical lens in which colonization produces a deep tangle of ecocide and genocide that targets not only species or populations but whole living assemblages, the ethics of agrarian development become far more complicated. Rural welfare in Paraguay was always tied to cotton welfare. And both were arms of US geopolitical interests in promoting a certain way of valuing human life, to the detriment of the Atlantic forest and the Aché Guarani and so many others who lived there. From an agribiopolitical perspective, the separation between genocide and deforestation is a historical peculiarity, a discursive trick that shielded the Green Revolution from the worst forms of criticism.

# CHAPTER SIXTEEN

# Immunizing Welfare

f the early phases of the Green Revolution unleashed extraordinary violence against people and other living things, it also matured over time into other sorts of killing. However impressive the cotton monocrop must have appeared when it dominated landscapes and annual GDP, like all monocrops, cotton was a fragile assemblage, increasingly vulnerable to the life projects of those creatures that agronomists characterize as pests.[1] The first of these intruders were fungal infections in the seeds and roots, and later aphids and caterpillars. These were nothing, however, in comparison to the boll weevil, or *picudo*, a voracious beetle that attacks cotton bolls just before they open, effectively destroying the harvest. In fact, part of Paraguay's comparative success with cotton in the early years was due to its isolation from weevil colonies, which were by then well established in much of the rest of the cotton-producing world.

As with cotton, the boll weevil's role in agribiopolitical history is both a global affair and one that played out differently in different places. The bug's historical significance is even memorialized by a statue in Enterprise, Alabama. In 1919, four years after Alabama's cotton crops were devastated by weevils, the statue was erected with the dedication, "In profound appreciation of the Boll Weevil and what it has done as the herald of prosperity." In

Enterprise, the appearance of the weevil led to crop diversification initiatives that (at least in the minds of the wealthy peanut growers who paid for the statue) changed their community for the better. The experience in Paraguay could not have been more different. Paraguay's response to the weevil invasion is a study in phytosanitary failure, not only because of the technical capacity of the agency in question, but because of the entire political apparatus that upheld it.[2]

In 1985, in response to weevil infestations in Brazil, Paraguay's Department of Plant Defense (the precursor to SENAVE), with help from the FAO, set up pheromone traps to capture weevils along the Brazilian border in Canindeyú and Alto Paraná.[3] These traps were the front line of a surveillance system, and farmers and agronomists were trained to catch and report weevil intruders. Those intruders finally arrived during the April harvest in 1991, and a general panic ensued as newspapers proclaimed the arrival of a "superbug" and ran articles on whether or not it was possible to "live with" boll weevils.[4] The weevils elicited a slate of agribiopolitical responses. There was a sudden scare about Brazilian cotton, which was being smuggled across the border to take advantage of artificially high prices at Paraguayan gins. Now that this foreign cotton might be harboring weevils, an order went out that any cotton crossing the border needed to be impounded and burned. Meanwhile, extension agents began telling farmers to set up buffers around cotton fields to stop the spread of bugs and to remove and burn all organic remains at the end of the harvest. Farmers also began using new, more potent insecticides, part of what became known as the "pesticide treadmill" of the Green Revolution.[5]

And just as the vitality of cotton plants and campesino farmers went hand in hand with the boom in national development, the increasing hardship of the cotton colonies coincided with the end of a developmental miracle, and eventually the end of rural welfare. It is hard to think about what happened to cotton colonies in the early 1990s without imaging, as Bertoni had, that the life force of the nation was linked to the vitality of its iconic plants. As the regime, economy, and crops all went into crisis, the agronomic response moved into a logical second phase: after decades of crop improvement, the ministry now focused on plant defense. In the waning years of the cotton nation, the Ministry of Agriculture underwent an inversion, from expansion to protection, from offensive colonization to defensive immunization, from killing forests and their indigenous inhabitants to killing bugs. Its failure in this immunizing task also spelled the end of whatever semblance of a rural welfare project Stroessner had promoted.

Campesino cotton growers in Paraguay describe the application of chemicals to plants as a form of medicine, *pohano*, from the verb root *poha* (to remedy). Although it can be qualified (for instance, *pohajuka*, literally "killer medicine," refers to poison), all pesticides are usually referred to by the simple "poha," the same name for mashed-up herbs one puts in mate in the morning. Pesticides make clearer than anything the intimate play between a politics of life and death, that one implies the other. In the same way that human medicine works to create life by negating it (think about life-giving *anti*biotics), the plant health industry relies on both hygienic techniques and powerful poisons.

Poha, in other words, includes the same internal tension as *pharmakon*, the Greek word for poison and remedy, which has come to inhabit a crucial place in the literature on biopolitics. As Roberto Esposito puts it, the pharmakon "relates to life from the ground of its reverse. More than affirm life, it negates its negation, and in the process ends up doubling it."[6] For Esposito, life involves two distinct but interconnected logics, which he calls "community" and "immunity."[7] Community refers to those aspects of reciprocal obligation that intensify the capacity for life, which can only be achieved through the connection with others. And yet too much community threatens life by making it indistinct, or unqualified. Community therefore also requires immunity, which functions by exclusion. We encountered this idea when talking about Elisabeth Förster's anti-Semitism, an example of immunity gone awry. Life, to Esposito, is a balance between community and immunity—too much of either is pathological. By extension, regulation is not merely about limiting or negating vital profusion, but rather part of life itself and therefore part of its aleatory quality. Nowhere does Esposito give the sense that he has something like a cotton colony in mind, or the dense agribiopolitical assemblages in which it thrives. But there is no reason why his notion of community and immunity can't be extended to human-plant relationships of Bertoni's cotton nation, and to campesino colonies, whose gardens became too similar to each other to resist the life projects of weevils.

All farmers act as both the doctors and the police of their gardens, and are adept at local phytosanitary practices, but monocrops require immunization at a scale that far surpasses individual farms. In Paraguay, many of these practices were first systematized by another son of Moisés Bertoni's, Arnaldo de Winkelried Bertoni. Winkelried was an entomologist and in the 1930s became the first professor of phytopathology at the national agriculture school established by his father.[8] Unlike his father and brother, Winkelried is the one that most people remember as the serious scientist, a careful cataloguer of insects who didn't let himself get swept up in national politics or problematic anthropological side projects. His huge collection of specimens is still kept in piles of shoeboxes in Paraguay's Museum of Natural History, a dusty building dedicated to national biodiversity right next to the SENAVE laboratories. In fact, all of the entomologists I've talked to in Paraguay revered him, and many saw him as epitomizing a core ethos of their discipline: a wonderment at all of the tiny creaturely variations of the natural world.[9] What went unsaid in some of our conversations was the core contradiction of almost all applied entomology: it uses that love of insects to find more efficient ways of killing them.

It was the generation of entomologists Winkelried trained that would have to contend with the boll weevil and the many other pests that followed Green Revolution monocrops into Paraguay. By then, the phytosanitary response was no longer one of farmers against pests, but of an entire state apparatus against an invading force. So while the Green Revolution is often told as a story of awesome advances in genetics and fertility, it was also a story about the coordinated intensification of systematic killing practices.[10] The fight against the boll weevil showed the Paraguayan state in its immunitary form, called to action to protect the increasingly vulnerable monocrops on which its rural welfare promises had become dependent. And its failure against weevils was also an indication of just how fragile that state had become.

## THE END OF WELFARE AGRICULTURE

When boll weevils arrived in Paraguay, Stroessner had just been deposed in a coup, and the Ministry of Agriculture was in deep crisis after several years of decline. In the mid-1980s, the Inter-American Development Bank (IADB), which had underwritten the Green Revolution through the STICA program, had halted almost all agricultural lending because its taste for strongmen had soured. But the problems at the heart of the Ministry of Agriculture weren't really felt until the year after the coup, when Hernando Bertoni, Stroessner's much-beloved minister, suddenly died. With him, so too did a particular vision of the nation-state, destructive and authoritarian though it was, that promoted rural welfare by linking it to crop development for small farmers.

With Hernando gone, the IADB returned to Paraguay to reform the Ministry of Agriculture according to an entirely new ideology of agrarian development. In less than a decade, from the beginning of the Latin American debt crisis through to the end of the Cold War, development agencies had almost completely abandoned productivist agricultural projects like STICA, and their related commitment to the welfare state. In the 1990s, they invested instead in neoliberal programs of good governance, anticorruption, privatization, and market liberalization.[11] Under the IADB's guidance, the cotton program became increasingly decentralized, and the cotton gins, now organized as a cartel known as CADELPA, took more control of the process.[12] The ministry reduced its own extension staff and contracted out most of its agrarian training and support programs to NGOs while the gins contracted their own technical support for farmers. Oversight of state-approved seed multipliers slipped as well, leading to a decline in the quality of the cotton produced by Reba-P279.

It was in this institutional environment that the weevils arrived and the massive chemical response began. Between 1990 and 1992, the average cost of pesticides per hectare doubled for smallholders. To make matters worse, cotton prices began to fall, not only because of a glut on global cotton markets, but also because of deteriorating quality of the fibers. Since CADELPA now controlled most credit to the countryside, they were shielded from the worst economic shocks, while the number of small farmers registering net losses on the harvest began to increase. Nonetheless, CADELPA made a series of fatal errors that made a bad situation far worse. The most notorious of these was the massive speculation, in 1993, on a new variety of seed from the US company Delta and Pine, which turned out to be vulnerable to a virus transmitted by aphids. Over 200,000 families of cotton growers lost their harvest. That fall, the rural organization known as the Federación Nacional Campesina organized what would become a massive, annual march on Asunción demanding support for smallholders. Cotton would hobble on for another decade, but it was never again more than a cycle of borrowing, protest, debt forgiveness and embezzlement.[13]

There are many chickens and eggs in this story, and as many ways of telling as there are political interests. One of my favorite agribiopolitical conspiracy theories appeared in ABC *Color* in October 1993, during the second planting since the arrival of weevils. Speculating on why campesinos hadn't all followed new phytosanitary protocols to burn the cotton leftovers from the previous season, one author found a backhanded way of blaming campesino ignorance:

There are long discussions, in both private and public institutions, trying to figure out why rural producers are not reacting to this important threat. . . . Sometimes it's attributed to culture, but it's also possible that they are sick, debilitated by things like the lack of iodine and iron in their blood that condemns them to live in a kind of permanent stupor. . . . Is it possible that the farmer who doesn't remove the remains of cotton plants is suffering from goiter . . . ? On that note, the minister of public health and social welfare is currently undertaking an evaluation of iodine deficiency in the countryside that could serve as a starting point.[14]

Iodine deficiency was indeed a problem in rural Paraguay, but in this article and countless others, it was also a convenient way to biologize poverty. This was one of the last articles that ABC *Color* published about cotton. The newspaper, whose interests were aligned primarily with those of the emergent rural elite, lost interest in the plant and the population on which it depended.

One of the most telling symptoms of the shift in agribiopolitical relations was the sudden change in the way the Ministry of Agriculture filed its annual reports. Until 1990, these reports were divided up into chapters on the performance of certain plants. The 1991 report was a panicked summary of ministerial disarray following Hernando's death. And from 1992 onward, the reports only talked about the efficiency of governance. For three years, while the weevils ravaged the eastern colonies, the ministry managed to produce annual reports about national agriculture without ever mentioning the crisis or even using the word "cotton."[15] The effect is striking, as though the state had finally effected a complete separation from plant life, as if the bureaucratic imperatives within Calle Última had become detached from the biological imperatives beyond them.

Of course, the rupture was not quite as complete as the hastily written reports suggest. But looking back two decades later, NGO workers and international experts who made their livelihoods in Paraguay trying to promote rural welfare describe the 1990s as an implosion of the Ministry of Agriculture. During our interviews, they described two decades of political chaos that made it impossible to properly attend to what was going on in the countryside.[16] These liberal development experts were loath to compliment the Stroessner regime in any way, but all were nostalgic for Hernando Bertoni, who to them represented a vision of state-led agriculture, and through it of support for the rural poor, that they clearly missed. At the Museum of Natural History, in a back room among Winkelried Bertoni's old insects, someone even managed to save Hernando's office desk, a relic of governmental coherence surrounded by the remains of scientific heroism.

In the wake of all of these scandals, Paraguayan agriculture policy remained disorganized and ever-changing. In fact, the rebuilding of the Ministry of Agriculture wasn't begun in earnest until Nicanor's administration in 2003–2004, the period of institutional reform we keep returning to. Pieces of the plant-protection apparatus, including the old abandoned (and not yet decontaminated) silos of the cotton program, were all consolidated as SENAVE in 2004. I met Inés Franceschelli in the shade of those silos, and it is also supposedly in their shade that many of the files of the Citizen Participation Unit were torched by SENAVE employees celebrating Lugo's ouster.[17] In the meantime, it's funny, but perhaps a little less surprising, that when antisoy activists in Lugo's government tried to build a regulatory instrument that would slow the spread of soybeans through eastern Paraguay, the soy that they envisaged, an invading life force from Brazil that overtook campesino colonies, appeared more like boll weevils than like cotton. In response, the state they mobilized was a phytosanitary state, a state that protected the cotton nation with the immunological apparatus at hand.

## IMMUNITY TO SOY

One day during the final months of the Government of Beans, Franceschelli told me that the Seed Department at SENAVE was trying to reconstitute the lost germplasm of Reba-P279. This was one of the clearest signs of the phytosanitary alliances that SENAVE was trying to promote. The irony was that during the Government of Beans, SENAVE was used not to protect the Green Revolution crop of the day (soy) but to protect an old crop against a new one. If the cotton nation had been built in part as a violent assertion of sovereignty over the eastern frontier and an extension of the living assemblage of the nation, it was the incompletion of this project and now the illness of the cotton colonies that allowed soy to move so quickly through the countryside. Even the responses occasionally resembled each other: the war against the boll weevil had required campesinos to create buffers around their fields, though in that case the purpose of the buffers was not to stop pesticide drift but rather to stop insect propagation. Both had made farmers aware of how the border was important not just for sovereignty in the abstract but intimately, for the health of their plants and their access to land, cash, and state services.

Barreras vivas stood for all of this. Yes, they prevented pesticide drift, but they were also immunological bulwarks against an invading species. During our responses to various denuncias, members of the Citizen Participation Unit would often point out the presence or absence of barreras as we entered particular colonies, commenting on them not just as a sign of sojeros' regulatory compliance but as a broad index of community health. A lack of barreras vivas meant not only that locals were being exposed to pesticide drift but also that they weren't well enough organized to directly confront the offending sojeros. Some inspectors told me that they would immediately get depressed when entering an old cotton colony where there were no barreras; they saw it as a sign of their imminent demise.

Treating soy in immunological terms meant turning it into death to cotton's life and, by extension, even Paraguayan life generally. This wasn't Lugo's primary project, nor was he its author. "La soja mata" was in place many years before Lugo even considered running for office, and before SENAVE became available to activists as a regulatory instrument. But in the crucible of Lugo's government, the phytosanitary approach to life and death served this project perfectly: SENAVE built on and reinforced a view of the Paraguayan (cotton) nation as a unitary biological assemblage organized around the great central heart of Asunción, under threat from external invaders bearing poisons, giant machinery, and Portuguese, pulling out the cotton and the campesinos and the Paraguayanness and leaving only beans. The role of SENAVE in this assemblage was to preserve the remnants of the cotton nation by keeping soy at bay with borders, barriers, inspectors, qualifying standards, laboratories, biosecurity protocols, carbon-copied inspection reports, rooms full of lawyers, and emissaries in pickup trucks.

It's easy in retrospect to see the contradictions of this operation. The apparatuses of plant protection had always been built to protect monocrops, not to repel them, to create conditions under which the most aggressive forms of agriculture could thrive. And yet in the age of monocrops, it is perhaps not surprising that battles over the shape of agriculture might end up taking on these Manichaean dimensions. After all, at the center of any agribiopolitical project lies a series of questions about who is killing what and whom and what extant forms of life can be encouraged to thrive at the expense of others. The more homogeneous one's conception of life becomes, the more its others come to be understood as death. And the self-proclaimed protectors of the cotton nation knew full well that their opponents saw things in even starker terms and had recourse to far more powerful instruments of violence with which to enforce their views.

Only months after the coup against Lugo, it became obvious that the Soy State would flip the agribiopolitical assemblage once again, turning soy into life and its opponents into an invading horde. In December 2013, Horacio Cartes deployed the police to protect soy from campesino protesters.[18] In what became a caricature of authoritarian agribiopolitics, blue-helmeted riot police stood around the edges of soy fields where there should have been a thick wall of elephant grass. One barrera viva had been replaced by another. Only this time, rather than protecting neighbors from pesticides, the barrera faced outward, protecting pesticides from neighbors.

With the police declared for soy, the stealthier elements of the Soy State would also deploy, hunting down, rooting out, and assassinating campesino leaders who might threaten to weaken it.[19] In each of these deaths, just as with all of the cases of poisoning, the causes were complicated and not easily reducible to soy expansion. But they weren't unrelated. In "Soy, Deforestation and Assassination," the activist paper *E'a* correlated deforestation maps with the location of assassinations and attempted assassinations of activists.[20] Ecocide, they concluded, goes hand in hand with genocide. By using the word "genocide" here, no one was trying to draw an equivalency between the violence against campesinos perpetrated along the soy frontier and the Indian hunting that had occurred in the same areas less than two generations previously. But the echo is nonetheless instructive: it helps to show that a new monocrop frontier was replicating what Patrick Wolfe calls the "logic of elimination," this time against the remnants of the cotton nation.[21]

# CHAPTER SEVENTEEN

# Dummy Huts and the Labor of Killing

D uring the soy conflicts of 2004 and 2005, just after Silvino Talavera's death and before the rise of the Government of Beans, the oddest structures began appearing on the edges of soy farms in conflict-ridden areas: tiny, empty houses. They looked something like campesino huts, only they were too small to really be lived in—at best they could be used for a bit of shade, since they often stood on the edges of land that had been stripped bare. The first of these that I ran across was just outside of Colonia Tekojoja, in a field I knew had recently been cleared by sojeros from a nearby town. It was conspicuously small, but also weirdly clean: the boards were freshly milled, and there were no shutters in the windows or anything else that indicated a person might occupy it. And there it sat, for several years, totally uninhabited: a dummy hut.

Sojeros built dummy houses like this one in order to strengthen their property claims, an improvised response to leftover land reform laws which insisted that land in colonies could only be owned by people who lived and worked there. According to the Estatuto Agrario, beneficiaries of land re-form had to stay on their allotted parcels, usually for twenty years, and any land that was abandoned in that time went back to being property of the state, to be redistributed again.[1] The legal restriction was there to deter the concentration of land in these colonies, where land prices were artificially low. The laws had rarely been enforced before the advent of soy, and these properties frequently changed hands. But as soon as sojeros began buying whole colonies in batches, at rates much higher than the state price, activists began to demand that sales be properly restricted; sojeros had had to find a way around the rules.[2] One way they experimented with fending off denunciation was by building fake houses that they could claim to be living in if they were ever questioned by the police.

The dummy houses were transitional structures, built by land claimants during a moment of legal uncertainty around which parts of property law would continue to apply. Over time they became superfluous, as most soy farmers settled on renting land, letting the campesinos living there subsist on meager rents until they chose to move on. The dummy huts disappeared or became tool sheds. But for a brief time they stood as an attempt by sojeros to say that soy didn't only kill; it also created life. To the extent that that life was fake, the huts evoked something else: a haunted landscape.

I choose the word "haunted" advisedly: the pretend houses pretended to harbor a certain kind of life, and their emptiness made the absence of that life all the more obvious. What was missing from the house was the life of labor and, by extension, the agribiopolitical assemblage that distributed land and labor in the production of rural welfare. When campesinos said that soy killed, they meant a lot of things, but this was its clearest sense: soy destroyed the promise of the relationship between work, citizenship, and welfare. Rental did much the same thing: it preserved a pretense of campesino livelihood but without work, and without the promise that the state would support them in thriving in the future.

And so the dummy huts leave us with a final dilemma. On the one hand, they help to mark the soy frontier off as a specific event, as a violent moment of displacement or elimination of life. On the other hand, as we've seen, the campesino life that came to haunt the huts was in many ways similar to the soy that surrounded it: a population drawn by the crop boom of a previous generation. Soy was at once an inversion of the relationship between agrarian labor and welfare promised by the land reform, and a mere continuation of the destruction wrought on the cotton frontier. Most political interventions—including Lugo's attempt to revive land reform promises of the 1970s—left out this second, politically uncomfortable part of the equation.[3] The task in this chapter is to find a way to bring it back in, to critique the way that soy kills without romanticizing what it kills, to show how its destruction is simultaneously novel and continuous with what came before. One way to do this is to be more specific about the ways in which killing works as a form of redistribution.

## LAND, LABOR, AND WELFARE

Land was always the primary currency of rural welfare in Paraguay, and the Institute for Rural Welfare spent most of its time and resources on redistributing properties. Giving out "land to the tiller" was not just about redistributing a vital resource—it was about a structural transformation in the rural economy such that it could support, if only minimally, large numbers of campesinos. The operative principle was that land held by smallholders was more productive per hectare, and that the wealth generated by small farms was better distributed than that produced on large farms.[4] The second currency of the equation "land to the tiller" was therefore labor: beyond the beneficiaries of land reform, who were expected to work their land in order to pay it off, smallholders were expected to provide further work for large numbers of family members and neighbors. Cotton colonies thus produced small urban settlements of people who could live on the cotton harvest, and around whom schools, churches, and small shops eventually thrived.

The recent literature on "land grabbing," in which Paraguayan soy figures prominently, chronicles the way that land reforms are being dismantled around the world.[5] These analyses show that as mechanized agriculture has spread, not only has land become concentrated in fewer and fewer hands, but the jobs associated with that land have also dwindled, undermining agriculture's primary mode of redistribution. Across Latin America, Asia, and certain parts of Africa, the spread of extensive monocrops like soy, corn, and palm oil undermines one of the progressive promises of the Cold War. Tania Li puts this in biopolitical terms, arguing that the new era of agriculture without work represents a betrayal of the biopolitical consensus of the mid-twentieth century, what she calls "make live" policies.[6] The old target populations of land reforms across the global south, she argues, have become surplus population to newfangled assemblages of agrarian capital that no longer need them.

This argument is consonant with a vitalist Marxist theory that was used during the Cold War to describe industrial mechanization and the deterioration of the welfare state. In several much-quoted passages, Marx used vitalist language to describe "living" human labor power, contrasting it with "dead" capital.[7] That line of reasoning became popular during the Cold War, after the biological vitalism of Bertoni and others had gone out of style. Li implicitly picks up on this line of argument in her interpretation of biopolitics, as do many campesino iterations of the slogan "la soja mata." For a time in Paraguay, *sojización* was synonymous with mechanization, because it entailed replacing workers with machines.[8] Similarly, campesinos often called soy fields "deserts," not because there was nothing living there but because there were no people. The argument that genetically modified organisms are "unnatural" operates on a similar vitalist premise: the machinic quality of engineered plants stirs anxieties around the decline not just of nature but of work itself as a privileged way of producing value.[9]

Perhaps it's not surprising then that soy farmers, like many others seeking to benefit from the productive powers unleashed by the life sciences in the last two decades, have developed their own vitalist language that makes "life as labor" sound anachronistic. While soy demands long, hard workdays of farmers and high personal and financial risk, many farmers I spoke to described the soy boom as though it were the beans themselves that did most of the work. "Soy is miraculous," one silo manufacturer told me at the Expo Santa Rita; "as long as soy keeps working [mientras la soja trabaja], we'll keep planting it." In a drought year, he had to acknowledge that there were great risks and setbacks in gambling on soy, but if the past two decades were any indication, he said, soy was not yet "exhausted." What's at stake in this agrarian neovitalism is not therefore just a difference in political ideology, or in the ethical calculus around violence and profit, but an ontological disagreement about what counts as life.

For soy farmers, life animates capitalist production, but it is a posthuman life, what Melinda Cooper calls "bioeconomics," in which all sorts of creatures produce surplus that can be financialized.[10] Indeed, bioeconomics often still includes welfare promises, as in the discourse of the so-called Second Green Revolution.[11] In this neoliberal version of the agrarian booms of the Cold War, the assemblage of biochemistry, smallholder labor, and the welfare state have been replaced with biotechnology, transnational capital (and private philanthropy), and the productivist state. Agrarian labor is minimized as a form of redistribution in favor of collective investment, rent, and taxation, while the ethical imperative of feeding the world continues to excuse some of the excesses of agrarian destruction. Laborers who do not have other ways to profit from a booming agrarian economy are merely expected to migrate and be absorbed by other labor markets.[12]

Between the humanist vitalism of the first Green Revolution, and the posthuman vitalism of the second, one factor remains constant: in each, the spark of life and of economic value resides in particular organisms. In the first, that organism is the human whose capacity for creativity lies at the core of the project, while plants are merely tools along the way. In the second, it is the plants themselves that are powerful and that need to be fostered and protected for the eventual betterment of people who passively eat what is being fed to them.

Neither of these vitalisms is very good at dealing with the complex connections between forms of life. It's telling, for instance, that Li believes it's possible to make live without ever letting die. "Both letting die, and making live, have a politics," she says, "but I reject the idea that the two are in some kind of functional equilibrium—that it is necessary to select some to die, in order for others to live."[13] Similarly, enthusiasts of the Second Green Revolution tend to assume that increased production, when it comes out in the wash, is always good because it implies overall growth, of food, of capital, of resources for industry. Both are a version of what Cary Wolfe describes as the problem of an "affirmative biopolitics" that finds itself incapable of differentiating between forms of life, and therefore of understanding the trade-offs necessary in the promotion of any specific form of life.[14]

In the context of Li's humanism, the aspiration is a noble one, but once we've moved beyond the human, once we've recognized the biopolitical as always already agribiopolitical, the equivalency at its heart is harder to sustain. What this suggests is not that the land-grab critique is wrong about the dismantling of welfare, but that in couching its politics in terms of the ontology of the first Green Revolution, it misses the larger story of destruction that the Green Revolution set in motion and is still ongoing. Life need not be conceptualized as a zero-sum game for us to better appreciate the way specific forms of thriving always depend on specific sorts of killing. A less abstract agribiopolitical history of the Green Revolution shows that the relationships between land, labor, and plants are far more tangled than they appear in simple recipes for economic development.

## LABOR AS A VITAL RELATION

It's not clear to me that campesinos being displaced by soy during this period were as committed to an abstract conception of labor power as the sociologists and agrarian economists who wrote about them. To campesinos, what haunted the dummy hut wasn't merely the possibility of more laboring bodies, but specific kinds of people who worked with soil and plants in particular ways; to say that soy killed was not only to ask how much labor was being lost on the soy frontier, but also what kinds of labor. And while this doesn't make the analytic task any easier, or the ethical road ahead any clearer, it does offer another insight into the agribiopolitical logic of the long Green Revolution, and one of the more complicated vital entanglements that it entails.

"Land to the tiller," as it was articulated in the Estatuto Agrario, derived value from agrarian labor primarily by transforming unused land into property. It began with the much-repeated line that Paraguay's problem was one of people with no land and land with no people.[15] The figure of land without people was itself ambivalent: on the one hand, it was explicitly meant as a condemnation of large properties, or *latifundios*, that were supposedly economically inefficient. Implicitly, though it also perpetuated the colonial trope of *terra nullius*, which disqualified indigenous modes of existence in the forest. Already then, rural welfare linked together the notion of agrarian redistribution with the ideology of colonial genocide.

Land reform worked like this: if colonists could find such unused land, they could stake a claim on it by manually introducing changes to the land that would be considered improvements, or *mejoras*. (Even in the absence of formal property titles or any other document, campesinos buying and selling plots of land from each other referred to the commodity being exchanged as mejoras.) The first mejora that could be recognized in this way was almost always deforestation. Indeed, the idea of deforestation as improvement was so entrenched that it was often a prerequisite for getting credit in areas where colonization was done by private companies rather than the state.[16] In other words the most basic way for campesinos to turn their work into property (and thus commodify it) was to cut and burn trees. From that point on, the planting of cotton and other cash crops organized campesino households into a further cycle of *mejoramiento*, in which families expected, at least once a year during the harvest, to be able to invest in the economic base of their households, including new buildings, new fields, vehicles, and quota payments to the IBR.[17]

As I've said, the creation of landed property was only one part of local economies, and almost no household got by working only on their own farms. To supplement this, and to better spread labor out through uneven agricultural cycles, there were several other forms of occasional labor, including *minga* (an exchange of labor between households), picking (which was counted as piecework), and, most importantly, *changa*, a kind of casual day labor.[18] Of all of these, changa was the one that most resembled wage labor, since it generally paid a set price for a set unit of time. When I was living in Vaquería in 2005, there was some variation in what different employers paid for more difficult work, but there was a well-established base rate that everyone knew: 8,000 guaranies (around $2) per day. In practice, one of the most common forms of changa on farms was *limpieza*, or cleaning, including all sorts of low-grade fieldwork, like clearing, hoeing, weeding, and brush burning, the sorts of immunological tasks that all small farms constantly undertake to prevent them from being overwhelmed by weeds.[19] It's the sort of work that was necessary to the production cycle, but could often be carried out on an ad hoc basis.

The specificity is important, because while I often heard the phrase "La soja nomomba'apoi ma'ave" (Soy doesn't make anybody work), I just as frequently heard "La soja nomochangai" (Soy doesn't produce changas). The fact is that despite the poor wages for often grueling work, changas remained a desirable form of work because campesinos retained control over other aspects of the labor arrangement. On the one hand, a *changuero* retained his or her independence. Many would say that it was preferable to be a changuero rather than a *tembiguái*, dependent on a boss.[20] If a family member got sick, if it rained, or if a cousin showed up wanting to go fishing, a changuero was under no obligation to go to work. If anything, the expectation flowed the other way: changa could work as an explicit form of redistribution in a tight-knit moral economy. It was not uncommon in Vaquería, for instance, for poorer households to ask their wealthier neighbors to give them changas, often by offering to clean their fields. The arrangement was one of the primary ways that large ranches organized patronage with local campesino colonies, offering changas to trusted families, but only in much rarer cases offering long-term contractual work.

Again, though, it would be wrong to think of the changa as a simple, interchangeable unit of labor time. Changas were also highly gendered, predominantly carried out by younger men. It was not only part of an economy that allowed cash to circulate locally, but was also part of a life stage for young men who aspired to establish homesteads of their own. Consequently the disappearance of changas also had gendered and generational effects on colonies, where young men found themselves traveling farther and farther in search of work, leaving spouses and young children at home with grandparents and sending remittances home to support farms that were no longer productive in their own right. As women joined this migrant labor force, a whole generation disappeared from the colonias.

So campesinos opposing soy remained committed to two ways of producing value through work while maintaining some control over it. The first was the mejora, a way of making and maintaining a claim on a piece of land, but not necessarily commodifying it completely so that they might sell or mortgage it.[21] The second was the changa, a kind of work that was relatively free of obligation, a right to work that eschewed the duty to work written into contracts.[22] Many campesinos made this clear to me when I asked them whether, if given the opportunity, they would like to be sojeros themselves. Most said no. Well aware of the way work was organized on modern soy farms, how mortgaged land and credit for machines and inputs drove sojeros to work eighteen-hour days in the summer, many campesinos were explicit that the sojero life was not the life for them.[23]

Meanwhile, campesinos' lack of property titles, and their changa work ethic, were both major impediments to the expansion of soybeans, and sojeros often expressed their annoyance about this in blatantly racist terms. Again and again, sojeros told me they thought campesinos were both lazy and economically irrational: "They only want changas," they would say to illustrate. As Kathi Weeks points out, the idea that the right to refuse work is a form of laziness has a long history in labor struggles.[24] But one can see where their frustration came from: as soy farms grew, and as their expanding monocrops became increasingly vulnerable to new kinds of pests, the fickle local labor force became increasingly hard to manage. Tensions were clearest in moments when a sudden flush of weeds or rust or insects put a crop at risk, and it was difficult to round up the manual labor necessary to hoe or spray down the intruders. On large soy farms, ad hoc changas were insufficient for cleaning fields. Every soy farmer I talked to about the disappearance of farm jobs insisted that their disagreements with changueros was one of the reasons why they eventually replaced most of their hired hands with expensive machinery.[25]

From the sojero point of view, taking over the campesino landscape for soy was therefore a process of acquiring these two forms of labor that sojeros wished were easier to control. The first was past deforestation, the process of improvement begun during the land reform, which they wished were more fully commodified as transferable property titles. After all, if they could simply buy the land outright, they wouldn't have had to erect the dummy huts. The second was the immunological work of cleaning weeds, limpieza, which they wished were easier to control than the recalcitrant changueros living nearby. What all of this suggests is that alongside the way of life, and the jobs, the dummy hut was haunted by the presence of other living beings, refigured as agricultural pests, which made so much agricultural labor necessary.

## THE ACQUISITION OF KILLING

The promotion of one form of life always comes at the expense of other forms or potential forms of life, but not always in ways that are predictable. The agribiopolitical question is not, therefore, whether soy kills, or whether soy's killing is justifiable for the good it produces, but how, specifically, soy kills, and how it is placed in dense webs of thriving and dying. One of the first things that jumps out about this specificity, and that we've seen hints of from the beginning of this book, is its speed. Soy's violence may have been slow, but its value derived specifically from the fact that, in relation to labor hours, it was less slow than the violence that came before. The machines that replaced changueros were all implements that intensified the labor of death: the bulldozer for clearing forest, the plow for killing weeds, the crop duster for killing pests, and the harvester for killing the crop. With any of these machines, a single person could now kill off much of the biomass in a relatively large area in a matter of hours, something that had been unimaginable in campesino communities only a few years before.

Consider, one last time, the Roundup Ready soybean, a technology so novel when it was introduced that it elucidated its own whole brand of agency panic, as though genetic modification itself would produce ecocide. And yet to soy farmers and most agronomists, genetic modification was merely one more technology in a long line of improvements that made farming more efficient. The mechanism was simple: as late as 1999, most soy farms still needed a steady supply of changueros, because while farmers could mechanize land clearing, planting, and harvesting, they still needed people to deal with weeds that sprang up after germination and before harvesting. A one hundred hectare field of soy could provide work of this sort for at least a dozen men on a regular basis, putting money back into circulation in nearby colonies.[26] Roundup Ready soy transformed this labor relation completely. Roundup kills most plants it encounters in a matter of days, so if there's one thing for which Roundup is extremely effective, it is cleaning a field in preparation for planting. For the first few decades of its manufacture, this was its primary use. Campesinos even used it periodically to kill particularly stubborn weeds before planting a garden, referring to it affectionately as *mata-todo*, or "kills everything." Monsanto made fortunes on Roundup, and when it faced patent expiration in the 1990s, its ingenious solution was to create a soybean that could resist applications of Roundup even once it was growing in the fields, thus replacing manual weeders with increased pesticide applications. The demand for Roundup skyrocketed, and the company could now make money both by selling seed and by contractually obliging farmers to buy their herbicides from them.[27]

The "miraculous" life of Roundup Ready soy derived from its resilience (and therefore self-selection) in the midst of industrial killing, by internalizing the relationship between killing and survival that had once been resolved with changas. It removed the need for changueros by creating the ultimate *pohajuka*, killer medicine, mata-todo. Once the changas were gone, and pesticide drift made rural life less livable, the small farms in the area became all the more vulnerable and could more easily be bought, or at least rented, from older family members while children left town to look for work elsewhere. The intensification of present forms of killing made it easier to commodify and appropriate the past forms of killing: the neighbor's property title. In this sense, Roundup Ready soy really was just a continuation of a logic of intensification and mechanization of killing begun during the Green Revolution.

Soy kills, but in most of Paraguay, it does not kill off a pristine environment nor a place of thriving, stable communities. Instead it co-opts and kills off some of the inhabitants of an already blasted landscape, a colonial scene of carnage of both humans and nonhumans.[28] The violence perpetrated against campesinos by sojeros was never equivalent to the violence of the land reform and the cotton boom, but it was continuous with it. Soy both built on previous forms of killing and inverted them, changing the very conceptions of life on which the cotton colonies, and the welfare state, had thrived. This is part of what happens on all frontiers. One wave replaces another and reorganizes economy, territory, and violence in a way that is incommensurate with but dependent on those that came before. And so the wave of soybeans that overwhelmed campesino colonies in the 2000s represented both a new kind of agribiopolitics and an elaboration of the cotton nationalism that had occurred before. The Second Green Revolution was an acceleration of the first, but also a qualitative shift, in which one assemblage of killing practices encountered, attacked, and supplanted another, less efficient one.

I've watched this process and its aftermath most closely in a handful of colonies in northern Caaguazú that I began visiting in 2004 and that, for a time, were considered one of the trenches of the battle against soy. Ña Costanza, the activist I introduced at the very beginning of this book, lived in one of these places, toward the end of a long road known as Carmelitas. Settled in the late 1970s, Carmelitas was a classic land reform colony, a long road dotted with houses every hundred meters or so, with mixed farms stretching back from the houses into the forest. In 2004, the family was still planting a bit of cotton, among other things, and the oldest son had recently moved out to go claim land in another settlement not far away. The year I arrived, Brasiguaios had begun buying up plots at the end of the road, and the following year they claimed three more, one of them right next door to Ña Costanza's house. She had been at the forefront of the attempt to stop any further takeover. She'd denounced the farmers to SENAVE, the Secretariat of the Environment, and the Ministry of Public Health and Social Welfare, and had formed a committee on the road to try to convince others not to sell their land.

In the midst of this, they sat down with two of the sojeros and offered a solution to the tension: they could plant soy so long as they stopped spraying their fields with tractors and instead hired neighbors to do the spraying as changueros (using backpacks as they did for cotton). The sojeros initially agreed to this, but the solution didn't last long. Whether because of increased cost or unmanageable labor relationships, they gave up after a year. Of the three farms targeted by protests, one replaced his soy with corn, another canceled his lease and left town, and the third doggedly remained, ultimately leading to a rapid expansion of soybeans up and down the road. Even though it failed, that fragile resolution clarified the stakes of what makes soy so powerful: for many, soy could stay so long as campesinos were invited to participate, to thrive even, in the labor of killing that soy required.

Over the next decade, many families in Carmelitas and nearby colonies offered up their land to soy farmers in different ways. The struggle to prevent the sale of untitled land had made it harder for them to move, even though some of them wanted to. One solution to all of these problems was to enter into an informal agreement whereby campesinos would be paid a wage to further improve their own land. The improvements included completing the bureaucratic process of titling the property (to make it easier to transfer ownership rights) and clearing land for the introduction of machinery.

In other words, unemployed ex-cotton growers were paid to remove what was left of their own cotton farms, particularly the shade trees, woodlots, orange groves, and charred stumps.

Sometimes called limpieza, *destronco* (detrunking), or *mecanización*, to soy farmers, of course, this paid service was just the final phase in the clearing of forest for agriculture, the finalization of a process that campesinos had already mostly accomplished. To campesino activists, however, it was something much more sinister. The symbolic significance of being paid to rip out the plants that they themselves had planted in the quest for a better life was lost on no one. Pointing to one neighbor who had recently finished his limpieza by knocking down his own house and hauling it away on a truck, my friend Antonio simply said, "They're paying him to kill himself." At the end of the process, the legal titling of the improvements was about acquiring the rights to sell or rent one's own self-killing. It seemed inevitable to Antonio and others that Carmelitas would soon be completely wiped out and replaced with a field of soy.

By 2019, though, when I returned to see who was left, I found something altogether stranger, a new kind of transitional structure. Driving down the road, it looked as though most of the houses were still there, along with gardens and a handful of fruit trees. But as I arrived at Ña Costanza's place, I could see soy about twenty meters back from the road. A small copse of trees still stood around her house, but beyond that and beyond the similar tree line behind all of her neighbors' houses, the soy stretched in one contiguous field as far as the eye could see. All of the old homesteads had been linked together in a giant rented field. The once-thriving community of cotton growers was now living in a thin strip along the road, having abandoned agriculture altogether. The dummy huts were gone, but sojeros were still shielded from questions about the legality of their property by a new kind of barrera viva composed of the vestiges of the old colony.

Ña Costanza lived there now with her husband, three grandchildren, and one of her twelve children. "What are you going to do?" she asked. "Soy won. There's nothing else." For Ña Costanza, as for so many others I visited, soy had become inevitable. The rental income, at about $3,000 per year for her relatively large property, was a temporary but stable way to produce a modicum of welfare for retired old homesteaders. Both she and her husband had recently recovered from cancer, which she attributed to the soy. Their cure, she said, was partly due to a newly available health care system, but mostly due to God. The middle generation of her family, like that of most on the road, was off somewhere else looking for domestic work or changas: in Asunción, São Paolo, Buenos Aires, and Madrid. A surprising number of them were off in the Chaco, the arid western half of Paraguay, which had become the new frontier of agricultural destruction. The expansion of ranching and of new drought-resistant soybeans into the Chaco in the past five years had turned it into the new frontier of forest destruction and genocide, much of it being carried out by campesinos displaced by soy in the east.[29]

Carmelitas now represented a new stage of the long Green Revolution. The dummy huts and rented fields were vestiges of the last frontier wave. But some of the laborers had moved onto a new frontier where they could still participate in agrarian killing, to new ways of intensifying production through the commodification of death. Regulation of the sort they once demanded from SENAVE no longer seemed necessary, since none expected their kids to remain there. The Government of Beans was a distant, sometimes painful memory of disappointment. The Soy State, at least, was quiet. Their resignation meant that soy could go back to being slow; no one needed to turn fumigations into events, because they no longer felt like they were at war. The frontier had passed over, leaving a new reality and a certain tranquility. Only when I asked about kids who had gone off to the Chaco did I sometimes hear the stories of soy's expansion. "I don't really know what goes on there," Ña Costanza said of one of her sons. "Once he called me in the middle of the night, crying. He said he was so scared, he'd never seen machines like that. They were killing everything, he said." But when I asked if he had come back, she indicated that he had stayed and that they had never talked about it again. "What are you going to do?" she said.

# Remains of Experiments Past

A mong the unexpected offspring of Paraguay's soy boom is a nascent tourism industry, creating destinations where people can consume fragments of the past. The Ministry of Tourism has rehabilitated Puerto Bertoni, turning the old nineteenth-century homestead overlooking the Paraná River into a scientific monument. People visiting that site might find that the portrait I've drawn of Moisés Bertoni is out of keeping with the official, twenty-first-century version of the man: at Puerto Bertoni, Moisés's legacy is all about conservation. The house sits in a 199-hectare preserve, a dense forest garden mixing native species and the eclectic imports that Bertoni himself planted. The jungle here still teems with birds and the occasional coati, and contains a small Mby'a village that can no longer live from hunting or agriculture. Tourist groups can make their way there by boat from the spectacular Yguazú falls in Brazil or Argentina, and encounter Bertoni as a forefather not of the Green Revolution in Paraguay, nor of an ambivalent nationalism, but of mainstream environmentalism.

Of course, as you move away from the river, following a few nineteenth-century European lampposts, standing Narnia-like in the middle of the forest, it doesn't take long to get to the soy. This property once covered 1,500 hectares, but it got whittled down by squabbling heirs and eventually sold off to local farmers. In the early 2000s, all but this small remaining piece was burned to the ground and replaced with a soy monocrop that stretches to Santa Rita and beyond. In fact, the approach to Puerto Bertoni by land is almost impossible to find, thin muddy tracks through a sea of beans. The contrast between forest and monocrop is appropriate, for both are legacies of a man who believed simultaneously in the cathedral of nature and in nationalist agricultural development.

But the contrast also turns diversity into a dualist caricature. Between these two versions is another Bertoni that we might coax out and try to let loose on the soy fields. In agronomy circles, *el sabio* is remembered in part for his decades-long battle against the use of fire for clearing cropland. He of course had no trouble with killing things. A tireless experimenter and plant breeder, committed to the modernization of export agriculture, at no point in his writings did he argue that one shouldn't kill an insect that is eating one's crops. He even admitted that the occasional use of fire was warranted. But in several essays that were ahead of their time, Bertoni argued that farmers should avoid burning brush as much as possible, because the long-term effects of such indiscriminate killing outweighed any of fire's short-term benefits for productivity. Instead, he offered a series of alternative methods, including the most radical, "planting without cleaning," a crop system that today is called permaculture or *agro-ecología*.[1]

Planting without cleaning focuses on companionship between crops, trees, soil, and debris. And though it creates intensively farmed plots with a minimum of killing, it definitely takes more time and care. As María Puig de la Bellacasa puts it, it implies a completely different biopolitics that eschews rapid solutions to agronomic problems and demands that a farmer work at the speed of the soil.[2] Despite his frenetic, perpetually dissatisfied intellect, Bertoni also advocated a similar, slow engagement with the world. His textbook on agronomy included advice about meditation, physical self-care, and continual learning.[3] Fire's long-term costs included not only the loss of soil microorganisms and beneficial insects but also climate stability, family well-being, and social cohesion.[4] It's not clear precisely what time frame he had in mind, but this is also Puig's point: to adopt soil's time is not to adjust to an investment window, but to slow down such that one falls out of phase with productivist reason. For that reason, agroecology is also not scalable in the same way as a monocrop, and can only be accomplished through emplaced commitments to long-term more-than-human relations. Beyond that, it tends to fall out of phase with governmental logics and international industrial imperatives.

Bertoni saw fire-free farming as an ethical, ecological, and economic imperative, and he was convinced that posterity would agree with him: "You can be sure, in the not-too-distant future, no one will clear their land with fire, no matter what the opposition to this may be at the outset. Nobody should harbor the least doubt about this: our descendants will not only stop committing this barbarity of burning fields, but they will have difficulty explaining how their ancestors could have believed for so long that it was the most rational thing to do."[5]

A century later, fire is still present in Paraguayan agriculture. In 2019, uncontrolled forest fires throughout Brazil, Bolivia and Paraguay (many of them deliberately set to make room for soy), briefly made international headlines as the newest characters of a global climate emergency.[6] Wildfires, like hurricanes and cracking ice sheets, have become narratively useful events in the discussion of climate change. But wildfires like these are merely extensions of practices of indiscriminate destruction that are now mostly practiced chemically and slip below the threshold of Anthropocenic outrage. Roundup and the other pesticides that go into supporting soybeans kill not just the plants that get in the way of soy but the dense aleatory webs of life on which the imagination plays.[7] It's hard to imagine how appalled Bertoni would be by the scale of biotic destruction in the Age of Monocrops.

If we can't all practice permaculture, though, how do we think and act beyond monocrops? Figuring out how to avoid the indiscriminate use of Roundup is not only a farmer's responsibility, nor is it the responsibility of the Paraguayan state. Both of these actors are merely part of larger assemblages in which all participants can practice what Donna Haraway calls an ethics of "eating well."[8] Eating well demands of everyone a food politics that is about thinking beyond simple stories that link farm to plate and becoming fully open to the tofu moments I talked about in chapter 6: the unsettling sense of a vast conspiracy animating the most mundane objects around us. Eating well is an excessive ethics that necessarily entails killing well. It is about giving up on the certainty that we know which forms of life are worth fostering or that any of them are beyond reproach.

It also means maintaining a biological, cultural, and analytic diversity not for the sake of diversity itself but for the vital possibilities that mixing always creates. The preserved Puerto Bertoni, where something called "nature" is temporarily shielded from the onslaught of monocrops, is itself a product of Anthropocene agribiopolitics. Despite this, one can still experience this anachronistic jungle mansion, where everything is allowed to thrive, as a place for imagining the world otherwise. As Manuel de Landa might put it, it is a place everywhere suffused with "an experimental attitude toward reality," a place for imagining other ways of assembling life.[9] Nothing could be more important for addressing the Anthropocene than keeping such experiments alive.

## WHAT WAS THE GOVERNMENT OF BEANS?

In the years after Lugo was removed from office, the worst fears of his supporters came to pass in mind-numbing succession. First were the little, cynical actions of the short-lived Liberal government of Federico Franco: the burning of the SENAVE archives, the deregulation of new GMOs, and the de facto suspension of pesticide regulations. And there were the deeper, more frightening moves to suppress the campesino movement, including the assassination of key witnesses to the massacre at Curuguaty. Lugo's coalition fell apart, and Horacio Cartes, the man who'd made his fortune laundering money from cigarette smuggling, handily won the next election, declared martial law in the north, and sent police to protect soy fields from demonstrators.[10] Five years later Cartes was succeeded by another Colorado Party strongman, the son of Stroessner's own private secretary, who easily won on a platform of law and order and an explicit promise not to bother the large agriculture sector with taxes or regulations.[11] Throughout the region, the governments of the left turn fell apart, each more spectacularly than the last, ushering in regimes for whom environmental deregulation was an unquestionable good.[12]

Soy of course did not stand still either. The international fight against Roundup eventually produced epidemiological evidence of its carcinogenic qualities, and a few high-profile legal cases seemed to spell the end of the most egregious uses of Roundup around the world.[13] As of this writing, it's unclear whether Monsanto or its new parent company, Bayer, can survive the coming onslaught of costly court rulings. But as with most phytosanitary interventions, this would do little to stop the advance of soy itself, which after all was much more than Roundup Ready soybeans and the chemicals that go with it. In fact, by 2012, Paraguayan soy fields had become so tangled with Roundup-resistant weeds that many farmers for a brief time had to scramble to find enough changueros to clean their fields before the stalks of resistant *capi'i pororo* and *lecherita* got caught up in the harvesters. For a while, passing soy fields on the highway I would see these new groups of people dotting the landscape, working away at a patch of stubborn grasses, and I'd wonder if the whole package of industrial relations was about to fly off on some other track. The dominant response, which eventually kicked in, was to find new, more potent chemical solutions to the problem. This began with new mixes of existing herbicides and new ways of timing the application of poisons. Crop breeders I spoke to were also looking forward to the development of beans that could genetically resist far stronger herbicides, such as 2,4-D and paraquat. In those spaces, the tactical victories in far-off courtrooms seemed less significant than the logic of expansion through more efficient forms of killing.

Meanwhile a second export commodity—beef—slowly caught up with soy in national importance and destructive force. In fact, though the Paraguayan beef industry had been around far longer, the sudden boom in meat production could also be understood as a way of adding value to soy, processing it through the bodies of cows before export. Feedlots sprang up throughout eastern Paraguay to produce meat at a much higher intensity than the ranches that used to compete for land with cotton colonies. And some of the beef displaced from the land best suited for soy was moved into less agriculturally desirable land. The new soy-beef complex pushed cattle farther into the Chaco, the arid plains west of the Paraguay River. As Ña Costanza's life became comparatively calm after being conquered by soy, the Chaco became the site of the most rapid deforestation in the world, and of new genocidal frontiers.[14]

For about three years after the coup, when I met up with the members of the Government of Beans who appear in these pages, I usually found people in mourning a certain dream of the state, and in shock at how easily it had all come undone.[15] It was hard to be an observer of Paraguay in those days without feeling that the momentum of industrial agriculture was unstoppable. And it was tempting to see the whole Lugo experience as a simple mistake, the mistake of thinking that states could be good for anything but intensifying agricultural violence. It's in that spirit that I backed the story of soy up 150 years to show the momentum the long Green Revolution. I hinted at deeper histories as well: the invention of monocrops, and phytosanitary governance in the seventeenth century. One could go further, to see all of the land now called Paraguay as a layering of colonial violence driven by a logic of acquisition and intensification that began with Spanish conquest.[16] Or further even, to the beginning of agriculture itself, and shortly thereafter the invention of the state form.[17]

But to say the Government of Beans was simply a mistake is also to concede too much coherence to the processes at work. After all, the state is also just a project of a bunch of people, suddenly availing themselves of new opportunities and tools, trying to encounter the world in a novel way. For the sincere among them, these encounters start as tofu moments—not moments of closure or of understanding, but as calls to action in a web that exceeds their ability to capture or to map. Those moments come without guarantees, of course, and they are always fraught and contradictory, but they are also alive with experimental possibility.[18]

Even though the state project failed, as perhaps it was bound to, everyone involved continued animating lives beyond monocrops. Andrés Wehrle, the agronomist who first drove Silvino Talavera to the hospital and later became the vice minister of agriculture under Lugo, went back to running his agroecology school in Pirapey. The Federación Nacional Campesina, long a supporter of modernist land reforms, began to experiment with new forms of collective agroecology in a handful of colonies. After the shake-up of campesino organizations that followed Lugo's ouster from power, CONAMURI began promoting organic mate production that was so successful that locals in one community close to Pirapey stopped renting their fields to sojeros and began planting yerba instead. Miguel Lovera rejoined the front lines of the fight against deforestation in the Chaco, trying to find ways to negotiate with ranchers to slow down their expansion and develop better relationships with Ayoreo neighbors. Inés Franceschelli started an NGO to promote seed diversity and a new urban farmers' market that is tiny in its impact, but that sparkles with a desire to eat well.

Perhaps most surprising was the afterlife of the case of Rubén Portillo in Yerutí, explored in chapter 10. After three years of trying to get the state to respond seriously to Portillo's death, lawyers from CODEHUPY took the case to the UN Human Rights Committee.[19] In a 2019 ruling, the committee found that Paraguay had violated its obligations under the International Covenant on Civil and Political Rights. The state had failed not only to protect Portillo from "the advance of soy monocultures and the abusive use of pesticides" but even to hold appropriate hearings after Portillo died.[20] The ruling itself, from a committee with no punitive authority, came and went after a handful of newspaper articles. Yet added to the pile of similar international denunciations, it set precedents for others to pick up and work with.

It's true that none of these tales of tactical sovereignty seem eventful in the way that Silvino Talavera's death or the election of Fernando Lugo or the massacre at Curuguaty were, creating palpable ruptures in Paraguayan time. They do not, on their own, call new actors into being, or generate new languages and narrative frames to accommodate them. But each of those events too was an amalgam of smaller gestures, too small to detect until their combination erupted into a flow of quasi-events that most people took to be natural. And because they were too small, we can only know them or try to know them retrospectively, as part of far-fetched conspiracies to push back against the wave of monocrops.

So I choose to remember the Government of Beans not merely after its failure but in the moments of tension that preceded that failure, that preceded the coup, just before everything became clear, somewhere back in chapter 12.

We are standing by the side of a road, with winter wheat stretching as far as the eye can see. Amada holds a clipboard in her hand and asks if this is a camino vecinal. Almost everything about the gesture feels empty, pedantic, and mundane. But it also resonates with possible futures. A camino vecinal, after all, isn't that much of a stretch. It's just a road where neighbors are responsible for each other's well-being and the well being of each other's crops. And that may be hard to achieve, but the form on the clipboard shows one step that might head in that direction.

If it is a camino vecinal, if Amada decides that this one little rule ought to apply here, who knows what might happen? If it is followed by lawyers who decide to read the form in a particular way, and political alliances that fall into place, or new weeds that push the farmers' calculus in a new direction, or some other tipping point in which large numbers of people suddenly decide to start eating well, then this little act of tactical sovereignty might turn out to have been worth it. If it is not a camino vecinal, then she chooses the response that puts no limits on the use of Roundup and other killing agents, makes no one stop to think about the effects that all this killing might be having on the health of those living nearby, on the likely survival of bird species, or on the temperature of the Earth. Then she causes the least trouble, in the short term, for everyone involved. She becomes part of the Soy State, and the colonial assemblage that it feeds in the fastest, most efficient manner. There's not much Amada can do here really. But given the tools at hand, she has found an opportunity to slow the whole thing down, even if only infinitesimally, and open up the realm of possibilities.

# NOTES

## INTRODUCTION

1. *Campesino* is often translated as "peasant," though in Paraguay it is as much an identity category as a class one. I use the Spanish throughout to avoid losing this specificity.

2. Hetherington, "Beans before the Law."

3. Ña Costanza is a pseudonym, as are all personal names in this book other than those of public figures.

4. See Zoomers, "Globalisation and the Foreignisation of Space"; Borras et al., "Land Grabbing and Global Capitalist Accumulation."

5. Borras et al., "The Rise of Flex Crops and Commodities." Oil palm and corn are similar crops in this way, as are industrial hogs, whose rendering creates no waste because it is converted into everything from pork chops to lip gloss. See Blanchette, *Porkopolis*.

6. du Bois, Tan, and Mintz, *The World of Soy*.

7. See Ash, Livezey, and Dohlman, *Soybean Backgrounder*. In 2006, it accounted for 65 percent of nonforage animal feeds globally.

8. See Eric Schroeder, "IGC: World Grains Output on Pace for Second Highest Total," *World Grain News*, October 2, 2017, https://www.world-grain.com/articles/8741-igc-world -grains-output-on-pace-for-second-highest-total.

9. Nixon, *Slow Violence and the Environmentalism of the Poor*.

10. Roundup is by far the most important pesticide used in soy farming. A broad-spectrum herbicide, Roundup is the brand name given by Monsanto to the generic glyphosate. Although Paraguayans now use many different generic versions of glyphosate, I refer to all of them as Roundup for continuity.

11. Morton, *Hyperobjects*. While I find the concept useful to a point, the way I use it departs somewhat from Morton's "object-oriented ontology" because, at least in the case of soy and the state, I treat the indeterminacy of objects as relational in a manner closer to actor-network theory.

12. According to the most recent report of the Intergovernmental Panel on Climate Change, land use accounts for 23 percent of global greenhouse gas emissions, with the worst contributors being deforestation and livestock-raising (see IPCC, *Climate Change and Land*). Transportation produces another 14 percent. These numbers are not particularly meaningful on their own, but the Food and Agriculture Organization's 2006 report on the meat industry's impact on climate change and biodiversity loss offers a comprehensive picture of why the industry is so particularly damaging. See Steinfeld et al., *Livestock's Long Shadow*.

13. See Kolbert, *The Sixth Extinction*; Muir, *The Broken Promise of Agricultural Progress*.

14. Moore, "The Capitalocene, Part I." This unevenness and the role that capital accumulation plays in generating new extractive economies have led Moore, among others, to use the word "Capitalocene" instead of "Anthropocene."

15. Steffen et al., "The Trajectory of the Anthropocene."

16. The clearest echo here is to Mitchell, *Carbon Democracy*.

17. Scott, *Seeing Like a State*, 183.

18. Levitsky and Roberts, *The Resurgence of the Latin American Left*.

19. For a nuanced assessment of Lugo's relationship to land reform and rural welfare, see Ezquerro-Cañete and Fogel, "A Coup Foretold."

20. In 2002, the Institute for Rural Welfare (IBR), was renamed the Instituto de Desarollo Rural y de la Tierra (INDERT). Although its mandate was updated and some of the titles changed to become more contemporary (most notably, dropping the word "welfare" in favor of "development"), the institution's functions changed very little. Because this book jumps back and forth in time, I refer to it throughout as IBR for the sake of continuity.

21. In this regard, Lugo's coalition was similar to the movements that had won power in the past decade in Brazil, Uruguay, and Argentina. The left turn in Latin America also had a more radical variant led by Venezuela and Bolivia.

22. The term "ecological modernization" is associated with thinkers such as Ulrich Beck (*The Risk Society*) and Anthony Giddens (*Modernity and Self-Identity*). See also Buttel, "Classical Theory and Contemporary Environmental Sociology." For histories of the rise of modernist government in environmental thinking, see especially Mathews, *Instituting Nature*; Agrawal, *Environmentality*.

23. See Abrahamsen, *Disciplining Democracy*; Guilhot, *The Democracy Makers*; Hetherington, *Guerrilla Auditors*.

24. During Lugo's government, this played out particularly in energy policy and the successful renegotiation of a usurious energy treaty between Brazil and Paraguay centered on the Itaipú Dam. For a full discussion, see Folch, *Hydropolitics*.

25. Coronil, *The Magical State*; Taussig, *The Magic of the State*; Das and Poole, *Anthropology in the Margins of the State*; Hansen and Stepputat, *States of Imagination*

26. Morton, *Hyperobjects*.

27. Robin, *The World According to Monsanto*.

28. This maddening double bind recapitulates one of the core debates in legal sociology and political science: public interest theories that suggest the state works in the interest of a collective good versus regulatory capture theories positing that regulatory apparatuses always respond to special interests (see Levine and Forrence, "Regulatory Capture").

29. Gudynas, "Extractivismos y corrupción"; Svampa and Viale, *Maldesarrollo*.

30. I elaborate on this notion of regulatory pragmatics in Hetherington, *Guerrilla Auditors*, inspired by Riles, *The Network Inside Out*; Hull, *Government of Paper*.

31. Das, "The Signature of the State."

32. On the future perfect construction of regulatory work, see Ballestero, *A Future History of Water*.

33. The term "out of phase" comes from Morton, *Dark Ecology, 7*.

34. Foucault, *The Birth of Biopolitics*; Campbell and Sitze, *Biopolitics*.

35. Cullather, *The Hungry World*.

36. On the Second Green Revolution, see Conway, *The Doubly Green Revolution*; Dano, *Unmasking the New Green Revolution in Africa*.

37. On the Human Development Index, measured by the UNDP, Paraguay increased its ranking more than any of its neighbors over the period in question, a ranking of some consequence, since it made it increasingly difficult for Paraguayans to access international development funding (see UNDP, *Paraguay*).

38. Tsing, "A Threat to Holocene Resurgence." Haraway, *Staying with the Trouble*, has suggested we call it the "plantationocene," a term I avoid because of the way the word "plantation" evokes a particular labor-intensive agribiopolitics that has never been applied to soybeans.

39. Shiva, *Monocultures of the Mind*.

40. For political economy, see especially the peasant studies and agrarian studies traditions (exemplified by works like Lapegna, *Soybeans and Power*, Fitting, *The Struggle for Maize*) and the critiques of global agrarian regimes (such as Patel, *Stuffed and Starved*; Moore, *Capitalism in the Web of Life*). For science and technology studies, see Mol, *The Body Multiple*; Law, *After Method*; Law and Mol, *Complexities*. For genealogies of life, see Cooper, *Life as Surplus*; Sunder Rajan, *Biocapital*; Povinelli, *Geontologies*; Murphy, *The Economization of Life*.

41. When I began planning this book I had three specific examples in mind of books that dealt with this problem of complexity: Raffles, *Insectopedia*; Tsing, *The Mushroom at the End of the World*; Fortun, *Promising Genomics*. Each of these books, while very different, innovates on the form of the chapter, allowing its objects and narratives to emerge as composites rather than as singular descriptions.

42. Mol, *The Body Multiple*.

43. On regulatory techniques and devices used in this way, see especially Law and Ruppert, "The Social Life of Methods: Devices"; Ballestero, *The Future History of Water*.

44. See Centre of Expertise on Resources, *Soy Supply Security for the Netherlands*.


## PART I. A CAST OF CHARACTERS

1. Ciancio, *La soja y el problema alimentario*. The claim is largely accepted in Paraguay, and he was recently the subject of a biography by González de Bosio, *Pedro Nicolás Ciancio*.

2. The contrast between civilization and barbarism was a key trope of Latin American liberalism, expressed most famously by Domingo Sarmiento, the Argentine president who had seen the war against Paraguay as a civilizing war (Sarmiento, *Facundo*).

3. Cited in González de Bosio, *Pedro Nicolás Ciancio*, 42. Unless otherwise noted, all translations are by the author.

4. It's not clear that Jefferson ever actually said this, but it was much quoted as a eulogy to the scientists of the Green Revolution (see Kloppenburg, *First the Seed*, 50).

5. Ciancio, *La soja y el problema alimentario*, 27.

6. See González de Bosio, *Pedro Nicolás Ciancio*, 17. It's not clear where Estigarribia got the soy wafers for his plan, but at the same time, the US began to promote soy production as a way to make up for dietary deficits among Allied troops in Europe. It was this project, feeding soy to soldiers, that made the US the world's largest soy producer and exporter, surpassing Manchuria, which had led the way to that point (Shurtleff and Aoyagi, *History of Soybeans and Soyfoods*).

7. Ciancio, *La soja y el problema alimentario*, 26.


## CHAPTER ONE. THE ACCIDENTAL MONOCROP

1. See Mora and Cooney, *Paraguay and the United States*. The abbreviation STICA stands for Servicio Técnico de Investigación Científica y Agrícola.

2. Also, 1943 was the year that the International Maize and Wheat Improvement Centre (CIMMYT) was built in Mexico, the flagship of what would later be called the Consultative Group on International Agricultural Research, or CGIAR.

3. The cotton program was also matched by a program in tobacco production aimed at the same small producers. For the sake of simplicity in this book, I'm only following cotton, which was the more successful of the two.

4. On the close diplomatic relations of Paraguay and the United States between 1954 (the year Stroessner took power, with tacit US support) and 1976, see Mora and Cooney, *Paraguay and the United States*. During this first phase of the dictatorship, the United States sent Paraguay unprecedented levels of military aid as well as technical support in agriculture.

5. Alarcón López, *El cultivo del trigo en el Paraguay*.

6. Latin American agronomists use the English word "farmer" to describe this style of agriculture.

7. Borlaug is a legend in agronomy circles, not only for his invention of high-yield wheat, but for heading the Latin American side of the Green Revolution from 1944 onward and mentoring thousands of students at CIMMYT in Mexico.

8. To put this in perspective, the deal promised the Soviet Union close to one quarter of the US's entire wheat crop. For an overview of the crucial realignment in agrarian commodities markets in 1972, see Friedman, "The Political Economy of Food"; Eckstein and Heien, "The 1973 Food Price Inflation."

9. Between subsidies given to American farmers to meet the increased demand, and skyrocketing prices, the greatest winner in all of this was American agriculture, which has maintained its global market dominance since then (McMichael, "Tensions between National and International Control").

10. Warnken, *The Development and Growth of the Soybean Industry*; Freire and Teixeira, "Soybeans and Soyfoods in Brazil," 236.

11. It's hard to get reliable figures for specific crops during this period. However, the agrarian census of 1981 reported that soybean territorial coverage went from 81,000 hectares in 1972 to 568,000 hectares in 1982. See Weisskoff, "The Paraguayan Agro-Export Model."

12. Weisskoff, "The Paraguayan Agro-Export Model."

13. Figure is extrapolated from Baer and Birch, "Expansion of the Economic Frontier." The same table lists soy exports at 0 percent in 1970.

14. Yerba mate (pronounced *mátay*) is a tea native to Paraguay that was once a significant export and is now consumed daily by almost all Paraguayans from a shared gourd as one of the country's primary social activities. Paraguayans also drink it cold as *terere*. It is sometimes written in English as maté, but I find this spelling distracting for those who know the drink and use the Spanish throughout this book.

15. Argentina is the best-known case, recruiting over five million European migrants between 1880 and 1920. By contrast, Paraguay only welcomed about twenty thousand immigrants in this period. Souchaud, *Pionniers brésiliens au Paraguay*, 64.

16. There are now many such colonies throughout eastern Paraguay. Colonias Unidas remains the oldest and largest.

17. To this day, the department of Itapúa, especially in the south, remains a landscape of mixed, medium-sized farms with diverse production.

18. See chapter 11 for a fuller account of the conditions for this opening.

19. Souchaud, *Pionniers brésiliens au Paraguay*.

20. The term "Brasiguaio" is often used pejoratively on both sides of the border (see Wagner, *Brasiguaios*). It does, however, mark a very clear identity category, and is just as often used by Brasiguaios themselves. Out of deference to them, I use the Portuguese spelling rather than the more common Spanish Brasiguayo.

21. I made three visits to soy research stations, agricultural fairs, and individual soy farms between 2010 and 2016, and I heard versions of this story a lot. It is also a common theme of cultural memorializing around the city of Santa Rita.

22. Census figures taken from Souchaud, *Pionniers brésiliens au Paraguay*, 131.

23. The modest ethnographic literature on this period corroborates this entirely. See Souchaud, *Pionniers brésiliens au Paraguay*; Wagner, *Brasiguaios*; Blanc, "Enclaves of Inequality."

24. Richards, "Soy, Cotton and the Final Atlantic Forest Frontier." As we'll see in later sections of the book, the national deforestation numbers are due not only to soy but also to cotton.

25. The severity of erosion made Paraguay into one of the world leaders in no-till planting. See Pieri et al., *No-Till Farming for Sustainable Rural Development*.

26. For instance, they began double planting, with farmers harvesting two crops of soybeans per year, with a short rotation of wheat or fallow in between. Increased rotations and an extended growing season increased pest pressure, and therefore the dependence on chemical pesticides, and so on.

27. Besky, "Exhaustion and Endurance in Sick Landscapes."

28. Smallholder cotton farming also presented more serious toxicological health risks, meaning that most international reports on pesticide use focused on that sector (see Dinham, *The Pesticide Hazard*).

29. Roundup Ready soy was first commercially available in the US in 1996 but did not reach Paraguay by way of Argentina until 1999.


## CHAPTER TWO. KILLER SOY

1. For a full recounting, see Viveros, "La guerra de una madre."

2. For reasons that we'll encounter in chapter 13, these claims were not backed up by official statistics, and few pesticide incidents were registered in the national health system. But the prevalence of the claim itself is an indicator of a moral indictment of the soy boom that was already well in place by 2003. By 2006, one NGO in Asunción, BASE Investigacio-

nes Sociales (BASE IS), was more systematically recording incidents like this as part of a larger campaign against agrotoxins (see Ayala, Gómez Hansen, and Palau, *Informe de la sociedad civil*).

3. The formulation "matters of concern" is from Latour, who uses it to differentiate from "matters of fact" that are settled (see Latour, "Why Has Critique Run Out of Steam?"). Marres, "Frontstaging Nonhumans," has been particularly helpful in thinking about how publics form around environmental matters of concern in the way that I describe here (see Hetherington, "How Can ANT Trace Slow-Moving Environmental Harms").

4. Nixon, *Slow Violence and the Environmentalism of the Poor*.

5. Auyero and Swistun, *Flammable*. This is also a basic tenet of the environmental justice and environmental racism literature (Harrison, *Pesticide Drift and the Pursuit of Environmental Justice*; Bullard, *Confronting Environmental Racism*).

6. Povinelli, *Economies of Abandonment*.

7. Povinelli, *Economies of Abandonment*, 144.

8. For narrative purposes, I have written about the trial as though only Hermann Schlender were on trial. In fact, Schlender and the second neighbor, Alfredo Lauro Laustenlager, were tried together.

9. Latour, *We Have Never Been Modern*.

10. Quoted from Tribunal de Sentencia de Encarnación, "Alfredo Lauro Laustenlager y Hermann Schlender producción de riesgos communes y homicidio culposo en Pirapey Km.35," Special Appeals Court, June 30, 2005.

11. From Tribunal de Sentencia de Encarnación, "Alfredo Lauro Laustenlager y Hermann Schlender producción de riesgos communes y homicidio culposo en Pirapey Km.35." Special Appeals Court, June 30, 2005.

12. In the environmental justice literature, this is usually called the deficit model of public knowledge (Wynne, "Knowledges in Context").

13. Viveros, "La guerra de una madre," 104. No one was ever charged in Serapio Villasboa's murder.

14. This formulation, and much of the discussion of distribution and rupture in this chapter, comes from Rancière, *Disagreement*.

15. Wagner-Pacifici, *What Is an Event?*

16. Stengers, *In Catastrophic Times*, 39.

17. Strathern, "Cutting the Network."

18. Schurman and Kelso, *Engineering Trouble*.

19. See Whatmore, *Hybrid Geographies*; Levidow and Carr, GM *Food on Trial*.

20. Stengers, *In Catastrophic Times*: 39.

21. Telesca, *Ligas agrarias cristianas*.

22. The Coordinadora Nacional de Mujeres Rurales e Indígenas (the National Organization of Rural and Indigenous Women), or CONAMURI, is a key actor in this book.

23. This group of international activists proved vital in publicizing the case and later in bringing resources to the national network. Among other things they founded a website for sharing information: www.lasojamata.net (later www.lasojamata.net.archived.website, last accessed October 6, 2019).

24. For Rancière, the emergence of a new language is a hallmark of the event. See Wagner-Pacifici, *What Is an Event?*; Papastergiadis, "A Breathing Space for Aesthetics and Politics."

25. This quote was not recorded but comes from field notes.

26. Hyperobjects, according to Morton, "inhabit a . . . causal system in which associations, correlations and probabilities are the only things we have to go on, for now. That's why it's so easy for Big Tobacco and global warming deniers: of course there is no direct proof of a causal link" (Morton, *Hyperobjects*, 39). In response, the human protagonists can't do much but try to play "catch-up with reality" (21).

## CHAPTER THREE. THE ABSENT STATE

1. In Argentina, the term "desert" has historically been used as a stand-in for *terra nullius*, the empty territory targeted for colonial conquest. In rural Paraguay, campesinos often used it the same way, to describe forests that they believed had no legitimate owner.

2. Increasingly, Expo Santa Rita is only the main stop on a full calendar of expos that work their way through eastern Paraguay.

3. Fogel and Riquelme, *Enclave sojero*. The two authors make a very strong nationalist statement in their introduction and respective chapters, but the other authors represent an interesting diversity of views, including a piece about anti-Brasiguaio racism inherent in Paraguayan nationalist rhetoric (see Albuquerque, "Campesinos Paraguayos y 'Brasiguayos'").

4. Riquelme, "Notas para el estudio de las causas y efectos de la migración," 135.

5. Many residents of Santa Rita object to this characterization, pointing out that the schools still follow the national curriculum, even if the teachers and students speak Portuguese as a first language, and that all official business at City Hall is conducted in Spanish.

6. The book spawned a long list of publications making similar claims. See Glaucer, *Extrangerización del territorio paraguayo*; Rojas, *Campesino rapé*; Rulli and Bravo, *Repúblicas unidas de la soja*; Palau et al., *Socio-Environmental Impacts*; Morínigo, *Auge de la producción rural y crisis campesina*; Doughman, *La chipa y la soja*; Cardozo et al., "Soy Expansion and the Absent State."

7. Fogel, "Efectos socioambientales del enclave sojero," 74.

8. Riquelme, "Notas para el estudio de los causas y efectos de la migración," 122.

9. Anderson, *Imagined Communities*.

10. Potthast-Jutkeit, *"Paraíso de Mohama"*; Williams, "Paraguayan Isolation under Dr. Francia."

11. Kraay and Wigham, *I Die with My Country*.

12. Huner, "How Pedro Quiñones Lost His Soul."

13. Roa Bastos, "Paraguay."

14. Because of extraordinary expropriations before the war (from the church, indigenous groups, and individual ranchers) and the death and exile of many landowners during the war, by 1870 the Paraguayan state effectively owned 98.4 percent of the national territory (Kleinpenning, *Rural Paraguay*, 119–121).

15. Pastore, *La lucha por la tierra*.

16. La Industria Paraguaya owned 2.65 million hectares, Barthes 881,000 hectares, and Matte Larangeira another 800,000 hectares (Kleinpenning, *Rural Paraguay*, 135). In the Chaco, to the west of the Paraguay River, Carlos Casado bought over five million hectares.

17. Barrett, *Lo que son los yerbales*; Kleinpenning, *Rural Paraguay*.

18. See Roa Bastos, "Una Isla Rodeada de Tierra," and Frutos, *Con el hombre y la tierra hacía el bienestar rural*. The latter formulation, of "land without people," like that of the desert, or terra nullius in other countries, was violent in its own right, a projection of emptiness onto land slated for colonization. See chapter 15.

19. The plan wasn't a new one: it had been attempted by nationalists in the 1930s but was only really successful in the 1960s, when many countries in the region were attempting something similar.

20. I am simplifying somewhat here. Throughout Paraguayan territory there were state and private colonization companies, both of which were accounted for in the Agrarian Statute of 1963. Private colonization, however, was much more prevalent in the border region (Cortéz, *Os brasiguaios*).

21. Cortéz, *Os brasiguaios*.

22. Conveniently, in Spanish and Portuguese, the words *frontera* and *fronteira* mean both "frontier" and "border."

23. Do Couto e Silva, cited in Cortéz, *Os brasiguaios*, 36–37.

24. The diplomatic resolution of this dispute sparked negotiations for creation of the gigantic binational hydro dam at Itaipú, which flooded the disputed territory, and the Treaty of Alliance and Cooperation (1975) that codified Brazilian interests in the border region (Menezes, *La herencia de Stroessner*; Folch, *Hydropolitics*).

25. Riquelme, "Notas para el estudio de las causas y efectos de la migración."

26. This racist characterization was in no way unusual but rather was an extension of discourses common in Argentina and Brazil and often internalized by Paraguayans themselves.

27. See Rulli and Bravo, *Repúblicas unidas de la soja*; Lapegna, *Soybeans and Power*.

28. As Warren Montag has argued, libertarian, anarchist, and critical theories of the state often implicitly make the state stand as death to the market's vitality (Montag, "Necro-Economics"). For a discussion of neovitalism in the soy economy, see chapter 17.

29. See Reeves, *Border Work*.

30. Anthropologists of finance and pharmaceuticals have shown how certain global industries can at times be structured entirely around arbitrage, the practice of speculating on price differences for the same product across different jurisdictions (Miyazaki, *Arbitraging Japan*; Petryna, *When Experiments Travel*).

31. C. E. Schuster, *Social Collateral*. The closer trading relationship with Brazil was, to some extent, at the expense of Argentina, who to that point was a closer partner. See Birch, "Pendulum Politics."

32. Weisskoff, "The Paraguayan Agro-Export Model."

33. Other countries would follow an analogous development strategy in the 1990s, most notoriously in the maquiladora industry along the US-Mexico border, allowing US firms to profit from cheap Mexican labor. (Paraguay would later establish its own maquiladora zone along the Brazilian border as well.)

34. Aguiar, *Stretching the Border*.

35. On how Brasiguaio life is constituted by the zone of differentiation created in the borderland, see Blanc, "Enclaves of Inequality."

36. The first description of this customs swindle occurs in Nickson, "Brazilian Colonization of the Eastern Border Region," 119. According to my interviews, the swindle was still going on until at least 2002. It did not always require the physical movement of the soybeans themselves but could be carried out simply on paper.


## CHAPTER FOUR. THE LIVING BARRIER

1. In fact, while I refer primarily to Silvia González in this section for narrative purposes, her work was coordinated through this NGO, the Centro de Estudios e Investigación de Derecho Rural y Reforma Agraria (CEIDRA). In her own retelling it is CEIDRA, and not she, that plays the hero. I gleaned most of this story from interviews with González but was later able to check them against an unpublished manuscript written by one of her colleagues (Martín Martínez, *Proceso político*) and the retellings of three soy lobbyists.

2. My previous book on Paraguay is an analysis of this cultural distance between new democrats and campesinos as it existed prior to Lugo's government (see Hetherington, *Guerrilla Auditors*).

3. Paraguay was still using several classes of organophosphates in the 1990s that had been banned in the rest of the world, and although the country had signed an agreement to harmonize pesticide regulations with its regional trading partners in the Mercosur, it remained

the only country not to have created a regulatory agency to do this. See Dinham, *The Pesticide Hazard.*

4. The Colorado Party is also a character in this drama, although we won't get to it in detail until chapter 7.

5. This is already an indication of an agribiopolitical strategy situated in an international rift between two separate agricultural regimes. One, led by the Food and Agriculture Organization, bases regulation on the Green Revolution imperatives of greater agrarian production; the other, led by groups such as Oxfam and the World Health Organization (WHO), begin from the imperative of protecting human health. See chapter 13.

6. Paraguay's proportional election system means that each party receives a number of seats proportional to the number of votes they get and fills them according to a predetermined ranked party list.

7. See Hetherington, *Guerrilla Auditors*, chapter 2.

8. See Ortega, *Cronología de denuncias de intoxicación*, 8–9.

9. Details of this text will become important later, including significant ambiguities in the first line. For the Spanish, see chapter 15.

10. December 3 marks the anniversary of the Dow Chemical explosion in Bhopal, India, and has been promoted as an action day by the International Pesticide Action Network since 1998.

11. Another political calculation influenced Cristaldo's decision to let this decree move ahead. During the election, Nicanor had promised to impose an export tax on unprocessed soybeans, something that was common in the region. Industry representatives understood in 2004 that the barrera viva was a small concession they might make in preparation for a longer fight against taxation. Nicanor failed to impose his tax, as have all four presidents who succeeded him.

12. Oscar Bogado, "Ley de plaguicidas reducirá 40% la producción agrícola," *Ultima Hora*, September 5, 2007, http://www.ultimahora.com/ley-plaguicidas-reducira-40-la-produccion -agricola-n59287.html.

13. The Partido Liberal Auténtico Radical, or PLRA, to whom I refer throughout as the Liberal Party or the Liberals.

14. This would change later, but for the first two years of his presidency SENAVE was controlled by liberal allies of the soy industry.

15. Density was an issue because farmers preferred to fulfill the barrera viva provision by planting a row of eucalyptus around their fields. This would make the barrera viva itself a profitable, low-maintenance crop, even though its evenly spaced trunks were not very effective at stopping pesticide drift.

16. Law 3742/09 did not explicitly repeal Regulatory Decree 2408/04.

1. "Nombramiento de Lovera en Senave es ilegal, aseguran," ABC *Color*, April 20, 2010, http://www.abc.com.py/edicion-impresa/economia/nombramiento-de-lovera-en -senave-es-ilegal-aseguran-92649.html; "Nombramiento de Lovera en Senave fue desa- certado, ratifican gremios," ABC *Color*, July 24, 2010, http://www.abc.com.py/edicion -impresa/economia/nombramiento-de-lovera-en---senave-fue-desacertado-ratifican -gremios-136131.html.

2. The same accusations were made of Lugo himself, although his public profile and his pastoral past shielded him from some of the more extreme and obviously disingenuous arguments.

3. Hetherington, *Guerrilla Auditors*.

4. Inter-American Development Bank, *Programa de diversificación y modernización*.

5. Paraguay had in fact signed the Codex in 1990 but was still not compliant. Comité Re- gional de Sanidad Vegetal del Cono Sur, *Estandar regional en protección fitosanitaria*.

6. See "Paraguai apresenta queixa contra Brasil," PR *Tribuna*, October 30, 2003, https:// www.tribunapr.com.br/noticias/economia/paraguai-apresenta-queixa-contra-brasil/. Ac- cording to interviews with soy farmers, even though the Paraná ban was rarely enforced, uncertainty was enough to change the incentives on the Paraguayan side of the border.

7. This was led by FECOPROD, the Federation of Production Cooperatives, which would later become one of the main components of the UGP.

8. In fact, disagreement about Monsanto royalty payments was one of the most important internal struggles in the UGP and continued until the royalty regime ended in 2013.

9. Third only to the US and China. See "Paraguay, 'Somos la mayor flota fluvial de Suda- mérica,'" January 23, 2016, Paraguay Fluvial Noticias, http://paraguayfluvial.com/paraguay -somos-la-mayor-flota-fluvial-de-sudamerica/.

10. Figures are from CAPECO, "Área de siembra, producción y rendimiento," n.d., accessed August 30, 2019, http://capeco.org.py/area-de-siembra-produccion-y-rendimiento/.

11. Bensaude-Vincent and Stengers, *A History of Chemistry*.

12. For an overview of this approach to governance, see Woolgar and Neyland, *Mundane Governance*. See also Ballestero, *A Future History of Water*; Ruppert and Law, "Devices."

13. Barad, *Meeting the Universe*.

14. Barad, *Meeting the Universe*, 337.

15. Barad, *Meeting the Universe*, 33.

16. Barad, *Meeting the Universe*, 33.

17. Barad, *Meeting the Universe*, 140.

## CHAPTER SIX. THE VAST TOFU CONSPIRACY

1. The reference comes from William Burroughs's *Naked Lunch*, a novel he famously described as "a frozen moment, when everyone sees what is at the end of every fork." Burroughs, *Naked Lunch*, 3.

2. These are only examples. Both Marco and Ale worked on two such projects, while Sofía worked on four separate projects and also accompanied me during several of my interviews and field studies.

3. There is some anachronism here as these are more current ways to describe the ISO's work. The term "technical nationalism" didn't emerge until 1969 (see Latimer, *Friendship among Equals*, 65). "Technical barriers to trade" is a term primarily associated with the World Trade Organization, which consolidated the work of the ISO in the 1980s under a set of more encompassing economic agreements.

4. FOCOSEP, *Informe final*, 7.

5. Law 2199/03 appointed the new director. The restructuring happened two years later with Law 2575/05.

6. All of this was predicated on the International Monetary Fund offering Paraguay a "standby loan" of $73 million to stabilize its currency. Despite Paraguay's continuing recession, the IMF was explicit that the loan was in anticipation of a turnaround in agricultural exports.

7. Gudynas, "Extractivismos y corrupción."

8. Bourdieu, "Rethinking the State."

9. This kind of casual, everyday bribery has its own ritual language that maintains plausible deniability for both the giver and receiver of the bribe, as the quid pro quo element of the transaction is strategically deferred in the idiom of the gift (Gupta, *Red Tape*; Smart, "The Unbearable Discretion of Street-Level Bureaucrats").

10. Melley, *Empire of Conspiracy*, 62.

11. Ricoeur, *Interpretation Theory*.

12. Marcus, *Paranoia within Reason*. The effort to reclaim conspiracy as a valuable form of political thought emerged in the 1990s as neoliberalism seemed to be dispersing authority in many political arenas (see also Stewart and Harding, "Bad Endings"; Lepselter, *Resonance of Unseen Things*).

13. The most common analytic frame used to discuss the Stroessner regime was a projection of Cold War anxieties about totalitarianism. See Hetherington, *Guerrilla Auditors*; Pietz, "The 'Post-colonialism' of Cold War Discourse."

14. Boccia Paz, González, and Palau Aguilar, *Es mi informe*.

15. Many critics of postcolonial neoliberalism have pointed to the rise of conspiracy theory to understand this moment, from sub-Saharan Africa (Comaroff and Comaroff, "Transpar-

ent Fictions") to the ex–Soviet Union (Humphrey, "Stalin and the Blue Elephant") to the US (Stewart and Harding, "Bad Endings").

16. See Mitchell, *Carbon Democracy*; Morton, *Hyperobjects*.

## PART II. AN EXPERIMENT IN GOVERNMENT

1. That event, known as Marzo Paraguayo, was a defining moment of the transition to democracy.

2. Levitsky and Roberts, *The Resurgence of the Latin American Left*.

3. This despite an earlier rift in the party that had created a breakaway movement centered on a very popular ex-general, Lino Oviedo. In the 2008 election, Oviedo, recently released from jail, came in a close third behind Lugo and Blanca Ovelar, the official Colorado candidate.

## CHAPTER SEVEN. CAPTURING THE CIVIL SERVICE

1. The political science literature that I draw on often makes a technical distinction between corruption (the use of public goods for private ends) and clientelism (the distribution of public goods for electoral ends). Like most anthropologists and Paraguayans, I favor a reading of corruption as the broad discourse of political accusation, which includes clientelism. See Smith, *A Culture of Corruption*; Gupta, "Blurred Boundaries"; Muir, "On Historical Exhaustion"; Ansell, "Clientelism, Elections, and the Dialectic of Numerical People."

2. The Liberal period was extremely tumultuous, cycling through twenty-two presidents in thirty-six years, including a brief revolutionary pause when the Febrerista Party took control in 1936–1937. See Lewis, *The Politics of Exile*.

3. For Mexico as a comparative example, see Hilgers, "Causes and Consequences of Political Clientelism"; Gutmann, *The Romance of Democracy*. For Argentina, see Stokes, "Perverse Accountability"; Auyero, *Poor People's Politics*.

4. This was by no means uniform, but it's hard for me to be precise about the practice. Bribery was difficult to collect data on, since few people would give details about their own bribe-taking practices. I relied on the anecdotes of bribe givers, two sting operations that happened during the study, and two old functionaries who told me they had taken bribes in the past but that they no longer did.

5. Setrini, "Twenty Years of Paraguayan Electoral Democracy."

6. See Nickson and Lambert, "State Reform and the 'Privatized State,'" 165.

7. Cortázar Velarde et al., *Serving Citizens*. This IADB report on civil service reform throughout Latin America reports an "index of civil service development" for 2004 that awarded Paraguay the lowest score after Honduras and El Salvador.

8. This is one of the most common forms of embezzlement in Paraguay, and the way that politically well-placed civil servants make their wealth, by receiving several salaries at once.

9. Paraguayan street-level politics very much resembles Javier Auyero's descriptions of clientelism in Buenos Aires (especially *Poor People's Politics* and *Routine Politics and Violence in Argentina*).

10. Gupta, "Blurred Boundaries."

11. Law 1626/2000, Art. 8.

12. In C. Schuster, *Clientelismo y el juego político*, 23–24.

13. Lilian Soto ran a major overhaul of civil service hiring practices under Lugo, and considered the freezer to be one of the worst violations of the rights of public workers. Under her mandate, the ministry ran a campaign called "Let's Unfreeze the Freezer," in which it sought to rehabilitate mistreated workers. She was personally appalled by my suggestion, during an interview, that freezer practices continued to be used, though less overtly, by some in Lugo's government.

14. For an excellent history of the rise of meritocracy in the US in the late nineteenth century that shows how this story not only serves as the basis for Weber's ideal-typical description of bureaucracy but also how this was imported into late twentieth-century Latin American state reforms, see Grindle, *Jobs for the Boys*.

15. See C. Schuster, *Clientelismo y el juego político*.

16. This is a pattern we can see broadly in anticorruption bureaucratic reform campaigns in countries as distinct as China, India, and Argentina, where the practices of the lower- and street-level bureaucrats are labeled as corrupt, while those of the professional classes are considered forms of social capital. See Osburg, "Making Business Personal."

17. Muir, "The Currency of Failure."

18. I've changed some of the details of this story so as not to impugn the actual people involved, who were never charged with any crimes. What is important here is not what actually happened but the climate in which people believed things to have happened.

19. Pereira's remarkable political trajectory and his ability to move between campesino organizations and technocratic ones epitomizes the double-bind of rural leaders that I explored in *Guerrilla Auditors*. There I argued that new democrats both rely on leaders like Pereira to give them a connection to the countryside and invariably treat them with suspicion for that very connection.

20. Among other things, Pereira was closely associated with a new conditional cash transfer program called Tekoporã, which, though purportedly universal in its application, was run by campesino organizations and often functioned as a clientelist tool.

21. See Pitt-Rivers, *The People of the Sierra*; Wolf, "Closed Corporate Peasant Communities"; Mintz and Wolf, "An Analysis of Ritual Co-parenthood."

22. Service and Service, *Tobatí*, 124–125.

23. Scott, "Corruption, Machine Politics and Political Change"; Powell, "Peasant Society and Clientelist Politics."

24. E.g., Germani, *Authoritarianism, Fascism, and National Populism.*

25. For this second wave of clientelism studies see particularly Auyero, *Poor People's Politics*; Abente Brun and Diamond, *Clientelism, Social Policy, and the Quality of Democracy.*


## CHAPTER EIGHT. CITIZEN PARTICIPATION

1. For a taste of what Asunción's development-induced traffic is like, see Melly, *Bottleneck.*

2. See Rama, *The Lettered City.* This was particularly true of Paraguay, whose first three dictators were all Francophiles. France itself didn't undergo a decentralizing reform until 1981.

3. Cheema and Rondinelli, *Decentralizing Governance*; Grindle, *Audacious Reforms.*

4. Van Cott, *The Friendly Liquidation of the Past.*

5. See Turner, "Paraguay as a Decentralized Unitary State."

6. Willis, Garman, and Haggard, "The Politics of Decentralization in Latin America."

7. Per diems for all Paraguayan functionaries varied by country of travel according to figures set before the crash of the Argentine peso in 2002. After 2002, per diem payments for travel to Argentina remained the same (jealously guarded by upper management), even though the actual travel costs plummeted.

8. The motivation here wasn't merely political zeal. In other technical agencies, I encountered two kinds of lab technicians: those whose experiments ended or died when the necessary equipment or inputs didn't show up in time, and those who would pay out of pocket to keep the lights on or to buy the growing medium necessary to keep an experiment going. The latter group were often younger, or at least more recently hired, and described their peers as having been worn down by the system.


## CHAPTER NINE. REGULATION BY DENUNCIATION

1. Marijuana production was on the rise at the time in Paraguay's northeast and has since become a far larger and more complicated industry that includes both small farmers and large plantations with near-slavery conditions. In some places there are clear overlaps between the oligarchs running the soy industry and those involved in the production and smuggling of marijuana, but in other places they are at odds, as marijuana production favors keeping some forest intact (to hide the produce).

2. Sofía Espíndola accompanied me on three follow-up visits as well.

3. The Guarani word used to describe colonization in the forest is *kuty* (cut).

4. See Guereña and Rojas Villagra, *Yvy jára*.

5. For a longer discussion of agrarian labor, see chapter 17.

6. This portion of her speech was often interrupted for clarification. The congressional hijinks around the approval of law 3407/09 had been discussed by campesino organizations over the previous year, and many leaders felt confused about what law was now in effect.

7. Biehl and Petryna, "Bodies of Rights."

8. Gilles Deleuze, from "O Abecedário de Gilles Deleuze," cited in Biehl and Petryna, "Bodies of Rights," 360.

9. Biehl and Petryna, "Bodies of Rights," 372.

10. The invocation of *realidad* is a common idiom on the Paraguayan left dating back to the Ligas Agrarias of the 1960s, which explicitly used the radical pedagogy of Paolo Freire to foment social change (Freire, *The Pedagogy of the Oppressed*). Since then, a common critique of the legal system is its failure to fully articulate this reality (Hetherington, *Guerrilla Auditors*).

11. As in so many colonial contexts, the image of the tribe and chief was largely an administrative fiction established by the INDI itself, and most of the communities I've visited have deeply divided power structures with different kinds of authority being vested in different people or factions. Although it went by different names, campesino authority was similarly divided between factions, even though activists in Asunción often talked about particular leaders as being "representatives of their community."

12. Only a registered inspector could sign them, and, technically, only these inspectors had permission to enter the farms at all. This was an underlying tension created by the unit model, in which inspectors often felt they were being used for their badge.

13. However, SENAVE did have the ability to call in prosecutors for the kinds of violations that amounted to criminal activities, including criminal acts against the environment. This is how the Rubén Portillo case, explored in chapter 10, moved forward.

14. I take the term "rendering technical" from Li, *The Will to Improve*.

15. And of course it didn't. When I returned a year later with Sofía, those who were present that day said there had never been any follow-up that they knew of. Someone had come, but they thought it was SEAM rather than SENAVE; no one was quite sure.

16. In previous work, I've called activists like him "guerrilla auditors" for the expertise they develop in bureaucratic documentation. See Hetherington, *Guerrilla Auditors*.


## CHAPTER TEN. CITATION, SAMPLE, AND PARALLEL STATES

1. This wouldn't be the last time I would see water collected in Fortín bottles, which often end up along the sides of roads and near fishing holes.

2. Kockelman, "Biosemiosis, Technocognition, and Sociogenesis."

3. See "Paraguay quintuplicó su importación de agrotóxicos en los últimos cuatro años," *E'a*, February 17, 2015, http://ea.com.py/v2/paraguay-quintuplico-su-importacion-de -agrotoxicos-en-los-ultimos-cuatro-anos/. A caveat is in order here. Although widely reported, as with most numbers in this book, these are affected by very variable reporting rates. In this case, the total volume increase was likely somewhat lower, while the percentage of imports officially reported likely rose.

4. I use oranges as my example here because on my two visits to SENAVE border inspectors, these were the most conspicuous samples being taken, and the practice of taking them home was a matter of some grumbling by other staff.

5. Latour, *The Making of Law*, 234.

6. On a the difference between legal judgments and scientific facts, see Latour, *The Making of Law*.

7. Portillo was the only one who died in the incident. For a fuller recounting, see "Recuento sobre las intoxicaciones en la colonia Yerutí," Base Investigaciones Sociales, March 17, 2011, http://www.baseis.org.py/base/leermas.php?noticia=332.

8. For more on the reporting system, see chapter 13. Calling in the case was quite unusual, and this doctor felt she received professional backlash from her superiors at the hospital.

9. "La ONU acusa a Paraguay de violar derechos humanos por el uso de agroquímicos." *El País*, August 16, 2019. https://radioatalaya.net/la-onu-acusa-a-paraguay-de-violar-derechos -humanos-por-el-uso-de-agroquimicos/.

10. The same was true of aldrin, a pesticide widely used to kill termites in cotton fields until 1993, when it was banned.

11. See Mopas, "Examining the CSI Effect through an ANT lens."

12. This case did have an afterlife, though, including a 2019 finding by the United Nations that the Paraguayan state's handling of it amounted to a violation of human rights. See the conclusion.


## CHAPTER ELEVEN. MEASUREMENT AS TACTICAL SOVEREIGNTY

1. Barad, *Meeting the Universe Halfway*.

2. Much of this discussion was previously published in two articles about the temporality of surveying (Hetherington, "Waiting for the Surveyor"; Hetherington, "Surveying the Future Perfect").

3. In fact, the same was true of property titles. As I've written elsewhere, after many years of demanding property titles from the IBR, several campesino organizations began to see those titles as a trap, inviting campesinos to mortgage their land. The instrument meant to secure land tenure, in other words, was often the instrument through which it was taken away (Hetherington, *Guerrilla Auditors*). But this didn't make the act of struggling for

property titles any less potent, as it was the idiom through which campesino activists engaged with bureaucrats.

4. Here the clipboard and the regulatory package in which it participates act as what Ballestero (*A Future History of Water*) calls a "regulatory device," an assemblage that enacts an ontological bifurcation between a simple road and a camino vicinal around which certain rights and responsibilities accrue.

5. I did not have the recorder on for this interchange, and I make no claim that I got the words right. But the spirit of the argument is right; this was only the first iteration of an argument I heard many times.

6. For a refresher on these legislative shenanigans, go back to chapter 3. The original Spanish of this much-debated error in Decree 2408/04 reads as follows: "En casos de cultivos colindantes a caminos vecinales, poblados objeto de aplicación de plaguicidas, se deberá contar con barreras vivas de protección a fin de evitar posibles contaminaciones, por deriva a terceros."

7. A year and many iterations of this argument later, Miguel Lovera would try to resolve it for good by issuing an executive resolution. "Caminos vecinales" would henceforth mean "a road that has people living on at least one of its sides or that habitually communicates one community with another, or one house with another, or one community with a road, or with an educational center, health center, temple, plaza or place of public gathering" (Resolución SENAVE 660/2011). This resolution was thrown out after the coup six months later, and inspectors went back to using the original text, including the ambiguous comma.

8. Das, "The Signature of the State," 234.

9. Asad, "Where Are the Margins of the State?," 287.

10. Hansen and Stepputat, *States of Imagination*, 301. This is in stark contrast to the bureaucratic ideal type laid out by Max Weber ("Bureaucracy"), in which the person of the bureaucrat disappears behind the function of his or her position and the caricature of indifference.

11. The ironies of the "heart of steel" would later be picked up by Stroessner's critics, but it was an effective corporeal mythology for his supporters.

12. Castro handed over the presidency of Cuba to his brother Raúl in February 2008, and Raúl oversaw an opening of the economy and a rapprochement with the US.

13. Kirchner died in October 2010. In June 2011, Chávez underwent an operation for colon cancer, and he died two years later. Lula da Silva's cancer diagnosis was announced in October 2011, in time to undergo treatment alongside Lugo in the same São Paolo hospital.

14. For the official story, see Andrés Colmán Gutiérrez, "Guerrilleros o terroristas: La historia de cómo nació el EPP," *Última Hora*, August 21, 2013, http://www.ultimahora.com /guerrilleros-o-terroristas-la-historia-como-nacio-el-epp-n715259.html. See Pereira, *El EPP*, for the theory that the EPP was invented. Although this thesis was popular during the first years of Lugo's government, most people later accepted that a small band of guerrillas had indeed formed in northern Caaguazú, Canindeyú, and especially the forests of Concepción.

1. Law 2532/2005, De Seguridad Fronteriza, regulated by presidential decree 7525/11.

2. As we saw in chapter 3, restrictions on the sale of land to Brazilian nationals had been removed by Stroessner to spur agricultural colonization of the border region and ease military tensions with Brazil.

3. The widely repeated story appeared first in *Última Hora*. See "Los productores advierten de una guerra civil en el campo," *Última Hora*, January 26, 2012, http://www.ultimahora .com/los-productores-advierten-una-guerra-civil-el-campo-n498626.html.

4. Lugo's office denied responsibility for the actual deployment of surveyors.

5. After four years in hiding, Cartes had returned after the 1989 coup to fight the charges. They were eventually overturned almost twenty-three years later, shortly before he announced his candidacy for president. Around the same time, WikiLeaks published documents showing that the CIA was still watching Cartes for connection to money laundering and drug trafficking. For an even-handed assessment of these various crimes and allegations, see "¿Quién es Horacio Cartes?," *ABC Color*, April 17, 2013, http://www.abc.com.py /especiales/paraguay-elige/quien-es-horacio-cartes-561729.html.

6. The Sindicato de Trabajadores de SENAVE, or SINTRASENAVE, the largest nontechnical union in the institution, operating primarily in the administrative section.

7. Marcos R. Velázquez, "Lovera barre a denunciantes de corrupción en el Senave," *ABC Color*, August 24, 2011, http://www.abc.com.py/edicion-impresa/economia/lovera-barre -a-denunciantes-de-corrupcion-en-el-senave-299500.html.

8. This is exactly what happened. Lugo and Perreira led Tekojoja into the next election with a new coalition called Frente Guazú, while most urban members formed a new group called Alianza Para el Progreso.

9. Resolución del SENAVE No. 660/11.

10. This was an application of Mercosur-wide phytosanitary guidelines meant to prevent the spread of soil diseases.

11. Three years after Lovera first tried to impose it, the soy moratorium was institutionalized and respected by all farmers in Paraguay, but that couldn't happen while Lovera was in charge.

12. "That bitch Perla" (*la perra Perla*) referred to Perla Alvarez, then head of CONAMURI and one of the key brokers between the rural organization and urban Luguistas.

13. "Presentan 12 argumentos para destituir a Lovera," *ABC Color*, June 8, 2012, http://www .abc.com.py/edicion-impresa/economia/presentan-12-argumentos-para--destituir-a- -lovera-411495.html.

14. See Que paso en Curuguaty, accessed February 12, 2020, http://quepasoencuruguaty. org. For another popular retelling, see Benegas, *La masacre de Curuguaty*.

15. CODEHUPY, *Informe Chokokue*.

16. Paraguay's original land registry was a single book, a declaration of assets by all of the country's major landholders, who declared their holdings after the war. Finca 30, or "farm 30," therefore refers to the thirtieth ranch to be registered in the postwar period.

17. Riquelme was a rich financier and one of Stroessner's longest-lasting cronies. His empire included supermarkets, food processors, glass factories, and banks, but, like most businesses of its scale, it was anchored in political connections and land ownership: massive ranches in Canindeyú and Alto Paraná.

18. CODEHUPY, *Informe Chokokue*, 51.

19. "Usucaption" is the legal name for a claim to property based on long-term use. Because of its centrality to the Marina Kue massacre, the term became well known in Paraguay.

20. The generous reading is that Filizzola believed the camp had been infiltrated by EPP, a suspicion that appears to have been completely unfounded.

21. Dante Leguizamón Morra and Hugo Valiente, "Por qué la acusación en el caso Marina Kue no puede garantizar un juicio justo," Qué pasó en Curuguaty, July 17, 2013, http://quepasoencuruguaty.org/opiniones/por-que-la-acusacion-en-el-caso-marina-kue-no-puede-garantizar-un-juicio-justo/.

22. Primarily the groups affiliated with Via Campesina, including the Mesa Coordinadora Nacional de Organiaciones Campesinas, CONAMURI, Organización Lucha por la Tierra, and the Movimiento Agrario Popular.

23. Ezquerro-Cañete and Fogel, "A Coup Foretold."

24. A large group of campesinos were tried, and four of them spent almost six years in jail before they were finally acquitted in 2018.

25. CODEHUPY, *Informe Chokokue*.

26. See "Policías custodian fumigación de sojales en zona vecinal de Canindeyú," *Última Hora*, December 3, 2013, http://www.ultimahora.com/policias-custodian-fumigacion-sojales-zona-vecinal-canindeyu-n746273.html; Jairo Marcos, "Paraguay, donde la tierra siembra desposesión y muerte," *Periodismo Humano*, accessed May 10, 2019, http://periodismohumano.com/temas-destacados/paraguay-donde-la-tierra-siembra-desposesion-y-muerte.html.

27. For a broad comparison of contexts, see Pitts et al., "21st Century Golpismo." In Brazil as well as in Argentina, Paraguay is often the butt of racist jokes, and the qualifier "Paraguayan" connotes something fake, corrupt, or backward. Although Paraguayans didn't invent it, as with the left turn, the subsequent right turn in Honduras, Paraguay, Argentina, Brazil, Venezuela and Bolivia all shared similarities, especially an oligarchy in charge of the media that opportunistically found ways to amplify corruption charges against sitting presidents. Only in Argentina did this work as an electoral strategy; in the other four countries something between a coup and an impeachment removed the left from power. Of these countries, only in Venezuela did the Left manage to hold tenuously to power.

28. She was not alone in seeing it this way, however. See especially Idilio Méndez Grimaldi's recounting of events in "Monsanto golpea en Paraguay: Los muertos de Curuguaty y el juicio político a Lugo," *Otramérica*, June 23, 2012, http://otramerica.com/radar/monsanto

-golpea-en-paraguay-los-muertos-de-curuguaty-y-el-juicio-politico-a-lugo/2082; as well as that of Atilio Borón, "¿Por qué derrocaron a Lugo?," *Aporrea*, June 23, 2012, https://www .aporrea.org/internacionales/a145567.html.

## PART III. AGRIBIOPOLITICS

1. White, *Breaking Silence*.

2. Stroessner had a great many godchildren, since asking men like him to be your child's *padrino* was common currency for cementing patrón-client relationships. Nonetheless, Filártiga's childhood stories about Stroessner give a sense of the intimacy between their families even before Stroessner became president.

3. Folidol is the trade name for ethyl parathion, an acutely toxic insecticide whose use is now restricted in most countries, including Paraguay.

4. March 1976 was a period of acute repression regionally following a military coup in Argentina.

5. White, *Breaking Silence*.

6. *One Man's War*, an HBO film about Filártiga's life, was released in 1991, the same year as *Silence of the Lambs*, which made Hopkins a major celebrity.

7. See White, *Breaking Silence*, 27–28.

8. See also Lang and Heasman, *Food Wars*; Cullather, *The Hungry World*.

9. Filártiga's agribiopolitical theories deserve their own study, one that would take us deep into some of the woolly contradictions of the Paraguayan left. For instance, in our interview he blamed soybeans for what he saw as an epidemic of homosexuality in the country and took personal credit for having warned the president of Bolivia, Evo Morales, about this problem. (In 2010, Morales gave the inaugural speech at the Americas Social Forum in Asunción in which he made similar comments. Together, both Filártiga and Morales recall a virulent strain of homophobia among Latin America's leftist cold warriors and among Paraguayan nationalists generally.) But I leave that tangent for others to explore, since I think it was less consequential for the Government of Beans itself. See "Evo culpa a los transgénicos de la homosexualidad y la calvicie," Paraguay.com, April 20, 2010, http://www.paraguay.com/newsletter /evo-culpa-a-los-transgenicos-de-la-homosexualidad-y-la-calvicie-20991/pagina/2.

## CHAPTER THIRTEEN. PLANT HEALTH AND HUMAN HEALTH

1. These would be followed by an unrelated set of scandals about corruption, abuse of power, and sexual assault that turned the university upside down.

2. The paper is not on the public record, but in interviews Insfrán refers to it as "Las enfermedades hematológicas y los transgénicos." The study compared cases of

these blood diseases as reported in several hospitals in the country to similar data from 1988.

3. There is no scientific consensus that suggests that GMOs themselves cause cancer except to the extent that they increase the use of pesticides. On the link between organophosphate-based insecticides and non-Hodgkin's lymphoma, see Dreiher and Kordysh, "Non-Hodgkin Lymphoma and Pesticide Exposure." On Roundup, see Zhang et al., "Exposure to Glyphosate-Based Herbicides and Risk for Non-Hodgkin Lymphoma."

4. Rachel Carson remains the best-known representative of this archetype. In soy politics, it is Dr. Andrés Carrasco, the Argentine molecular biologist known for his crusade against glyphosate, who was pilloried in Argentina. Both Carson and Carrasco died early of cancer.

5. Graciela Vizcay Gómez, "Piden sancionar a médico paraguayo que probó el daño de los agrotóxicos," Rebelión, February 4, 2015, http://www.rebelion.org/noticia.php?id=195057.

6. The symposium, held on September 25 and 26, was called "Controversia científica: Transgénicos, plaguicidas y salud humana." It assembled thinkers and activists from as far away as Norway in a who's who of anti-GMO science. The conference opened with a eulogy to Andrés Carrasco, delivered by Joel Filártiga.

7. The interview was published without an author as "Entrevista con Dr. José Luis Insfrán," in an environmental periodical, *Green Tour Magazine* in 2015. The publication had no volume or issue numbers. And though Insfrán gave us a hard copy of the magazine, that issue no longer appears on the magazine's website, www.greentourmagazine.com.

8. In 2015, fully 37 percent of CONACYT's funding went to agriculture, while health sciences only received 22 percent of funding. Figures from Portillo, *Agronegocios y la facultad de ciencias agrarias de la UNA*, 107. In 2019, the soy lobby won a further victory when Eduardo Felippo became head of CONACYT. Felippo had previously been an industrial lobbyist and had no scientific training. He promised to run the institution "like a company," so that all science conducted in the country would lead to direct financial benefit. See "Estudiantes exigen salida de Felippo del Conacyt," *ABC Color*, December 26, 2019, https://www.abc.com.py/edicion-impresa/locales/2019/12/27/estudiantes-exigen-salida-de-felippo-del-conacyt/.

9. "Piden datos de pesquisa del uso de agroquímicos," *Agrositio*, March 24, 2019, https://www.agrositio.com.ar/noticia/202883-piden-datos-de-pesquisa-del-uso-de-agroquimicos.

10. "Estadísticas—2010," Ministerio de Salud Publica y Bienestar Social, Centro Nacional de Toxicologia, internal document provided by Vigilancia staff.

11. These problems emerged in many interviews with local health clinic staff.

12. Given its famed anticommunism, it's ironic that Paraguay is one of the countries that most benefited from Cuban medical expertise throughout the second half of the twentieth century. See Huish and Kirk, "Cuban Medical Internationalism."

13. Many people are also critical of this approach for being patronizing to rural women, intrusive on domestic space, and tangential to the treatment of serious illness that most people wished the state were more forthcoming in providing. But overall, the increase in health resources in rural areas was welcomed by everyone I spoke to.

14. Although the protocol and the office existed prior to 2010, it was under Martínez that the office expanded and the protocol reformed to explicitly include pesticide poisoning.

15. This was a standard way to deal with workplace safety cases, just as it was for fatal car accidents involving wealthy drivers.

16. For reasons covered in chapter 9, I'm skeptical that the tests for agrochemicals were actually carried out, and I haven't been able to find corroboration. But this is a moot point, since I am also skeptical that, had they been carried out, the tests would have found traces of pesticides in wells that were far from the fields. By contrast, detecting E. coli in water is very straightforward.

17. In Argentina, the resource in question was also soy; in Brazil and Venezuela it was oil, in Bolivia natural gas, and in Ecuador it was oil and mining. See especially Gudynas, "Extractivismos y corrupción"; Svampa and Vialle, *Maldesarrollo*.

18. Cueto, *Missionaries of Science*.

19. This characterization of Foucauldian biopolitics is from Sunder Rajan, *Biocapital*, 12.

20. Foucault, *Society Must Be Defended*, 247.

21. This expanded version was often called "integrated land reform," a project that began with redistribution but then tried to inscribe state institutions and welfare services in the new communities created by this redistribution.

22. Foucault, *The Birth of Biopolitics*, chapter 1.

23. Miller, *Mastering the Market*; Kaplan, *Provisioning Paris*.

24. Brooke and Otter, "Concluding Remarks," 285.

25. Ebbels, *Principles of Plant Health and Quarantine*, 9.

26. Harwood, *Europe's Green Revolution and Its Successors*.

27. The classic statement is Latour's *We Have Never Been Modern*, which critiqued European epistemology as a vestige of the Enlightenment. The agribiopolitical story doesn't refute that one but does suggest more nuance in relation to state-led agriculture.

28. Esposito, *Bíos*, 16. In particular, Esposito refers to Rudolph Kjellen as the first person to employ the term "biopolitics" in his book *The State as a Form of Life* (1927).

29. Saraiva, *Fascist Pigs*.

30. See Moore, *Capitalism in the Web of Life*.

31. Saraiva, *Fascist Pigs*, 12. The figure of "bare life" is perhaps the most extreme version of this, where the figure of the biological human signifies the outside of the social (see Agamben, *Homo Sacer*).

32. On multispecies ethnography, see especially Haraway, *When Species Meet*; Kirksey and Helmreich, "The Emergence of Multispecies Ethnography"; Tsing, *The Mushroom at the End of the World*. For comparable moves in the history of science, see Saraiva, *Fascist Pigs*; Murphy, *The Economization of Life*.

1. Among these are the country's largest conservation organization, the National Library of Agriculture, and a museum preserving his home along with 199 hectares of trees in the heart of soy country.

2. The great exceptions to this are Danilo Baratti and Patrizia Candolfi, Swiss historians on whose work I have leaned heavily in this chapter. See Baratti and Candolfi, *Vida y obra del sabio Bertoni*.

3. Quoted by Herbert Baldus (1954) in Baratti and Candolfi, *Vida y obra del sabio Bertoni*, 153. A similar quote appears in Chase-Sardi, *El derecho consuetudinario indígena*, 95.

4. One important exception to this is Bertoni's taxonomic descriptions of plants, and his name appears in the history, for instance, of yerba mate and stevia (*Stevia Rebaudiana* [Bertoni]), both native to Paraguay.

5. By the end of the war, adult women also outnumbered men by a ratio of 2:1. There is a large debate among historians about the actual figures here. See Whigham and Potthast, "The Paraguayan Rosetta Stone"; Kleinpenning, "Strong Reservations."

6. Gómez Florentín, *El Paraguay de la post guerra*, 17.

7. Kleinpenning, *Rural Paraguay*.

8. For an overview of this period, see Gómez Florentín, *El Paraguay de la post guerra*.

9. Cecilio Báez was the most well-known proponent of this view, and frequent intellectual antagonist to Bertoni. Báez, who served as president in 1905–1906, was only one in a long line of urban elites who believed that racial cretinism was what made Paraguayans vulnerable to dictatorship and war (see Rivarola, *Obreros, utopias y revoluciones*, 156).

10. The formal rural economy over those decades was centered on the *yerbal* system for collecting and drying the leaves of semiwild yerba mate. Yerbales were European-owned firms that controlled millions of hectares of yerba-rich forest, which was harvested by indentured laborers. See Barrett, *Lo que son los yerbales*.

11. Bertoni began lecturing on the topic as early as 1909, but the books, totaling 1,289 pages, were published between 1922 and 1927. See Baratti, "Moisés Santiago Bertoni y la generación nacionalista-indigenista paraguaya."

12. His vision of the Guarani's cultural virtues closely mirrored the Tolstoyan patriarchal ideology with which he had built Puerto Bertoni. Perhaps the best indication of the way he projected his own utopian desires onto racial characteristics is his later argument that his study of skull shapes suggested that the Guarani somehow got their superior brain size from "Alpine Man," the race proper to Switzerland. See Bertoni, *Resúmen de prehistoria y protohistoria de los países guaraníes*.

13. A few years later, Manuel Domínguez, an admirer of Bertoni's, would call this valor "the soul of the race." Many other young scholars of this generation were deeply impressed by

Bertoni's vision, including Justo Benítez and Efraím Cardozo, who would go on to write the official history of the nation in the 1930s and 1940s. See Baratti, "Moisés Santiago Bertoni."

14. Mestizaje was a racist mirror of eugenics, in that it promoted assimilation to rather than purification of a national genetic ideal. If purist eugenics dominated Southern Cone politics, mestizaje was much more common in Mexico and Andean countries.

15. See Vasconcelos *La raza cósmica*. Baratti and Candolfi suggest that Vasconcelos was influenced directly by Bertoni (*Vida y obra del sabio Bertoni*, 164–166).

16. On eugenics and horse breeding, see Stokes, *The Right to Be Well Born*. On hybrid corn and race, see Hartigan, "Mexican Genomics and the Roots of Racial Thinking."

17. Chesterton, *The Chaco War*, 10.

18. The fact that the war was conducted in Guarani (rather than Spanish) to confuse Bolivian troops is a cornerstone of Paraguayan nationalist history.

19. Chesterton, *The Grandchildren of Solano López*.

20. As Baratti and Candolfi put it, Bertoni's theories came to be understood as a form of "inverted Nazism," which lauded racial mixing over purity but to similar fascist ends (*Vida y obra del sabio Bertoni*, 154).

21. Its special status as a refuge for fascists lasted well into the 1990s, when a small but important contingent of white South Africans arrived, following the end of apartheid.

22. Grosz, *The Nick of Time*. I'm glossing over centuries of terminological and metaphysical arguments here, and Bergson refused the term "vitalism" altogether. In Driesch, vital force was called "entelechy" and was thought of as an organizing principle. In Bergson, élan vital accounted for the passage of time, whereas in Nietzsche it is will to power that usually holds this position.

23. Jones, *The Racial Discourses of Life Philosophy*.

24. Stauffer, "Haeckel, Darwin and Ecology."

25. In fact, Bertoni's first move away from mechanism was toward a kind of scientific spiritualism, which he only called vitalism many years later.

26. Bertoni, "La Vida," 139.

27. Canguilhem, *Knowledge of Life*.

28. Martínez Cuevas, *Los eslabones del oro blanco*.

29. Bertoni, *El algodón y el algodonero*, 6.

30. On Nietzsche's (mis)reading of Darwin, see Grosz, *The Nick of Time*; Pearson, *Germinal Life*.

31. I take much of my reading of the relationship between Nietzsche and Förster from Ben MacIntyre's excellent book on Elisabeth Förster, *Forgotten Fatherland*. To be clear, Bertoni and Förster didn't know each other directly, and Förster's New Germany was defunct by 1889, long before Bertoni became a national figure.

32. For detailed quotations from these letters, see MacIntyre, *Forgotten Fatherland*.

33. Hence Nietzsche's affirmative view of life contains the seeds of a far more destructive view. See Esposito, *Bíos*; Wolfe, *Before the Law*.

34. Esposito, *Bíos*.

35. Esposito, *Bios*, 106.

36. MacIntyre, in *Forgotten Fatherland*, is not as convinced as Nietzsche was that Bernhard was the intellectual mastermind behind the New Germany experiment. Elisabeth seems to have been both smarter and more determined than her husband and promoted this vision for fifty years after his death.

37. Bertoni, "La Vida," 145.

38. Saraiva, *Fascist Pigs*.

39. One sign of Moisés's restless political sensibilities is evident in the fact that all of his thirteen children were named after Swiss national heroes, great scientists, or Russian anarchists. Guillermo Tell, his first son, was also one of Paraguay's leading scientists at the time. He and his father had a falling out in the early 1910s, with the son coming to despise his father's megalomania and isolationism. In 1915, Guillermo became involved in national politics, a move that clearly upset his father. See Baratti and Candolfi, *Vida y obra del sabio Bertoni*, 91.

40. Lewis, *The Politics of Exile*.

41. Pastore, *La lucha por la tierra*.

42. Baratti and Candolfi, *Vida y obra del sabio Bertoni*.

43. Lipman, "Vitalism and Reductionism in Liebig's Physiological Thought."

44. See de Gregori, "Muck and Magic or Change and Progress."

45. Deleuze is the most obvious boundary thinker here, since he makes explicit his debt to prewar vitalism while strictly refusing any ontological distinction between the organic and the nonorganic. See Bennett, *Vibrant Matter*.

46. For this somewhat controversial reading, see Deleuze, *Foucault*.


## CHAPTER FIFTEEN. COTTON, WELFARE, AND GENOCIDE

1. Cullather, *The Hungry World*, 10.

2. Mora and Cooney, in *Paraguay and the United States*, claim that the US had been lobbying for this since 1941, but were unable to concretize the deal until 1943, once the tide seemed to be turning against Germany in the war. The grant was very generous by contemporary standards, and would set the tone for Cold War development in the years to come as American geopolitical concerns moved from fighting fascism to fighting communism.

3. See Russell, *War and Nature*.

4. Alarcón López, *El cultivo del trigo en el Paraguay*. The story of wheat self-sufficiency often came up in interviews with scientists as the signature achievement of Paraguayan agronomy.

5. Paraguay was far from the only country to use cotton for national development in this period, and the woes that would later befall the crop also affected other countries. See Murray, *Cultivating Crisis*.

6. This is so not because cotton was the most important economic product (though it was one of them) but rather because it was so key in enrolling campesinos into the dictatorship's state project.

7. Weisskoff, "The Paraguayan Agroexport Model." Again, this was not only due to cotton, but also included the beginnings of the soy crop and the construction of the Itaipú dam.

8. Hetherington, "Privatizing the Private."

9. Gudeman, *The Anthropology of Economy*.

10. See Pollan, *The Botany of Desire*.

11. On the flourishing of companion species, see Haraway, *When Species Meet*.

12. Tsing, "A Threat to Holocene Resurgence," 52.

13. See "Semillas de algodón en Paraguay," *ABC Color*, January 18, 2006, http://www.abc.com.py/edicion-impresa/suplementos/abc-rural/semillas-de-algodon-en-paraguay-881034.html.

14. On how to see evolution as an accumulation of deaths, see Kohn, *How Forests Think*.

15. Pavetti and Saito, "Changes in Land Use and Ecosystem Services."

16. Thiele, "The Dynamics of Farm Development in the Amazon."

17. As part of the construction of the Itaipú dam, Paraguay built a national steel plant, ACEPAR, that consumed millions of tons of charcoal. When Paraguay began restricting and later banned the sale of exotic hardwoods, they just went in the ovens as well.

18. Richards, "Soy, Cotton and the Final Atlantic Forest Frontier." Over the next decade, as soy took over, this was reduced again to 9,000 square kilometers.

19. The 1992 Rio Earth Summit was a watershed in international environmental organizing that laid the groundwork for the meetings on greenhouse gas reductions first established in Kyoto in 1997.

20. These appeared over the course of the year in *ABC Color*'s weekly "Rural" supplement and *Última Hora*'s "Correo Rural."

21. The Aché were not the only indigenous group to be pushed to the brink of annihilation by cotton, and later soy colonialism, and the process is still going on. The Aché are, however, the most notorious case from this period. On Paraguay's ongoing genocidal frontier in the Chaco, see Bessire, *Behold the Black Caiman*.

22. Their reduction to a small reservation provided the setting for one of anthropology's classic elegies to a dying culture, Clastres's *Chronique des Indiens Guayaki*.

23. Münzel, *The Aché Indians*; Arens, *Genocide in Paraguay*; Arens, *The Forest Indians in Stroessner's Paraguay*; Maybury-Lewis and Howe, *The Indian Peoples of Paraguay*.

24. Münzel, *The Aché Indians*.

25. Arens, *Genocide in Paraguay*.

26. Wiesel, "Now We Know."

27. Wiesel, "Now We Know," 167.

28. See Maybury-Lewis and Howe, *The Indian Peoples of Paraguay*; Hill and Hurtado, *Aché Life History*; Reed and Renshaw, "The Aché Guarani." Hitchcock, Flowerday, and Koperski, "The Aché of Paraguay," gives an overview of the debate that is generous to both sides.

29. Reed and Renshaw, "The Aché Guarani."

30. There are of course sharper ideological reasons why settler states prefer not to think of their histories as genocidal. But the specific way that the conversation around genocide was structured in the postwar international order has been particularly good at eliding criticism of violence against indigenous people on agrarian frontiers. The attempts to change this conversation on which this chapter draws are especially strong in North American indigenous studies, where scholars argue that the logic of settler colonialism requires the erasure of preexisting groups, whether or not that logic specifically intends to do so. Patrick Wolfe calls this "the logic of elimination" that amounts to "structural genocide" ("Settler Colonialism"). See also Huseman and Short, "A Slow Industrial Genocide"; Stevenson, *Life beside Itself*; Smith, *Sexual Violence and Indian Genocide*. All of these authors argue that the restricted use of the word "genocide" has helped to obscure colonial violence in different ways, most recently the way that environmental destruction, or ecocide, goes hand in hand with the eradication of groups of people (see especially Short, *Redefining Genocide*).

31. In the Aché case, advocates of using the term included Bartomeu Melià and Miguel Chase-Sardi, whom we met in chapter 14 (see Melià and Münzel, "Ratones y jaguares"; Bejarano, *¿Genocidio en el Paraguay?*). In this tradition, the same word, in combination with "ethnocide" and "ecocide," gets used to describe the combined environmental and social atrocities of both colonialism and Cold War capitalist expansion. See Galeano, *Las venas abiertas*; Girardi, "Capitalismo, ecocidio, genocidio."

## CHAPTER SIXTEEN. IMMUNIZING WELFARE

1. On monocrops as fragile, see Besky, "Exhaustion and Endurance."

2. There are a lot of versions out there of what happened to the cotton crop. I've reconstructed this story from a reading of ABC Color and *Última Hora* weekly rural supplements, as well as interviews with farmers and agronomists.

3. Marengo and Whitcomb, "Discovery of the Boll Weevil."

4. The term *súperplaga* was especially popular in ABC Color. Nikiphoroff, in *El subdesarrollo rural paraguayo*, mentions attempts at controlling boll weevils as early as 1985, and Marengo and Whitcomb, "Discovery of the Boll Weevil," claim the pests arrived in 1990. National newspapers ABC Color and *Última Hora* very clearly put the moment in April 1991, predicting devastation for the following year's crop.

5. Murray, *Cultivating Crisis*.

6. Esposito, *Bíos*, 331.

7. The argument presented here is developed in Esposito's trilogy of works on life, *Bíos*, *Communitas*, and *Immunitas*.

8. Like his brother Guillermo Tell, Winkelried had a falling out with his father and moved to Asunción in 1917.

9. The few people I met who knew him say he was a sensitive person, apolitical, and extremely dedicated to his science.

10. This process, sometimes referred to as "deskilling," is a pervasive feature of Green Revolution rescaling. See Stone, "Agricultural Deskilling."

11. On the relationship between neoliberalism and the end of welfare agriculture, see Li, "To Make Live or Let Die?"

12. CADELPA stands for the Camara Algodonera del Paraguay.

13. Nikiphoroff, *El subdesarrollo rural paraguayo*. For an astonishing exposé of how CADELPA continued to profit from failing "cotton reactivation" programs for the next decade, see Areco, *Ladrones y señores*.

14. Supplemento Rural, ABC Color, October 13, 1993, 4.

15. The ministry, to be fair, did create a program for weevil mitigation, which left its own reports in the archives. But it is striking that the top-level reports about the ministry in these years never mention them, and talk only about governance structures.

16. This was a theme during three interviews with international experts who had arrived during the 1980s from the US and Germany and ended up staying in Paraguay working for development NGOs. It was also a universal feeling of the older generation of crop scientists I interviewed who had begun their careers in the wheat and cotton programs of Hernando Bertoni. All of these interviewees, of course, had benefited from the previous arrangement, even if they didn't all subscribe to its ideology.

17. Along with another of Lovera's initiatives, the Registry of Indigenous Seeds.

18. See "Policías custodian fumigación de sojales en zona vecinal de Canindeyú," *Última Hora*, December 3, 2013, http://www.ultimahora.com/policias-custodian-fumigacion-sojales-zona-vecinal-canindeyu-n746273.html.

19. The human rights organization CODEHUPY documented six murders of rural activists in the year following the Curuguaty massacre and the coup (see CODEHUPY, *Informe Chokokue*).

20. "Soja, deforestación y asesinatos," *E'a*, August 8, 2014, http://ea.com.py/v2/soja
-deforestacion-y-asesinatos/. The article picks up a central theme from CODEHUPY's report
on campesino assassinations (*Informe Chokokue*).

21. Wolfe, "Settler Colonialism."

## CHAPTER SEVENTEEN. DUMMY HUTS AND THE LABOR OF KILLING

1. Specifically, land reform beneficiaries were expected to pay off their titles over
ten years (though they could speed this up if they wished to), after which they were
awarded a title that could not be sold for a further ten years. Until these rights became
fully transferrable, most land in colonies were held as *derecheras*, nontransferrable
rights. The Estatuto Agrario is the land reform law passed by Stroessner in 1963 and
amended in 2002.

2. See Hetherington, *Guerrilla Auditors*, for a longer description of the legal wrangling
around land titles in this period, and the complex strategies for maintaining the appearance
of legality in a very gray area of property law.

3. According to Gudynas ("Extractivismos y corrupción"), this was a pervasive feature of
Latin America's left turn.

4. On scale and productivity, see Carter, "Identification of the Inverse Relationship"; Berry
and Cline, *Agrarian Structure and Productivity*. Studies of rural labor in Paraguay using this
calculus have found that despite far poorer infrastructure and markets for small farmers
than large ones, the smallest farms still produce thirteen times as much value per hectare
as the largest, while employing almost twenty times as many laborers (Toledo, "Farm Size
Productivity Relationships in Paraguay").

5. For a general overview, see Kay, "Agrarian Reform and the Neoliberal Counter-Reform
in Latin America"; Zoomers, "Globalisation and the Foreignisation of Space"; Borras et al.,
"Land Grabbing and Global Capitalist Accumulation." For the Paraguayan case, see Ezquerro-
Cañete, "Poisoned, Dispossessed and Excluded"; Elgert, "'More Soy on Fewer Farms'"; Palau
et al., *Socio-Environmental Impacts of Soybean in Paraguay*.

6. As Li ("To Make Live or Let Die?") points out, this transition is not only agricultural, but
an extension of the neoliberal dynamic of jobless growth globally.

7. Marx here was repurposing an older trope in political economy (see Schabas, "Adam
Smith's Debts to Nature"), stating that capital (including machinery) is "dead labor, that,
vampire-like, only lives by sucking living labor, and lives the more, the more labor it sucks"
(Marx, *Capital*, 233). This vitalist argument is quite different than the prewar argument of
Bertoni and others who saw life force as literally biological. In the Marxist equivalent, life
is fundamentally humanist, and as the idea was picked up by Braverman and others after
World War II, it appeared as an abstraction linked to the human production of value.

8. Again, there is a lot of elision in common usage. But just as fields of wheat are often called fields of soy, for years campesinos I knew took all introductions of heavy machinery into agrarian terrain as a precursor to planting soy.

9. Whatmore, *Hybrid Geographies*.

10. Cooper (*Life as Surplus*) uses the term "bioeconomics" critically, much as Sunder Rajan (*Biocapital*) uses the word "biocapital." Bioeconomics also increasingly has a celebratory valence, as used especially in the EU to describe new economic forms arising from the financialization of living processes.

11. Richards, "Contradictions of the 'New Green Revolution.'"

12. For a critique of the World Bank version of this as particularly revealing of this "escape valve," see Li, "Reading the *World Development Report*."

13. Li, "To Make Live or Let Die?," 67.

14. Wolfe, *Before the Law*, 58–59.

15. "Hombres sin tierra y tierras sin hombres" was a favorite slogan of Juan Manuel Frutos.

16. This was especially the case in the eastern border region, where Brazilian settlers received land and credit from Brazilian colonization firms. Campesinos always had more difficulty accessing formal credit.

17. For a discussion of how this economic form works in campesino communities throughout Latin America, see Gudeman, *The Anthropology of Economy*.

18. There were, of course, many forms of work that occupied people in and around the rhythms of the cotton harvest (for instance, peddling, teaching, healing, and cutting hair), but they tended to be thought of as derivative of agricultural production. Even this hierarchy tends to invisibilize other forms of labor that support agriculture as well, including unremunerated domestic and care work mostly carried out by women.

19. On the relationship between cleanliness and weeds in Latin American agrarian imaginaries, see Carse, "Dirty Landscapes."

20. "Tembiguái" literally means someone who is defined by their work, but it has a long pejorative history and was associated in the nineteenth century with slavery. See Huner, "How Pedro Quiñones Lost His Soul."

21. This game of protecting land by resisting formalization was part of a larger regional struggle. On one side, development banks and influential economists argued that incomplete land titling was the single greatest obstacle to agrarian development, while Via Campesina, the international federation of peasant organizations, advised local groups to resist land titling altogether. For an overview, see Hetherington, *Guerrilla Auditors*.

22. Sharecropping, which was more prominent in earlier phases of soy colonization, followed a similar logic. Following the autonomist Marxist tradition, we might say that campesinos have a propensity for resisting both private property and the organization of work. See Weeks, *The Problem with Work*, 96–101.

23. A common joke about soy was that it was a *brasilero jukaha*, a Brazilian-killer, which could refer either to the way they were constantly exposed to agrochemicals or to the way they worked themselves to death.

24. See Weeks, *The Problem with Work*, 98. This also evokes the tradition of "weapons of the weak" popularized by James Scott, *Weapons of the Weak*.

25. There was an evident tension around changes in rural labor among all soy farmers I spoke to. For instance, many of them claimed that their neighbors bought new tractors and combines because they were attracted to flashy expensive machines. But every one of them told me that they bought machines only reluctantly, that they would personally have preferred to give work, but that the labor force around them was too unreliable.

26. I know of only one farm, which cultivates a hundred hectares of organic soy, that still does all of this work by hand and is able to recruit sufficient changueros for the job.

27. For an overview of Monsanto's corporate strategy, see Robin, *The World According to Monsanto*.

28. On blasted landscapes, see Tsing, *The Mushroom at the End of the World*.

29. See Franceschelli and Lovera, "Report on Livestock Development in Paraguay." On the genocidal aspects of intensification of production in the Chaco, see Bessire, *Behold the Black Caiman*.


## CONCLUSION

1. See especially Bertoni, *El rozado sin quemar*; Bertoni, *Agenda y mentor agrícola*. Although these sorts of practices have been around since the late nineteenth century, they have never been adopted by mainstream food producers. Now though, even the IPCC says that addressing climate change will require a transition to more agroecological practices of the sort that Bertoni advocated (IPCC, *Climate Change and Land*).

2. In *Matters of Care*, Puig calls this an "alterbiopolitics." See also Lyons, *Vital Decomposition*.

3. Bertoni, *Agenda y mentor agrícola*.

4. Bertoni, *Agenda y mentor agrícola*, 459–467.

5. Bertoni, *El rozado sin quemar*, 11.

6. See Sarah Gibbens, "The Amazon Is Burning at Record Rates and Deforestation Is to Blame," *National Geographic*, August 21, 2019, https://www.nationalgeographic.com/environment/2019/08/wildfires-in-amazon-caused-by-deforestation/.

7. Kosek, "Industrial Materials."

8. Haraway (*When Species Meet*, 295) takes this formulation from Derrida's influential essay about animal responses. See also Wolfe, *Before the Law*.

9. De Landa, *A Thousand Years of Nonlinear History*, 273; Jensen, "Here Comes the Sun?"

10. J. Marcos and M. A. Fernández, "Paraguay, donde la tierra siembra desposesión y muerte," *Periodismo Humano*, May 8, 2014, http://www.desplazados.org/paraguay-donde-la-tierra-siembra-desposesion-y-muerte/.

11. Mario Abdo Benítez won the presidential election for the Colorado Party in April 2018, capturing nostalgia for the dictatorship and its clientelist version of welfare politics. Although distancing himself from Stroessner the man, he openly praised the social and economic advances of Stronismo. See "Abdo Benítez resalta obras del stronismo y el progreso del país gracias a la ANR," *Última Hora*, January 24, 2018, https://www.ultimahora.com/abdo-benitez-resalta-obras-del-stronismo-y-el-progreso-del-pais-gracias-la-anr-n1130233.html.

12. In fact, by late 2019, the regional pendulum had swung so hard to the right that Paraguay's Colorado Party looked quite moderate by comparison to the new regimes established in parliamentary coups in Brazil and Bolivia.

13. In 2015, the World Health Organization declared glyphosate a carcinogen, and though the findings remained controversial, the declaration completely changed the international discourse about Roundup, leading to several very costly court findings of liability for Monsanto and its parent company, Bayer.

14. See Franceschelli and Lovera, "Report on Livestock Development in Paraguay."

15. Even most of the soy farmers I had come to befriend during this process found the hard turn toward authoritarianism that followed the Lugo experiment to be somewhat dispiriting, though every one of them preferred this to the regulatory uncertainty they had felt under Lugo, and most simply saw it as confirmation of a corrupt Paraguayan culture.

16. Moore, "The End of the Road?"

17. Scott, *Against the Grain*; Morton, *Dark Ecology*.

18. Hall, "The Problem of Ideology."

19. Santi Carneri, "La Onu acusa a Paraguay de violar los derechos humanos por el uso de agroquímicos," *El País*, August 16, 2019, https://elpais.com/internacional/2019/08/15/america/1565888297_356651.html.

20. See Pacto Internacional de Derechos Civiles y Políticos, "Dictamen aprobado por el Comité al tenor del artículo 5, párrafo 4, del Protocolo Facultativo, respecto de la comunicación núm. 2751/2016," August 9, 2019, 7.

# BIBLIOGRAPHY

Abente Brun, Diego, and Larry Diamond. *Clientelism, Social Policy, and the Quality of Democracy*. Baltimore, MD: Johns Hopkins University Press, 2014.

Abrahamsen, Rita. *Disciplining Democracy: Development Discourse and Good Governance in Africa*. London: Zed, 2000.

Agamben, Giorgio. *Homo Sacer: Sovereign Power and Bare Life*. Stanford, CA: Stanford University Press, 1998.

Agrawal, Arun. *Environmentality: Technologies of Government and the Making of Subjects*. Durham, NC: Duke University Press, 2005.

Aguiar, José Carlos G. *Stretching the Border: Smuggling Practices and the Control of Illegality in South America*. Santiago: Global Consortium on Security Transformation, 2010.

Alarcón López, Emiliano. *El cultivo del trigo en el Paraguay*. Asunción: El Lector, 2010.

Albuquerque, José L. C. "Campesinos Paraguayos y 'Brasiguayos' en la frontera este del Paraguay." In *Enclave sojero: Merma de soberanía y pobreza*, edited by R. B. Fogel and M. Riquelme, 149–182. Asunción: CERI, 2005.

Anderson, Benedict. *Imagined Communities: Reflections on the Origin and Spread of Nationalism*. London: Verso, 1983.

Ansell, Aaron. "Clientelism, Elections, and the Dialectic of Numerical People in Northeast Brazil." *Current Anthropology* 59, suppl. 18 (2018): S128–S137.

Areco, Esteban. *Ladrones y señores: Los dueños del cartel del algodón*. Asunción: AGR Servicios Gráficos, 2001.

Arens, Richard. *The Forest Indians in Stroessner's Paraguay: Survival or Extinction?* London: Survival International, 1978.

Arens, Richard. *Genocide in Paraguay*. Philadelphia: Temple University Press, 1976.

Asad, Talal. "Where Are the Margins of the State?" In *Anthropology in the Margins of the State*, edited by V. Das and D. Poole, 279–288. Santa Fe, NM: School of American Research Press, 2004.

Asdal, Kristin, Tone Druglitro, and Steve Hinchliffe. *Humans, Animals and Biopolitics: The More-Than-Human Condition*. London: Routledge, 2016.

Ash, Mark S., Janet Livezey, and Erik N. Dohlman. *Soybean Backgrounder*. Washington, DC: US Department of Agriculture, Economic Research Service, 2006.

Auyero, Javier. *Poor People's Politics: Peronist Survival Networks and the Legacy of Evita*. Durham, NC: Duke University Press, 2001.

Auyero, Javier. *Routine Politics and Violence in Argentina: The Gray Zone of State Power*. Cambridge, UK: Cambridge University Press, 2007.

Auyero, Javier, and Débora Alejandra Swistun. *Flammable: Environmental Suffering in an Argentine Shantytown*. New York: Oxford University Press, 2009.

Ayala Amarilla, Oscar, Idalina Gómez Hansen, and Mariela Palau. *Informe de la sociedad civil sobre el cumplimiento del PIDESC en Paraguay en el contexto rural (2000–2005)*. Asunción: BASE Investigaciones Sociales, 2006.

Baer, Werner, and Melissa H. Birch. "Expansion of the Economic Frontier: Paraguayan Growth in the 1970s." *World Development* 12, no. 8 (1984): 783–798.

Baer, Werner, and Melissa H. Birch. *Privatization in Latin America: New Roles for the Public and Private Sectors*. Westport, CT: Praeger, 1994.

Ballestero, Andrea. *A Future History of Water*. Durham, NC: Duke University Press, 2019.

Barad, Karen Michelle. *Meeting the Universe Halfway: Quantum Physics and the Entanglement of Matter and Meaning*. Durham, NC: Duke University Press, 2007.

Baratti, Danilo. "Moisés Santiago Bertoni y la generación nacionalista-indigenista paraguaya." *Bulletin Société Suisse des Américanistes*, no. 66–67 (2002): 41–47.

Baratti, Danilo, and Patrizia Candolfi. *Vida y obra del sabio Bertoni: Moisés Santiago Bertoni, 1857–1929: Un naturalista suizo en Paraguay*. Asunción: Helvetas, 1999.

Barrett, Rafael. *Lo que son los yerbales*. Asunción: OM Bertani, 1910.

Barry, Andrew. "Materialist Politics: Metallurgy." In *Political Matter: Technoscience, Democracy, and Public Life*, edited by S. Whatmore and B. Braun, 89–118. Minneapolis: University of Minnesota Press, 2010.

Bavington, Dean. *Managed Annihilation: An Unnatural History of the Newfoundland Cod Collapse*. Vancouver: University of British Columbia Press, 2010.

Beck, Ulrich. *Risk Society: Towards a New Modernity*. London: Sage, 1992.

Beckert, Sven. *Empire of Cotton: A Global History*. New York: Knopf, 2014.

Bejarano, Ramón César. *¿Genocidio en el Paraguay?* Asunción: Toledo, 1974.

Benegas, Julio. *La masacre de Curuguaty: Golpe sicario en el Paraguay*. Asunción: Arandurã, 2015.

Bennett, Jane. *Vibrant Matter: A Political Ecology of Things*. Durham, NC: Duke University Press, 2010.

Bensaude-Vincent, Bernadette, and Isabelle Stengers. *A History of Chemistry*. Cambridge, MA: Harvard University Press, 1996.

Berry, R. Albert. *Poverty, Economic Reform, and Income Distribution in Latin America*. Boulder, CO: Rienner, 1998.

Berry, R. Albert, and William R. Cline. *Agrarian Structure and Productivity in Developing Countries*. Baltimore, MD: Johns Hopkins University Press, 1979.

Bertoni, Moisés Santiago. *Agenda y mentor agrícola*. Puerto Bertoni: Ex Silvis, 1927.

Bertoni, Moisés Santiago. *El algodón y el algodonero*. Puerto Bertoni: Ex Silvis, 1927.

Bertoni, Moisés Santiago. *El rozado sin quemar*. Puerto Bertoni: Ex Silvis, 1924.

Bertoni, Moisés Santiago. *La civilización guaraní*. Part I, *Etnología: Origen, extensión y cultura de la raza Karaí-Guaraní y protohistoria de los Guaraníes*. Puerto Bertoni: Ex Silvis, 1922.

Bertoni, Moisés Santiago. *La civilización guaraní*. Part II, *Religión y moral: La religión guaraní y la moral guaraní*. Puerto Bertoni: Ex Silvis, 1924.

Bertoni, Moisés Santiago. *La civilización guaraní*. Part III, *Etnografía: Conocimientos*. Puerto Bertoni: Ex Silvis, 1927.

Bertoni, Moisés Santiago. "La vida." *Revista de la Sociedad Científica del Paraguay* 2, no. 3 (1927): 139–146.

Bertoni, Moisés Santiago. *Resumen de prehistoria y protohistoria de los países guaraníes*. Asunción: O'Leary, 1914.

Besky, Sarah. "Exhaustion and Endurance in Sick Landscapes: Cheap Tea and the Work of Monoculture in the Dooars, India." In *How Nature Works: Rethinking Labor on a Troubled Planet*, edited by S. Besky and A. Blanchette, 23–40. Albuquerque: University of New Mexico Press, 2019.

Bessire, Lucas. *Behold the Black Caiman: A Chronicle of Ayoreo Life*. Chicago: University of Chicago Press, 2014.

Biehl, João, and Adriana Petryna. "Bodies of Rights and Therapeutic Markets." *Social Research: An International Quarterly* 78, no. 2 (2011): 359–386.

Birch, Melissa. "Pendulum Politics: Paraguay's National Borders, 1940–1975." In *Changing Boundaries in the Americas: New Perspectives on the U.S.-Mexican, Central American, and South American Borders*, edited by L. A. Herzog, 203–228. La Jolla, CA: Center for US-Mexican Studies, UCSD, 1992.

Blanc, Jacob. "Enclaves of Inequality: Brasiguaios and the Transformation of the Brazil-Paraguay Borderlands." *Journal of Peasant Studies* 42 (2014): 145–158.

Blanchette, Alex. "Herding Species: Biosecurity, Posthuman Labor, and the American Industrial Pig." *Cultural Anthropology* 30, no. 4 (2015): 640–669.

Blanchette, Alex. *Porkopolis: American Animality, Standardized Life, and the "Factory" Farm*. Durham, NC: Duke University Press, 2020.

Boccia Paz, Alfredo, Myrian Angélica González, and Rosa Palau Aguilar. *Es mi informe: Los archivos secretos de la policía de Stroessner*. Asunción: CDE, 1994.

Borras, Saturnino M., Jr., Jennifer C. Franco, S. Ryan Isakson, Les Levidow, and Pietje Vervest. "The Rise of Flex Crops and Commodities: Implications for Research." *Journal of Peasant Studies* 43, no. 1 (2016): 93–115.

Borras, Saturnino M., Jr., Cristóbal Kay, Sergio Gómez, and John Wilkinson. "Land Grabbing and Global Capitalist Accumulation: Key Features in Latin America." *Canadian Journal of Development Studies/Revue Canadienne d'Études du Développement* 33, no. 4 (2012): 402–416.

Bosso, Christopher J. *Pesticides and Politics*. Pittsburgh: University of Pittsburgh Press, 1987.

Bourdieu, Pierre. "Rethinking the State: Genesis and Structure of the Bureaucratic Field." In *State/Culture: State-Formation after the Cultural Turn*, edited by G. Steinmetz, 53–75. Ithaca, NY: Cornell University Press, 1999.

Bratsis, Peter. "The Construction of Corruption, or Rules of Separation and Illusions of Purity in Bourgeois Societies." *Social Text* 4, no. 77 (2003): 9–33.

Brooke, John L., and Christopher Otter. "Concluding Remarks: The Organic Anthropocene." *Eighteenth-Century Studies* 49, no. 2 (2016): 281–302.

Bullard, Robert D. *Confronting Environmental Racism: Voices from the Grassroots*. Boston: South End Press, 1993.

Burroughs, William S. *Naked Lunch*. New York: Grove, 1959.

Buttel, Frederick H. "Classical Theory and Contemporary Environmental Sociology: Some Reflections on the Antecedents and Prospects for Reflexive Modernization Theories in the Study of Environment and Society." In *Environment and Global Modernity*, edited by Gert Spaargaren, Arthur P. J. Mol, and Frederick H. Buttel, 17–39. London: Sage, 2000.

Campbell, Timothy C., and Adam Sitze, eds. *Biopolitics: A Reader*. Durham, NC: Duke University Press, 2013.

Canguilhem, Georges. *Knowledge of Life*. New York: Fordham University Press, 2008.

Cardozo, Mario L., Danilo Salas, Isabel Ferreira, Teresa Mereles, and Laura Rodríguez. "Soy Expansion and the Absent State: Indigenous and Peasant Livelihood Options in Eastern Paraguay." *Journal of Latin American Geography* 15, no. 3 (2016): 87–104.

Carse, Ashley. "Dirty Landscapes: How Weediness Indexes State Disinvestment and Global Disconnection." In *Infrastructure, Environment, and Life in the Anthropocene*, edited by Kregg Hetherington, 97–114. Durham, NC: Duke University Press, 2019.

Carter, Michael R. "Identification of the Inverse Relationship between Farm Size and Productivity: An Empirical Analysis of Peasant Agricultural Production." *Oxford Economic Papers* 36, no. 1 (1984): 131–145.

Centre of Expertise on Resources. *Soy Supply Security for the Netherlands: Anticipating Future Global Challenges through Strategic Responses*. The Hague: Centre for Strategic Studies, 2015.

Chase-Sardi, Miguel. *El derecho consuetudinario indígena: Y su bibliografía antropológica en el Paraguay*. Asunción: Centro de Estudios Antropológicos, Universidad Católica, 1990.

Cheema, G. Shabbir, and Dennis A. Rondinelli. *Decentralizing Governance: Emerging Concepts and Practices*. Washington, DC: Brookings Institution, 2007.

Chesterton, Bridget María. *The Chaco War: Environment, Ethnicity, and Nationalism.* London: Bloomsbury, 2016.

Chesterton, Bridget María. *The Grandchildren of Solano López: Frontier and Nation in Paraguay, 1904–1936.* Santa Fe: University of New Mexico Press, 2013.

Ciancio, Pedro Nicolás. *La soja y el problema alimentario del Paraguay.* Asunción: Imprenta Nacional, 1950.

Clastres, Pierre. *Chronique des Indiens Guayaki.* Paris: Plon, 1972.

Clastres, Pierre. *Society against the State.* New York: Urizen, 1977.

CODEHUPY. *Informe Chokokue, 1989–2013.* Asunción: CODEHUPY, 2014.

Comaroff, Jean, and John Comaroff. "Transparent Fictions; or, The Conspiracies of a Liberal Imagination: An Afterword." In *Transparency and Conspiracy: Ethnographies of Suspicion in the New World Order,* edited by H. G. West and T. Sanders, 287–300. Durham, NC: Duke University Press, 2003.

Comité Regional de Sanidad Vegetal del Cono Sur. *Estandar regional en protección fitosanitaria.* Buenos Aires, 2003.

Conway, Gordon. *The Doubly Green Revolution: Food for All in the Twenty-First Century.* Ithaca, NY: Comstock, 1998.

Cooper, Melinda. *Life as Surplus: Biotechnology and Capitalism in the Neoliberal Era.* Seattle: University of Washington Press, 2008.

Coronil, Fernando. *The Magical State: Nature, Money, and Modernity in Venezuela.* Chicago: University of Chicago Press, 1997.

Cortázar Velarde, Juan Carlos, Mariano Lafuente, Mario Sanginés, Christian Schuster, Koldo Echebarría, Francisco Longo, Luciano Strazza, and Mercedes Iacoviello. *Serving Citizens: A Decade of Civil Service Reforms in Latin America (2004–13).* Washington, DC: Inter-American Development Bank, 2014.

Cortéz, Cácia. *Os brasiguaios.* São Paolo: Brasil Agora, 1995.

Cueto, Marcos. *Missionaries of Science: The Rockefeller Foundation and Latin America.* Bloomington: Indiana University Press, 1994.

Cullather, Nick. *The Hungry World.* Cambridge, MA: Harvard University Press, 2010.

Dano, Elenita C. *Unmasking the New Green Revolution in Africa: Motives, Players and Dynamics.* Penang: Third World Network, 2008.

Das, Veena. "The Signature of the State: The Paradox of Illegibility." In *Anthropology in the Margins of the State,* edited by V. Das and D. Poole, 225–252. Santa Fe, NM: School of American Research Press, 2004.

Das, Veena, and Deborah Poole, eds. *Anthropology in the Margins of the State.* Santa Fe, NM: School of American Research Press, 2004.

de Gregori, Thomas R. "Muck and Magic or Change and Progress: Vitalism versus Hamiltonian Matter-of-Fact Knowledge." *Journal of Economic Issues* 37, no. 1 (2003): 17–33.

de Landa, Manuel. *A Thousand Years of Nonlinear History.* New York: Zone, 1997.

Deleuze, Gilles. *Foucault.* Paris: Minuit, 1986.

Dinham, Barbara. *The Pesticide Hazard: A Global Health and Environmental Audit.* London: Zed, in association with the Pesticides Trust, 1993.

Doughman, Richard. *La chipa y la soja: La pugna gastro-politica en la frontera agroexportadora del este paraguayo*. Asunción: Base Investigaciónes Sociales, 2011.

Dreiher, Jacob, and Ella Kordysh. "Non-Hodgkin Lymphoma and Pesticide Exposure: 25 Years of Research." *Acta Haematologica* 116, no. 3 (2006): 153–164.

du Bois, Christine M., Chee Beng Tan, and Sidney Wilfred Mintz. *The World of Soy*. Urbana: University of Illinois Press, 2008.

Ebbels, D. L. *Principles of Plant Health and Quarantine*. Wallingford, UK: CABI, 2003.

Eckstein, Albert, and Dale Heien. "The 1973 Food Price Inflation." *American Journal of Agricultural Economics* 60, no. 2 (1978): 186–196.

Elgert, Laureen. "'More Soy on Fewer Farms' in Paraguay: Challenging Neoliberal Agriculture's Claims to Sustainability." *Journal of Peasant Studies* 43, no. 2 (2016): 537–561.

Esposito, Roberto. *Bíos: Biopolitics and Philosophy, Posthumanities*. Minneapolis: University of Minnesota Press, 2008.

Esposito, Roberto. *Communitas: The Origin and Destiny of Community*. Cultural Memory in the Present. Stanford, CA: Stanford University Press, 2010.

Esposito, Roberto. *Immunitas: The Protection and Negation of Life*. Cambridge, UK: Polity, 2011.

Evans, Peter, and James E. Rauch. "Bureaucracy and Growth: A Cross-National Analysis of the Effects of 'Weberian' State Structures on Economic Growth." *American Sociological Review* 64, no. 5 (1999): 748–765.

Ezquerro-Cañete, Arturo. "Poisoned, Dispossessed and Excluded: A Critique of the Neoliberal Soy Regime in Paraguay." *Journal of Agrarian Change* 16, no. 4 (2016): 702–710.

Ezquerro-Cañete, Arturo, and Ramón Fogel. "A Coup Foretold: Fernando Lugo and the Lost Promise of Agrarian Reform in Paraguay." *Journal of Agrarian Change* 17, no. 2 (2017): 279–295.

Fitting, Elizabeth. *The Struggle for Maize: Campesinos, Workers, and Transgenic Corn in the Mexican Countryside*. Durham, NC: Duke University Press, 2010.

FOCOSEP. *Informe final, periodo 2006–2009*. Asunción: Republica del Paraguay y Union Europea, 2009.

Fogel, Ramón B. "Efectos socioambientales del enclave sojero." In *Enclave Sojero: Merma de soberania y pobreza*, edited by R. B. Fogel and M. Riquelme, 35–112. Asunción: CERI, 2005.

Fogel, Ramón B. "El Movimiento de los Carperos." *Novapolis* 5 (2012): 11–30.

Fogel, Ramón B., and Marcial Riquelme, eds. *Enclave Sojero: Merma de soberanía y pobreza*. Asunción: CERI, 2005.

Folch, Christine. *Hydropolitics: The Itaipú Dam, Sovereignty, and the Engineering of Modern South America*. Princeton, NJ: Princeton University Press, 2019.

Fortun, Michael. *Promising Genomics: Iceland and deCODE Genetics in a World of Speculation*. Berkeley: University of California Press, 2008.

Foucault, Michel. *The Birth of Biopolitics: Lectures at the Collège de France, 1978–1979*. New York: Springer, 2008.

Foucault, Michel. *The History of Sexuality*. New York: Pantheon, 1978.

Foucault, Michel. *Society Must Be Defended: Lectures at the Collège de France, 1975–76.* New York: Picador, 2003.

Franceschelli, Inés, and Miguel Lovera. "Report on Livestock Development in Paraguay." In *What's at Steak?* Amsterdam: Global Forest Coalition, 2016.

Freire, Paulo. *Pedagogy of the Oppressed.* New York: Bloomsbury, 1970.

Freire de Sousa, Ivan Sergio, and Rita de Cassia Milagres Teixeira Vieira. "Soybeans and Soyfoods in Brazil: Sketch of an Expanding World Commodity." In *The World of Soy,* edited by Christine M. Du Bois, Chee Beng Tan, and Sidney Wilfred Mintz, 234–256. Urbana: University of Illinois Press, 2008.

Friedmann, Harriet. "The Political Economy of Food: The Rise and Fall of the Postwar International Food Order." *American Journal of Sociology* 88 (1982): S248–S286.

Frutos, Juan Manuel. *Con el hombre y la tierra hacia el bienestar rural.* Asunción: Cuadernos Republicanos, 1982.

Galeano, Eduardo H. *Las venas abiertas de América Latina.* Montevideo: Universidad Nacional de la República, 1971.

Germani, Gino. *Authoritarianism, Fascism, and National Populism.* New Brunswick, NJ: Transaction, 1978.

Giddens, Anthony. *Modernity and Self-Identity: Self and Society in the Late Modern Age.* Stanford, CA: Stanford University Press, 1991.

Gilbert, Geoff. *Responding to International Crime.* Amsterdam: Nijhoff, 2006.

Girardi, Giulio. "Capitalismo, ecocidio, genocidio: El clamor de los pueblos indígenas." *Realidad: Revista de Ciencias Sociales y Humanidades,* no. 41 (1994): 669–698.

Glauser, Marcos. *Angaité's Responses to Deforestation: Political Ecology of the Livelihood and Land Use Strategies of an Indigenous Community from the Paraguayan Chaco.* Münster: LIT, 2019.

Glauser, Marcos. *Extrangerización del territorio paraguayo.* Asunción: BASE Investigaciones Sociales, 2009.

Gómez Florentín, Carlos. *El Paraguay de la post guerra (1870–1900).* Asunción: El Lector, 2013.

González, Erasmo. *El gobierno de 1936 y su proyecto de identidad nacional.* Asunción: El Lector, 2012.

González de Bosio, Beatriz. *Pedro Nicolás Ciancio: El introductor de la soja al Paraguay.* Asunción: El Lector, 2013.

Grindle, Merilee Serrill. *Audacious Reforms: Institutional Invention and Democracy in Latin America.* Baltimore, MD: Johns Hopkins University Press, 2000.

Grindle, Merilee Serrill. *Jobs for the Boys: Patronage and the State in Comparative Perspective.* Cambridge, MA: Harvard University Press, 2012.

Grosz, E. A. *The Nick of Time: Politics, Evolution, and the Untimely.* Durham, NC: Duke University Press, 2004.

Gudeman, Stephen. *The Anthropology of Economy: Community, Market, and Culture.* Malden, MA: Blackwell, 2001.

Gudeman, Stephen, and Alberto Rivera. *Conversations in Colombia: The Domestic Economy in Life and Text.* Cambridge, UK: Cambridge University Press, 1990.

Gudynas, Eduardo. "Buen Vivir: Germinando alternativas al desarrollo." *América Latina en movimiento*, no. 462 (2011): 1–20.

Gudynas, Eduardo. "Extractivismos y corrupción en América del Sur Estructuras, dinámicas y tendencias en una íntima relación." *RevIISE: Revista de Ciencias Sociales y Humanas* 10, no. 10 (2017): 73–87.

Gudynas, Eduardo. "The New Bonfire of Vanities: Soybean Cultivation and Globalization in South America." *Development* 51, no. 4 (2008): 512–518.

Guereña, Arantxa, and Luis Rojas Villagra. *Yvy jára: Los dueños de la tierra en Paraguay.* Asunción: Oxfam, 2016.

Guilhot, Nicolas. *The Democracy Makers: Human Rights and International Order.* New York: Columbia University Press, 2005.

Gupta, Akhil. "Blurred Boundaries: The Discourse of Corruption, the Culture of Politics, and the Imagined State." *American Ethnologist* 22, no. 2 (1995): 375–402.

Gupta, Akhil. *Postcolonial Developments: Agriculture in the Making of Modern India.* Durham, NC: Duke University Press, 1998.

Gupta, Akhil. *Red Tape: Bureaucracy, Structural Violence, and Poverty in India.* Durham, NC: Duke University Press, 2012.

Gutmann, Matthew C. *The Romance of Democracy: Compliant Defiance in Contemporary Mexico.* Oakland: University of California Press, 2002.

Hall, Stuart. "The Problem of Ideology: Marxism without Guarantees." In *Critical Dialogues in Culture Studies*, edited by D. Morley and K.-H. Chen, 24–46. London: Routledge, 1996.

Hansen, Thomas Blom, and Finn Stepputat. "Sovereignty Revisited." *Annual Review of Anthropology* 35 (2006): 295–315.

Hansen, Thomas Blom, and Finn Stepputat. *States of Imagination: Ethnographic Explorations of the Postcolonial State, Politics, History, and Culture.* Durham, NC: Duke University Press, 2001.

Haraway, Donna Jeanne. *Staying with the Trouble: Making Kin in the Chthulucene.* Durham, NC: Duke University Press, 2016.

Haraway, Donna Jeanne. *When Species Meet.* Minneapolis: University of Minnesota Press, 2008.

Harrison, Jill Lindsey. *Pesticide Drift and the Pursuit of Environmental Justice.* Cambridge, MA: MIT Press, 2011.

Hartigan, John, Jr. *Care of the Species: Races of Corn and the Science of Plant Biodiversity.* Minneapolis: University of Minnesota Press, 2017.

Hartigan, John, Jr. "Mexican Genomics and the Roots of Racial Thinking." *Cultural Anthropology* 28 no. 3 (2013): 372–395.

Harwood, Jonathan. *Europe's Green Revolution and Its Successors: The Rise and Fall of Peasant-Friendly Plant Breeding.* New York: Routledge, 2012.

Hetherington, Kregg. "Beans before the Law: Knowledge Practices, Responsibility, and the Paraguayan Soy Boom." *Cultural Anthropology* 28, no. 1 (2013): 65–85.

Hetherington, Kregg. *Guerrilla Auditors: The Politics of Transparency in Neoliberal Paraguay.* Durham, NC: Duke University Press, 2011.

Hetherington, Kregg. "How Can ANT Trace Slow-Moving Environmental Harms as They Become Eventful Political Disruptions?" In *Routledge Companion to Actor Network Theory*, edited by A. Blok, I. Farias, and C. Roberts, 328–336. London: Routledge, 2019.

Hetherington, Kregg. "Introduction: Keywords for the Anthropocene." In *Infrastructure, Environment, and Life in the Anthropocene*, edited by K. Hetherington, 1–13. Durham, NC: Duke University Press, 2019.

Hetherington, Kregg. "Peasants, Experts, Clients, and Soybeans: The Fixing of Paraguay's Civil Service." *Current Anthropology* 59, suppl. 18 (2018): S171–S181.

Hetherington, Kregg. "Privatizing the Private in Rural Paraguay: Precarious Lots and the Materiality of Rights." *American Ethnologist* 36, no. 2 (2009): 224–241.

Hetherington, Kregg. "Promising Information: Democracy, Development, and the Re-mapping of Latin America." *Economy and Society* 41, no. 2 (2012): 127–150.

Hetherington, Kregg. "Regular Soybeans: Translation and Framing in the Ontological Politics of a Coup." *Indiana Journal of Global Legal Studies* 21, no. 1 (2014): 55–78.

Hetherington, Kregg. "Surveying the Future Perfect: Anthropology, Development and the Promise of Infrastructure." In *Infrastructures and Social Complexity: A Companion*, edited by P. Harvey, C. B. Jensen, and A. Morita, 58–68. London: Routledge, 2017.

Hetherington, Kregg. "Waiting for the Surveyor: Development Promises and the Temporality of Infrastructure." *Journal of Latin American and Caribbean Anthropology* 19, no 2 (2014): 195–211.

Hilgers, Tina. "Causes and Consequences of Political Clientelism: Mexico's PRD in Comparative Perspective." *Latin American Politics and Society* 50, no. 4 (2008): 123–153.

Hill, Kim, and A. Magdalena Hurtado. *Aché Life History: The Ecology and Demography of a Foraging People*. New York: Aldine de Gruyter, 1996.

Hitchcock, Robert K., Charles Flowerday, and Thomas E. Koperski. "The Aché of Paraguay and Other 'Isolated' Latin American Indigenous Peoples: Genocide or Ethnocide?" In *Genocide of Indigenous Peoples: A Critical Bibliographic Review*, edited by Robert Hitchcock, 173–194. London: Taylor and Francis, 2011.

Huish, Robert, and John M. Kirk. "Cuban Medical Internationalism and the Development of the Latin American School of Medicine." *Latin American Perspectives* 34, no. 6 (2007): 77–92.

Hull, Matthew S. *Government of Paper: The Materiality of Bureaucracy in Urban Pakistan*. Berkeley: University of California Press, 2012.

Humphrey, Caroline. "Stalin and the Blue Elephant: Paranoia and Complicity in Post-Communist Metahistories." In *Transparency and Conspiracy: Ethnographies of Suspicion in the New World Order*, edited by H. G. West and T. Sanders, 175–203. Durham, NC: Duke University Press, 2003.

Huner, Michael. "How Pedro Quiñones Lost His Soul: Suicide, Routine Violence, and State Formation in Nineteenth-Century Paraguay." *Journal of Social History* (2019). https://doi.org/10.1093/jsh/shz044.

Inter-American Development Bank. *Programa de diversificación y modernización del sector agropecuario*. Washington, DC: Inter-American Development Bank, 1994.

Intergovernmental Panel on Climate Change. *Climate Change and Land: An IPCC Special Report On Climate Change, Desertification, Land Degradation, Sustainable Land Management, Food Security, and Greenhouse Gas Fluxes in Terrestrial Ecosystems*. 2019. https://www.ipcc.ch/srccl/.

Isaacman, Allen F. *Cotton Is the Mother of Poverty: Peasants, Work, and Rural Struggle in Colonial Mozambique, 1938–1961*. Portsmouth, NH: Heinemann, 1996.

Jansen, Kees, and Esther Roquas. "Biosafety Regulation and Global Governance: The Problem of Absentee Expertise in Latin America." In *Food for the Few: Neoliberal Globalism and Biotechnology in Latin America*, edited by G. Otero, 91–114. Austin: University of Texas Press, 2008.

Jensen, Casper Bruun. "Here Comes the Sun? Experimenting with Cambodian Energy Infrastructures." In *Infrastructure, Environment, and Life in the Anthropocene*, edited by K. Hetherington, 216–235. Durham, NC: Duke University Press, 2019.

Johnson, Walter. *River of Dark Dreams*. Cambridge, MA: Harvard University Press, 2013.

Jones, Donna V. *The Racial Discourses of Life Philosophy: Negritude, Vitalism, and Modernity*. New Directions in Critical Theory. New York: Columbia University Press, 2010.

Kanie, Norichika, and Peter M. Haas. *Emerging Forces in Environmental Governance*. New York: United Nations University Press, 2004.

Kaplan, Steven Laurence. *Provisioning Paris: Merchants and Millers in the Grain and Flour Trade during the Eighteenth Century*. Ithaca, NY: Cornell University Press, 2018.

Kay, Cristóbal. "Agrarian Reform and the Neoliberal Counter-Reform in Latin America." In *The Spaces of Neoliberalism: Land, Place and Family in Latin America*, edited by Jacquelyn Chase, 25–52. Bloomfield, CT: Kumarian, 2002.

Kirksey, S. E., and S. Helmreich. "The Emergence of Multispecies Ethnography." *Cultural Anthropology* 25, no. 4 (2010): 545–576.

Kleinpenning, J. M. G. *Man and Land in Paraguay*. Amsterdam: CEDLA, 1987.

Kleinpenning, J. M. G. *Rural Paraguay, 1870–1932*. Amsterdam: CEDLA, 1992.

Kleinpenning, J. M. G. "Strong Reservations about 'New Insights into the Demographics of the Paraguayan War.'" *Latin American Research Review* 37, no. 3 (2002): 137–142.

Kloppenburg, Jack Ralph. *First the Seed: The Political Economy of Plant Biotechnology, 1492–2000*. 2nd ed. Madison: University of Wisconsin Press, 2004.

Kockelman, Paul. "Biosemiosis, Technocognition, and Sociogenesis." *Current Anthropology* 52, no. 5 (2011): 711–739.

Kohn, Eduardo. *How Forests Think: Toward an Anthropology beyond the Human*. Oakland: University of California Press, 2013.

Kolbert, Elizabeth. *The Sixth Extinction: An Unnatural History*. New York: Henry Holt, 2014.

Kosek, Jake. "Industrial Materials: Labor, Landscapes, and the Industrial Honeybee." In *How Nature Works: Rethinking Labor on a Troubled Planet*, edited by Sarah Besky and Alex Blanchette, 149–168. Albuquerque: University of New Mexico Press, 2019.

Kraay, Hendrik, and Thomas Whigham. *I Die with My Country: Perspectives on the Paraguayan War, 1864–1870*. Lincoln: University of Nebraska Press, 2004.

Lang, Tim, and Michael Heasman. *Food Wars*. London: Earthscan, 2004.

Lapegna, Pablo. *Soybeans and Power: Genetically Modified Crops, Environmental Politics, and Social Movements in Argentina*. Oxford: Oxford University Press, 2016.

Lash, Scott. "Lebenssoziologie Georg Simmel in the Information Age." *Theory, Culture and Society* 22, no. 3 (2005): 1–23.

Latimer, Jack. *Friendship among Equals: Recollections from ISO's First Fifty Years*. Geneva: International Organization for Standardization, 1997.

Latour, Bruno. *The Making of Law: An Ethnography of the Conseil d'État*. Cambridge, UK: Polity, 2010.

Latour, Bruno. *Pandora's Hope: Essays on the Reality of Science Studies*. Cambridge, MA: Harvard University Press, 1999.

Latour, Bruno. *We Have Never Been Modern*. Cambridge, MA: Harvard University Press, 1993.

Latour, Bruno. "Why Has Critique Run Out of Steam? From Matters of Fact to Matters of Concern." *Critical Inquiry* 30, no. 2 (2004): 225–248.

Law, John. *After Method: Mess in Social Science Research*. London: Routledge, 2004.

Law, John, and Annemarie Mol. *Complexities: Social Studies of Knowledge Practices, Science and Cultural Theory*. Durham, NC: Duke University Press, 2002.

Law, John, and Annemarie Mol. "Globalisation in Practice: On the Politics of Boiling Pigswill." *Geoforum* 39, no. 1 (2008): 133–143.

Law, John, and Evelyn Ruppert. "The Social Life of Methods: Devices." *Journal of Cultural Economy* 6, no. 3 (2013): 229–240.

Leguizamón, Amalia. "Modifying Argentina: GM Soy and Socio-Environmental Change." *Geoforum* 53 (2014): 149–160.

Lemarchand, René. "Political Clientelism and Ethnicity in Tropical Africa: Competing Solidarities in Nation-Building." *American Political Science Review* 66, no. 1 (1972): 68–90.

Lepselter, Susan. *Resonance of Unseen Things*. Ann Arbor: University of Michigan Press, 2016.

Levidow, Les, and Susan Carr. *GM Food on Trial: Testing European Democracy*. Genetics and Society. New York: Routledge, 2010.

Levine, Michael E., and Jennifer L. Forrence. "Regulatory Capture, Public Interest, and the Public Agenda: Toward a Synthesis." *Journal of Law, Economics, and Organization* 6 (1990): 167–198.

Levitsky, Steven, and Kenneth M. Roberts. *The Resurgence of the Latin American Left*. Baltimore, MD: Johns Hopkins University Press, 2013.

Lewis, Paul H. *Political Parties and Generations in Paraguay's Liberal era, 1869–1940*. Chapel Hill: University of North Carolina Press, 1993.

Lewis, Paul H. *The Politics of Exile: Paraguay's Febrerista Party*. Chapel Hill: University of North Carolina Press, 1968.

Li, Tania. "Reading the *World Development Report 2008: Agriculture for Development*." *Journal of Peasant Studies* 36, no. 3 (2009): 591–592.

Li, Tania. "To Make Live or Let Die? Rural Dispossession and the Protection of Surplus Populations." *Antipode* 41 (2010): 66–93.

Li, Tania. *The Will to Improve: Governmentality, Development, and the Practice of Politics.* Durham, NC: Duke University Press, 2007.

Lien, Marianne E. *Becoming Salmon: Aquaculture and the Domestication of a Fish.* California Studies in Food and Culture. Oakland: University of California Press, 2015.

Lipman, Timothy O. "Vitalism and Reductionism in Liebig's Physiological Thought." *Isis* 58, no. 2 (1967): 167–185.

Lyons, Kristina. *Vital Decomposition: Soil Practitioners and Life Politics.* Durham, NC: Duke University Press, 2020.

Macintyre, Ben. *Forgotten Fatherland: The Search for Elisabeth Nietzsche.* London: Macmillan, 1992.

MacKenzie, Donald. "Finding the Ratchet: The Political Economy of Carbon Trading." *Post Autistic Economics Review* 42 (2007): 8–17.

Marcus, George E. *Paranoia within Reason: A Casebook on Conspiracy as Explanation,* vol. 6. Chicago: University of Chicago Press, 1999.

Marengo, R. M., and W. H. Whitcomb. "Discovery of the Boll Weevil, *Anthonomus grandis* Boheman in Paraguay (Coleoptera: Curculionidae)." *Insecta Mundi* 412 (1991). https://digitalcommons.unl.edu/insectamundi/412.

Marrero-Guillamón, Isaac. "The Politics and Aesthetics of Assembling: (Un)building the Common in Hackney Wick, London." In *Urban Cosmopolitics: Agencements, Assemblies, Atmospheres,* edited by A. Blok and I. Farias, 125–145. London: Routledge, 2016.

Marres, Noortje. "Frontstaging Nonhumans: Publicity as a Constraint on the Political Activity of Things." In *Political Matter: Technoscience, Democracy, and Public Life,* edited by Sarah Whatmore and Bruce Braun, 177–210. Minneapolis: University of Minnesota Press, 2010.

Martínez Cuevas, Efraín. *Los eslabones del oro blanco: La historia del algodón en el Paraguay.* Asunción: La Rural Ediciones, 1984.

Martini, Carlos, and Fátima Myriam Yore. *La corrupción como mecanismo de reproducción del sistema político paraguayo: Apuntes para una radiografía de la impunidad.* Asunción: CIDSEP/UC, 1998.

Martín Martínez, Mariluz. *Proceso político, legislativo y social de la regulación del uso de agrotóxicos en Paraguay.* Asunción: CEIDRA, 2009.

Marx, Karl. *Capital: A Critique of Political Economy.* New York: International Publishers, 1967.

Mathews, Andrew S. *Instituting Nature: Authority, Expertise, and Power in Mexican Forests.* Cambridge, MA: MIT Press, 2011.

Maybury-Lewis, David, and James Howe. *The Indian Peoples of Paraguay: Their Plight and Their Prospects.* Peterborough, NH: Cultural Survival, 1979.

McMichael, Philip. "Tensions between National and International Control of the World Food Order: Contours of a New Food Regime." *Sociological Perspectives* 35, no. 2 (1992): 343–365.

Melià, Bartomeu, and Christine Münzel. "Ratones y jaguares: Reconstrucción de un genocidio a la manera de los Axe-Guayaki del Paraguay oriental." In *Las culturas condenadas,* edited by A. Roa Bastos, 62–85. Mexico City: Siglo XXI, 1978.

Melley, Timothy. *Empire of Conspiracy: The Culture of Paranoia in Postwar America.* Ithaca, NY: Cornell University Press, 2000.

Melly, Caroline. *Bottleneck: Moving, Building, and Belonging in an African City.* Chicago: University of Chicago Press, 2017.

Méndez Grimaldi, Idilio. *Los herederos de Stroessner.* Asunción: Arandurã, 2007.

Menezes, Alfredo da Mota. *La herencia de Stroessner: Brasil-Paraguay, 1955–1980.* Asunción: Schauman, 1990.

Miller, Judith A. *Mastering the Market: The State and the Grain Trade in Northern France, 1700–1860.* Cambridge, UK: Cambridge University Press, 1999.

Mintz, Sidney W., and Eric R. Wolf. "An Analysis of Ritual Co-parenthood (Compadrazgo)." *Southwestern Journal of Anthropology* 6, no. 4 (1950): 341–368.

Mitchell, Timothy. *Carbon Democracy: Political Power in the Age of Oil.* London: Verso, 2011.

Miyazaki, Hirokazu. *Arbitraging Japan: Dreams of Capitalism at the End of Finance.* Oakland: University of California Press, 2013.

Mol, Annemarie. *The Body Multiple: Ontology in Medical Practice.* Durham, NC: Duke University Press, 2002.

Montag, Warren. "Necro-Economics: Adam Smith and Death in the Life of the Universal." *Radical Philosophy*, no. 134 (2005).

Moore, Jason W. *Capitalism in the Web of Life: Ecology and the Accumulation of Capital.* New York: Verso, 2015.

Moore, Jason W. "The Capitalocene, Part I: On the Nature and Origins of Our Ecological Crisis." *Journal of Peasant Studies* 44, no. 3 (2017): 594–630.

Moore, Jason W. "The End of the Road? Agricultural Revolutions in the Capitalist World-Ecology, 1450–2010." *Journal of Agrarian Change* 10, no. 3 (2010): 389–413.

Mopas, Michael. "Examining the 'CSI Effect' through an ANT Lens." *Crime, Media, Culture* 3, no. 1 (2007): 110–117.

Mora, Frank O., and Jerry Wilson Cooney. *Paraguay and the United States: Distant Allies.* Athens: University of Georgia Press, 2010.

Morínigo, José Nicolás. *Auge de la producción rural y crisis campesina.* Asunción: Fondec, 2009.

Morton, Timothy. *Dark Ecology: For a Logic of Future Coexistence.* New York: Columbia University Press, 2016.

Morton, Timothy. *Hyperobjects: Philosophy and Ecology after the End of the World.* Minneapolis: University of Minnesota Press, 2013.

Muir, Cameron. *The Broken Promise of Agricultural Progress: An Environmental History.* London: Routledge, 2014.

Muir, Sarah. "The Currency of Failure: Money and Middle-Class Critique in Post-Crisis Buenos Aires." *Cultural Anthropology* 30, no. 2 (2015): 310–335.

Muir, Sarah. "On Historical Exhaustion: Argentine Critique in an Era of 'Total Corruption.'" *Comparative Studies in Society and History* 58, no. 1 (2016): 129–158.

Münzel, Mark. *The Aché Indians: Genocide in Paraguay.* Copenhagen: International Work Group for Indigenous Affairs, 1973.

Murphy, Michelle. *The Economization of Life.* Durham, NC: Duke University Press, 2017.

Murray, Douglas L. *Cultivating Crisis: The Human Cost of Pesticides in Latin America.* Austin: University of Texas Press, 1994.

Nading, Alex M. *Mosquito Trails: Ecology, Health, and the Politics of Entanglement.* Oakland: University of California Press, 2014.

Nagel, Beverly Y. "'Unleashing the Fury': The Cultural Discourse of Rural Violence and Land Rights in Paraguay." *Comparative Studies in Society and History* 41, no. 1 (1999): 148–181.

Netz, Reviel. *Barbed Wire: An Ecology of Modernity.* Middletown, CT: Wesleyan University Press, 2004.

Newell, Peter. "Bio-hegemony: The Political Economy of Agricultural Biotechnology in Argentina." *Journal of Latin American Studies* 41, no. 1 (2009): 27–57.

Nickson, Andrew. "Brazilian Colonization of the Eastern Border Region of Paraguay." *Journal of Latin American Studies* 13, no. 1 (1981): 111–131.

Nickson, Andrew. "Paraguay's Archivo del Terror." *Latin American Research Review* 30 (1995): 125–130.

Nickson, Andrew, and Peter Lambert. "State Reform and the 'Privatized State' in Paraguay." *Public Administration and Development* 22, no. 2 (2002): 163–174.

Nikiphoroff, Basilio. *El subdesarrollo rural paraguayo: La problemática algodonera: Estrategias para el desarrollo.* Colección Futuro verde. Asunción: Fundación Moisés Bertoni, Intercontinental Editora, 1994.

Nixon, Rob. *Slow Violence and the Environmentalism of the Poor.* Cambridge, MA: Harvard University Press, 2011.

Ortega, Jaquelina. *Cronología de denuncias de intoxicación y derechos humanos ante el avance de los agronegocios.* Asunción: BASE Investigaciones Sociales, 2008.

Osburg, John. "Making Business Personal: Corruption, Anti-corruption, and Elite Networks in Post-Mao China." *Current Anthropology* 59, suppl. 18 (2018): S149–S159.

Palau Viladesau, Tomás, Luis Rojas, Milena Pereira, and Richard Doughman. *Socio-Environmental Impacts of Soybean in Paraguay.* São Paolo and Asunción: Repórter Brasil and BASE Investigaciones Sociales, 2010.

Papastergiadis, Nikos. "A Breathing Space for Aesthetics and Politics: An Introduction to Jacques Rancière." *Theory, Culture and Society* 31, no. 7–8 (2014): 5–26.

Pastore, Carlos. *La lucha por la tierra en el Paraguay.* Montevideo: Antequera, 1972.

Patel, Raj. "The Long Green Revolution." *Journal of Peasant Studies* 40, no. 1 (2013): 1–63.

Patel, Raj. *Stuffed and Starved: Markets, Power and the Hidden Battle for the World Food System.* London: Portobello, 2007.

Patel, Raj, and Jason W. Moore. *A History of the World in Seven Cheap Things: A Guide to Capitalism, Nature, and the Future of the Planet.* Berkeley: University of California Press, 2017.

Pavetti, Alicia, and Osamu Saito. "Changes in Land Use and Ecosystem Services in Paraguay." *Japanese Society of Civil Engineers* 40 (2012): 331–337.

Pearson, Keith Ansell. *Germinal Life: The Difference and Repetition of Deleuze.* Cambridge, UK: Cambridge University Press, 1999.

Peck, James, and Adam Tickell. "Neoliberalizing Space." *Antipode* 34, no. 3 (2002): 380–404.

Pereira, Hugo. *El EPP, defensa reaccionaria de un modelo de desarrollo desigual y excluyente.* Asunción: ServiLibro, 2015.

Perkins, John. *Geopolitics and the Green Revolution: Wheat, Genes and the Cold War.* Oxford: Oxford University Press, 1997.

Petryna, Adriana. *When Experiments Travel: Clinical Trials and the Global Search for Human Subjects.* Princeton, NJ: Princeton University Press, 2009.

Pieri, Christian, Guy Evers, John Landers, Paul O'Connell, and Eugene Terry. *No-Till Farming for Sustainable Rural Development.* Washington, DC: World Bank, 2002.

Pietz, William. "The 'Post-colonialism' of Cold War Discourse." *Social Text* 19–20 (fall 1988): 55–75.

Pitt-Rivers, Julian. *The People of the Sierra.* Chicago: University of Chicago Press, 1954.

Pitts, Bryan, Rosemary Joyce, Russell Sheptak, Kregg Hetherington, Marco Castillo, and Rafael Ioris. "21st Century Golpismo: A NACLA Roundtable: Six Latin Americanist Scholars Reflect on the Ousters of Presidents Manuel Zelaya, Fernando Lugo, and Dilma Rousseff." *NACLA Report on the Americas* 48, no. 4 (2016): 334–345.

Pollan, Michael. *The Botany of Desire: A Plant's Eye View of the World.* New York: Random House, 2001.

Portillo, Ana. *Agronegocios y la Facultad de Ciencias Agrarias de la UNA.* Asunción: BASE Investigación Sociales, 2018.

Potthast-Jutkeit, Bárbara. *"Paraíso de Mahoma" o "País de las mujeres"? El rol de la familia en la sociedad paraguaya del siglo XIX.* Asunción: Instituto Cultural Paraguayo-Alemán, 1996.

Povinelli, Elizabeth A. *Economies of Abandonment: Social Belonging and Endurance in Late Liberalism.* Durham, NC: Duke University Press, 2011.

Povinelli, Elizabeth A. *Geontologies: A Requiem to Late Liberalism.* Durham, NC: Duke University Press, 2016.

Powell, John Duncan. "Peasant Society and Clientelist Politics." *American Political Science Review* 64, no. 2 (1970): 411–425.

Puig de La Bellacasa, María. *Matters of Care: Speculative Ethics in More Than Human Worlds.* Minneapolis: University of Minnesota Press, 2017.

Raffles, Hugh. *Insectopedia.* New York: Vintage, 2010.

Rama, Angel. *The Lettered City: Post-contemporary Interventions.* Durham, NC: Duke University Press, 1996.

Rancière, Jacques. *Disagreement: Politics and Philosophy.* Minneapolis: University of Minnesota Press, 1999.

Reed, Richard, and John Renshaw. "The Aché Guaraní: Thirty Years after Maybury-Lewis and Howe's Report on Genocide in Paraguay." *Tipití: Journal of the Society for the Anthropology of Lowland South America* 10, no. 1 (2012): 1.

Reeves, Madeleine. *Border Work: Spatial Lives of the State in Rural Central Asia.* Ithaca, NY: Cornell University Press, 2014.

Richards, Donald G. "Contradictions of the 'New Green Revolution': A View from South America's Southern Cone." *Globalizations* 7, no. 4 (2010): 563–576.

Richards, Peter D. "Soy, Cotton, and the Final Atlantic Forest Frontier." *Professional Geographer* 63, no. 3 (2011): 343–363.

Ricoeur, Paul. *Interpretation Theory: Discourse and the Surplus of Meaning*. Fort Worth: Texas Christian University Press, 1976.

Riles, Annelise. *The Network Inside Out*. Ann Arbor: University of Michigan Press, 2000.

Riquelme, Marcial. "Notas para el estudio de los causas y efectos de las migraciones brasilenas en el Paraguay." In *Enclave sojero: Merma de soberania y pobreza*, edited by R. B. Fogel and M. Riquelme, 113–148. Asunción: CERI, 2005.

Rivarola, Milda. *Obreros, utopías y revoluciones: Formación de las clases trabajadoras en el Paraguay liberal, 1870–1931*. 2nd ed. Asunción: Servilibro, 2010.

Roa Bastos, Augusto. "Paraguay, una isla rodeada de tierra." *El Correo de la UNESCO*, August 1977.

Robin, Marie-Monique. *The World According to Monsanto: Pollution, Corruption, and the Control of the World's Food Supply*. New York: New Press, 2010.

Rojas, Luis. *Campesino rapé*. Asunción: BASE Investigaciones Sociales, 2015.

Rondinelli, Dennis A., James S. McCullough, and Ronald W. Johnson. "Analysing Decentralization Policies in Developing Countries: A Political-Economy Framework." *Development and Change* 20, no. 1 (1989): 57–87.

Rulli, Javiera, and Elizabeth Bravo, eds. *Repúblicas unidas de la soja: Realidades sobre la producción de soja en America del Sur*. Buenos Aires: Grupo de Reflexión Rural, 2007.

Russell, Edmund. *War and Nature: Fighting Humans and Insects with Chemicals from World War I to Silent Spring*. Cambridge, UK: Cambridge University Press, 2001.

Saraiva, Tiago. *Fascist Pigs: Technoscientific Organisms and the History of Fascism*. Cambridge, MA: MIT Press.

Sarmiento, Domingo Faustino. *Facundo; or, Civilization and Barbarism*. 1845; New York: Penguin, 1998.

Schabas, Margaret. "Adam Smith's Debts to Nature." *History of Political Economy* 35, no. 5 (2003): 262–281.

Schurman, Rachel, and Dennis D. Kelso. *Engineering Trouble: Biotechnology and Its Discontents*. Oakland: University of California Press, 2003.

Schuster, Caroline E. *Social Collateral: Women and Microfinance in Paraguay's Smuggling Economy*. Oakland: University of California Press, 2015.

Schuster, Christian. *Clientelismo y el juego político de profesionalizar el empleo público en Paraguay: Documento de trabajo*. Asunción: CADEP, 2013.

Scott, James C. *Against the Grain: A Deep History of the Earliest States*. New Haven: Yale University Press, 2017.

Scott, James C. "Corruption, Machine Politics, and Political Change." *American Political Science Review* 63, no. 4 (1969): 1142–1158.

Scott, James C. *Seeing Like a State: How Certain Schemes to Improve the Human Condition Have Failed*. Yale Agrarian Studies. New Haven, CT: Yale University Press, 1998.

Scott, James C. *Weapons of the Weak: Everyday Forms of Peasant Resistance*. New Haven, CT: Yale University Press, 1985.

Service, Elman Rogers, and Helen S. Service. *Tobatí: Paraguayan Town*. Chicago: University of Chicago Press, 1954.

Setrini, Gustavo. "Twenty Years of Paraguayan Electoral Democracy: From Monopolistic to Pluralistic Clientelism." Working Paper #3. Asunción: CADEP, 2010.

Shiva, Vandana. *Monocultures of the Mind: Perspectives on Biodiversity and Biotechnology*. London: Palgrave Macmillan, 1993.

Short, Damien. *Redefining Genocide: Settler Colonialism, Social Death and Ecocide*. London: Zed, 2016.

Shurtleff, William, and Akiko Aoyagi. *History of Soybeans and Soyfoods in South America (1884–2009): Extensively Annotated Bibliography and Sourcebook*. Lafayette, CA: Soyinfo Center, 2009.

Smart, Alan. "The Unbearable Discretion of Street-Level Bureaucrats: Corruption and Collusion in Hong Kong." *Current Anthropology* 59, suppl. 18 (2018): S37–S47.

Smith, Andrea. "Sexual Violence and American Indian Genocide." *Journal of Religion and Abuse* 1, no. 2 (1999): 31–52.

Smith, Daniel Jordan. *A Culture of Corruption: Everyday Deception and Popular Discontent in Nigeria*. Princeton, NJ: Princeton University Press, 2010.

Souchaud, Sylvain. *Pionniers brésiliens au Paraguay*. Paris: Karthala, 2002.

Stauffer, Robert C. "Haeckel, Darwin, and Ecology." *Quarterly Review of Biology* 32, no. 2 (1957): 138–144.

Steffen, Will, Wendy Broadgate, Lisa Deutsch, Owen Gaffney, and Cornelia Ludwig. "The Trajectory of the Anthropocene: The Great Acceleration." *Anthropocene Review* 2, no. 1 (2015): 81–98.

Steinfeld, Henning, Pierre Gerber, T. D. Wassenaar, Vincent Castel, Mauricio Rosales, and Cees de Haan. *Livestock's Long Shadow: Environmental Issues and Options*. Rome: Food and Agriculture Organization, 2006.

Stengers, Isabelle. *In Catastrophic Times: Resisting the Coming Barbarism*. London: Open Humanities Press, 2015.

Stevenson, Lisa. *Life beside Itself: Imagining Care in the Canadian Arctic*. Oakland: University of California Press, 2014.

Stewart, Kathleen, and Susan Harding. "Bad Endings: American Apocalypsis." *Annual Review of Anthropology* 28 (1999): 285–310.

Stokes, Susan C. "Perverse Accountability: A Formal Model of Machine Politics with Evidence from Argentina." *American Political Science Review* 99, no. 3 (2005): 315–325.

Stokes, William Earl Dodge. *The Right to Be Well Born: Or, Horse Breeding in Its Relation to Eugenics*. London: Hardpress, 1917.

Stone, Glenn Davis. "Agricultural Deskilling and the Spread of Genetically Modified Cotton in Warangal." *Current Anthropology* 48, no. 1 (2007): 67–103.

Strathern, Marilyn. "Cutting the Network." *Journal of the Royal Anthropological Institute* 2, no. 3 (1996): 517–535.

Sunder Rajan, Kaushik. *Biocapital: The Constitution of Postgenomic Life*. Durham, NC: Duke University Press, 2006.

Svampa, Maristella, and Enrique Viale. *Maldesarrollo: La Argentina del extractivismo y el despojo*. Buenos Aires: Katz, 2015.

Taussig, Michael T. *The Magic of the State*. New York: Routledge, 1997.

Telesca, Ignacio. *Ligas agrarias cristianas: Orígenes del movimiento campesino en Paraguay*. Asunción: CEPAG, 2004.

Thiele, Graham. "The Dynamics of Farm Development in the Amazon: The Barbecho Crisis Model." *Agricultural Systems* 42, no. 3 (1993): 179–197.

Toledo, Ricardo. "Farm Size-Productivity Relationships in Paraguay's Agricultural Sector." In *Losing Ground in the Employment Challenge: The Case of Paraguay*, edited by A. Berry, 85–100. New Brunswick, NJ: Transaction, 2010.

Tsing, Anna Lowenhaupt. *The Mushroom at the End of the World: On the Possibility of Life in Capitalist Ruins*. Princeton, NJ: Princeton University Press, 2015.

Tsing, Anna Lowenhaupt. "A Threat to Holocene Resurgence Is a Threat to Livability." In *The Anthropology of Sustainability*. London: Springer, 2017.

Turner, Brian. *Community Politics and Peasant-State Relations in Paraguay*. Lanham, MD: University Press of America, 1993.

Turner, Brian. "Paraguay as a Decentralized Unitary State: What Does It Mean?" Paper presented at the annual conference of the Latin American Studies Association, Guadalajara, Mexico, 1997.

UNDP. *Paraguay: Human Development Report*. New York: United Nations Development Program, 2018.

USDA. *Paraguay Biotechnology Annual*. Buenos Aires: Global Agriculture Information Network, 2007.

Van Cott, Donna Lee. *The Friendly Liquidation of the Past: The Politics of Diversity in Latin America*. Pitt Latin American Series. Pittsburgh: University of Pittsburgh Press, 2000.

Viveros, Diana. "La guerra de una madre contra los agroquímicos." In *Los desterrados no van al supermercado: Crónicas del país que alimenta al mundo pero tiene hambre*, edited by J. Acuña and J. Heilborn. Asunción: Kultural, 2017. https://elsurti.com/madre-vs -agroquimicos/.

Wagner, Carlos. *Brasiguaios: Homens sem pátria*. Petrópolis: Vozes, 1990.

Wagner-Pacifici, Robin. *What Is an Event?* Chicago: University of Chicago Press, 2017.

Warnken, Philip F. *The Development and Growth of the Soybean Industry in Brazil*. Ames: Iowa State University Press, 1999.

Weber, Max. "Bureaucracy." In *From Max Weber: Essays in Sociology*, edited by H. H. Gerth and C. W. Mills, 196–244. New York: Routledge, 2009.

Weeks, Kathi. *The Problem with Work: Feminism, Marxism, Antiwork Politics, and Postwork Imaginaries*. Durham, NC: Duke University Press, 2011.

Weisskoff, Richard. "The Paraguayan Agroexport Model of Development." *World Development* 20, no. 10 (1992): 1531–1540.

West, Harry G., and Todd Sanders. *Transparency and Conspiracy: Ethnographies of Suspicion in the New World Order*. Durham, NC: Duke University Press, 2003.

Whatmore, Sarah. *Hybrid Geographies: Natures, Cultures, Spaces*. London: Sage, 2002.

Whatmore, Sarah, and Bruce Braun. *Political Matter: Technoscience, Democracy, and Public Life*. Minneapolis: University of Minnesota Press, 2010.

Whigham, Thomas. "Paraguay and the World Cotton Market: The 'Crisis' of the 1860s." *Agricultural History* 68, no. 3 (1994): 1–15.

Whigham, Thomas L., and Barbara Potthast. "The Paraguayan Rosetta Stone: New Insights into the Demographics of the Paraguayan War, 1864–1870." *Latin American Research Review* 34, no. 1 (1999): 174–186.

White, Richard Alan. *Breaking Silence: The Case That Changed the Face of Human Rights*. Washington, DC: Georgetown University Press, 2004.

Wiesel, Elie. "Now We Know." In *Genocide in Paraguay*, edited by Richard Arens, 165–168. Philadelphia: Temple University Press, 1976.

Williams, John Hoyt. "Paraguayan Isolation under Dr. Francia: A Re-evaluation." *Hispanic American Historical Review* 52, no. 1 (1972): 102–122.

Willis, Eliza, Christopher da C. B. Garman, and Stephan Haggard. "The Politics of Decentralization in Latin America." *Latin American Research Review* 34, no. 1 (1999): 7–56.

Wolf, Eric R. "Closed Corporate Peasant Communities in Mesoamerica and Central Java." *Southwestern Journal of Anthropology* 13, no. 1 (1957): 1–18.

Wolfe, Cary. *Before the Law: Animals in a Biopolitical Context*. Chicago: University of Chicago Press, 2012.

Wolfe, Patrick. "Settler Colonialism and the Elimination of the Native." *Journal of Genocide Research* 8, no. 4 (2006): 387–409.

Woolgar, Steve, and Daniel Neyland. *Mundane Governance: Ontology and Accountability*. Oxford: Oxford University Press, 2013.

World Bank. *World Development Report: The State in a Changing World*. Washington, DC: World Bank, 1997.

Wynne, Brian. "Knowledges in Context." *Science, Technology, and Human Values* 16, no. 1 (1991): 111–121.

Zoomers, Annelies. "Globalisation and the Foreignisation of Space: Seven Processes Driving the Current Global Land Grab." *Journal of Peasant Studies* 37, no. 2 (2010): 429–447.

Zhang, Luoping, Iemaan Rana, Emanuela Taioli, Rachel M. Shaffer, and Lianne Sheppard. "Exposure to Glyphosate-Based Herbicides and Risk for Non-Hodgkin Lymphoma: A Meta-Analysis and Supporting Evidence." *Mutation Research* 781 (2019): 186–206.

219; and monocrops, 171; panics over, 79–80; symposium on, 164, 245n6; as technology, 211; vitalist arguments against, 206. *See also* Roundup Ready soybeans

genocide, 191–93, 202, 208, 215, 220, 250nn21–22, 251nn30–31

Gerardo (SENAVE inspector), 97–98, 100–103, 107, 112, 117–18, 136, 138, 152

González, Silvia, 54–57, 59, 61, 62, 65, 82, 89, 104, 121, 147, 232n1

González Macchi, Luís Ángel, 57

Government of Beans, 8–12; conceptual difficulties, 16–18; contemporary views of, 215, 220; culture of, 103; and Curuguaty massacre, 151; and denuncias, 119; end of, 12, 152–55; epidemiology of, 168; gestures made by, 129; historical contexts, 220–21; and judicialization, 114; legitimacy of, 142; limits of, 121, 145; and living barriers, 132; and measurement, 69, 75–76, 132; multiplicity of, 16–18; and parallel infrastructures, 114, 119–20; and pesticide regulation, 65; possibility of, 140; and Latin American left turn, 224n21; temporal issues, 105; and violence, 143. *See also* Lugo, Fernando, coalition government; SENAVE

great acceleration, 7

Green Revolution, First: biopolitics of, 13, 170, 173, 185, 208; Ciancio and, 20; conditions enabling, 13; and the ISO, 73; and killing, 193, 194, 197; and monocrops, 189; negative impacts of, 13–14; Rockefeller Foundation and, 170; and Second Green Revolution, 212; soy and, 7; and the United States, 23–24, 185; vitalism of, 207. *See also* agribiopolitics, Green Revolution and; STICA program

Green Revolution, long, 160, 215, 220

Green Revolution, Second, 14, 206–7, 212

Green Revolution in Paraguay: Moisés Santiago Bertoni and, 178; environmental destruction of, 190–91; and Filártiga, 159–60; IADB and, 64; and land redistribution, 47; and Nazism, 192; STICA program, 185, 249n2; and wheat, 25. *See also* cotton farming

Guarani language: Brasiguaios and, 49; campesinos and, 33, 101, 185; and class divides, 91–92; mestizos and, 48; as national language, 46; politicians and, 44, 57, 62; prejudices against, 49; and soy, 6, 45; tekojoja, 82

Guarani peoples, 103, 176, 247n12. *See also* Aché Guarani genocide

Gudynas, Eduardo, 75, 169, 253n3

Haeckel, Ernst, 178–79

Hansen, Thomas Blom, 141, 241n10

Haraway, Donna, 189, 218

hardwoods, 190, 250n17

health: human versus plant, 163–66, 168, 170, 172–73, 183, 245n2

herbicide-resistant weeds, 30

Huner, Michael, 46

hyperobjects: and causality, 230n26; definition of, 6–7, 224n11; soy as, 6–7, 17–18, 42, 113; states as, 9

immunity, 180–81, 196–97, 201

immunological institutions, 181

InBIO agency, 164

indigenous peoples: Aché Guarani, 191–93, 250nn21–22, 251n31; Moisés Santiago Bertoni's history of, 176, 247n11; Guarani, 103; Mby'a, 108–9, 137, 140, 216; tribe and chief fictions, 115, 239n11

La Industria Paraguaya, 47, 150, 231n16

inequality: criminal courts and, 37

Insfrán, José Luís, 163–64, 244–45n2, 245nn6–7

Institute for Rural Welfare (IBR): and border security laws, 145; campesino activists and, 119; cotton program, 24; creation of, 47, 73; Finca 30 petitions, 150–51; and Government of Beans, 8; measurement and surveying work, 133, 135; and property, 134–35, 205, 240n3; renaming of, 224n20; and state building, 114

Institute of Technology and Standardization (INTS), 71, 73–74, 76, 235n5

Inter-American Development Bank (IADB): civil service reports, 236n7; conspiracy theories about, 79; and the Green Revolution, 64, 197; investments in Paraguay, 74; and the ISO, 73; and Stroessner regime, 64, 73

International Monetary Fund (IMF), 74, 235n6

International Standards Organization (ISO), 73, 76, 235n3

intra-actions, 68–69, 132

Itaipú electric dam, 26, 49, 51, 231n24, 250n7

Itapúa, 27–28, 47, 53, 186, 227n17

Japan and Japanese, 26, 27

Jazmín (Lugo supporter), 81, 83

Jefferson, Thomas, 20, 226n4

Jones, Donna, 178

judicialization, 113–14

ka'aguy (forest), 46–49

Karajakái: Citizen Participation Unit in, 106–12, 121, 136–40, 222; deforestation, 137; health clinic, 166–69; pesticide impacts, 110–11, 166–67; sojero state-building, 169; *See also* Canindeyú

killing: and agribiopolitics, 201; and agriculture, 188–91, 194; applied entomology and, 197; and food politics, 218; and the Green Revolution, 194, 197; machines for, 211; of pests, 194; in "planting without cleaning," 217; soy's forms of, 212; and thriving, 207. *See also* ecocide; genocide

Kirchner, Cristina, 11, 82, 241n13

Kirchner, Néstor, 141, 241n13

Kockelman, Paul, 122

labor, 208–10; casual day, 209–10, 215; of death, 211; land improvements, 201, 207–8, 254n21; and mechanization, 210, 255n25; occasional forms of, 208–9, 254n18

lab technicians, 238n8

land: concentration of, 205, 253n6; grabs, critiques of, 205, 207; improvements, 201, 207–8, 213–14, 254n21; reform, 40, 47–48, 134–35, 170–71, 203, 208, 213, 246n11, 253n1; sale restrictions, 144, 242n2; scarcity of, 1, 4; state ownership and sales, 47, 231n14; surveys of, 133–35; takeovers causing migration, 5; untitled, 213; without people, 208. *See also* Institute for Rural Welfare (IBR)

Latin American left turn: Brazil and, 82, 113–14; collapse of, 219; and Government of Beans, 224n21; leftist leaders with health problems, 141–42, 241n13; political interventions, 204, 253n3; and right turn, 243n27

Latour, Bruno, 35, 124, 229n3, 246n27

Li, Tania, 205–7, 253n6

liberalism: Latin American, 19, 226n2

Liberal Party, 82; and February Revolution, 182; during Lugo era, 60, 82, 83; origins of, 87; in power, 87, 236n2; and 2013 election, 146

life as labor, 205–6, 253n6

Liga Nacional de Carperos, 145, 151

Ligas Agrarias, 39–40, 239n10

Lilian (rural doctor), 167–69

limpieza, 214

living barriers: and boll weevil buffers, 200–201; campesino support for, 59; Cartes era, 152–53; Citizen Participation Unit enforcement, 131–32, 135, 137–38, 201; and community

health, 201; density issue, 233n15; farms lacking, 130–31; functions of, 53, 200–201; laws mandating, 53, 58, 147; legal battles over, 59–61; measurements of, 132–33; and road classifications, 137–38, 241n7; and Silvino Talavera's death, 53; soy industry responses, 58–59; as state presence symbol, 61

living borders doctrine, 48–49

logic of elimination, 202

López, Francisco Solano, 176–77

Lovera, Miguel, 62–63, 72, 85–86, 221; and SENAVE, 85–86, 89–95, 99, 121, 123, 146–49, 241n7

Lugo, Fernando: appeal of, 82; and appointments, 60, 62, 72; cancer of, 141; electoral victory, 8, 60, 81–83; impeachment, 151–53; and Marxism, 234n2; plots against, 76; and soy anxieties, 68; supporters of, 8, 75; 2013 election, 147, 242n8. *See also* Government of Beans

Lugo, Fernando, coalition government: civil service reforms, 237n13; class alliances enabling, 91–92; clientelism of, 92, 93–94; confianza language, 89–90; coup against, 2, 12, 153–55; end of, 219; and EPP, 142; experimental governance, 136; and the freezer, 90; immunological approach to soy, 201; infighting, 147; Law of Border Security decree, 144–45, 242n4; and Marina Kue massacre, 151; new democrats, 60, 92; Sixto Pereira, 93–94, 237nn19–20; press attacks on, 149; public health reforms, 165–66; research funding, 164, 245n8; tactical sovereignty of, 140–41; unraveling of, 148; and violence, 142–43. *See also* Curuguaty, massacre in; new democrats; Tekojoja Party

Lula da Silva, Luiz Inácio, 82, 141, 241n13

Lunardelli, Geremia, 48

machinery-soy associations, 206, 254n8

MacIntyre, Ben, 248n31, 249n36

March to the East, 48, 186

Marcus, George, 78

marijuana, 51, 106, 142, 238n1

Marina Kue, 150–51, 243nn19–20

Martínez, Esperanza, 166–67, 170–71

Marxism, 205–6, 253n7

Marzo Paraguayo, 81, 236n1

masculine identities, 187, 209

mass extinctions, 7

Matte Larangeira, 47, 231n16

Mby'a indigenous people, 108–9, 137, 140, 216

pesticide regulation (*continued*)
61, 233n16; legislation for, 54–56, 59, 232n3; and nostalgia, 12; suspension of, 219. *See also* SENAVE

pesticides: agribiopolitics of, 196; aldrin, 240n10; and cancer, 245n3; and cotton, 196; cotton versus soy, 14; cypermethrin, 30; and double planting, 228n26; the environment and, 110, 154; Folidol, 244n3; humans and, 5, 110–11, 154; in Karajakái, 110–11; lindane, 126–27; monitoring of, 30, 55; monocrop dependence on, 30; organophosphates, 32, 36, 232n3, 245n3; smells from, 5, 34–35, 110; soy farmer beliefs about, 41–42; sprays of, 4–5; stronger, 219–20. *See also* Roundup; Talavera, Silvino

Petryna, Adriana, 113–14

phytosanitary interventions, 30. *See also* pesticides

phytosanitary politics, 160

phytosanitary regulation, 13, 171; boll weevil control, 196–97; and border control, 147, 242n10; soy moratorium, 147–48. *See also* SENAVE

Pink Tide. *See* Latin American left turn

pioneer citizens, 108, 114–15, 119, 150, 188

Pirapey, 33, 39–40, 44, 47, 221

plant biology, 183

plant health regimes, 171. *See also* health: human versus plant

"planting without cleaning," 217, 255n1

Plaza de la Democracia, 81, 236n1

Plaza Uruguaya, 42

police, 77–78, 81, 142, 219, 235n9. *See also* Curuguaty, massacre in

pollution, 5

Portillo, Rubén, 125–26, 128, 221, 239n13, 240n7

Povinelli, Elizabeth, 35

Project for Strengthening the Competitiveness of Paraguay's Export Sector, 74–75

protocols, 121–22, 124, 127–28, 138

public health reforms, 165–68, 170–71, 245nn13–14, 246n14

Puerto Bertoni, 216–18

Puig de la Bellacasa, María, 217

quasi-events, 35, 111, 113, 154, 222

realidad invocations, 239n10

regulations: ADM and, 67; changing, 56; decrees versus laws, 61; and judgment, 11; and life, 196; as responses, 113; the state and the everyday, 68. *See also* SENAVE

regulatory capture, 10, 225n28

regulatory devices, 241n4

regulatory pragmatics, 11

Ricoeur, Paul, 78

rights, 113–14

Rio Earth Summit, 191, 250n19

Riquelme, Blas N., 150, 243n17

Riquelme, Marcial, 45, 48, 52

Roa Bastos, Augusto, 46, 231n18

Rockefeller Foundation, 23–24, 170. *See also* STICA program

Roundup, 29–30, 34, 42, 211–12, 219, 224n10, 256n13

Roundup Ready soybeans, 30–31; ban on, 10, 64, 80; commercial availability of, 228n29; as genetic event, 38; impact on labor, 211–12; Paraguayan crop dominance, 10, 64; royalties, 50, 65, 234n8

Rousseff, Dilma, 153

rural activists, 2, 6, 8

rural healthcare reform, 165–66, 245n13

rural welfare: agrarian redistribution and colonial genocide, 208; and colonization, 48, 111; and cotton, 190, 193; as distant promise, 111–12; end of, 153, 195; and killing, 190; and land, 43, 47, 133–34; living barriers, 133; Lugo's promises for, 1, 8, 37; Ministry of Public Health, 166; pesticides and, 17; repurposing of, 116; revival hopes, 8, 153; SENAVE and, 94–95, 100, 114, 119; and sovereignty, 45; Stroessner regime and, 24, 116. *See also* Citizen Participation Unit; Institute for Rural Welfare (IBR)

San Pedro, 24, 47, 186

Santa Rita, 44–45, 48–50, 230n2, 230n5

Saraiva, Tiago, 182

Schlender, Hermann, 32–33, 58. *See also* Talavera, Silvino

seccional system, 116

Secretariat of the Environment (SEAM), 58, 60, 100

SENAVE, 12–13; agribiopolitics of, 201; archive burning, 219; the author and, 71, 85–86, 96; budget problems, 146; Cartes era, 152–54; centralization problems, 99; chemical importer busts, 123; citations and administrative indictments, 118–20, 128; clientelist hiring practices, 86, 90–91; Colorado Party and, 86–87; confianza (trust) language, 89–90; countryside presence, 99; creation of, 63–66, 200; and criminal activities, 239n13; Darío, 93–94, 146; and decentralization, 98–99; embezzlement at, 102, 146; and global capitalism, 15; and

9 781478 006893